THE MACMILLAN SERIES OF ILO STUDIES

Iftikhar Ahmed (*editor*)
BIOTECHNOLOGY: A HOPE OR A THREAT?

Richard Anker and Catherine Hein (*editors*)
SEX INEQUALITIES IN URBAN EMPLOYMENT IN THE THIRD WORLD

W. R. Böhning
STUDIES IN INTERNATIONAL LABOUR MIGRATION

Enyinna Chuta and Carl Liedholm
EMPLOYMENT AND GROWTH IN SMALL-SCALE INDUSTRY

Ghazi M. Farooq and George B. Simmons (*editors*)
FERTILITY IN DEVELOPING COUNTRIES

David J. C. Forsyth
TECHNOLOGY POLICY FOR SMALL DEVELOPING COUNTRIES

Dharam Ghai, Azizur Rahman Khan, Eddy Lee and Samir Radwan (*editors*)
AGRARIAN SYSTEMS AND RURAL DEVELOPMENT

Jeffrey James and Susumu Watanabe (*editors*)
TECHNOLOGY, INSTITUTIONS AND GOVERNMENT POLICIES

Vali Jamal and John Weeks
AFRICA MISUNDERSTOOD OR WHATEVER HAPPENED TO THE RURAL-URBAN GAP?

Nicolas Jéquier and Yao-Su Hu
BANKING AND THE PROMOTION OF TECHNOLOGICAL DEVELOPMENT

Azizur Rahman Khan and Dharam Ghai
COLLECTIVE AGRICULTURE AND RURAL DEVELOPMENT IN SOVIET CENTRAL ASIA

Ng Sek-Hong and Victor Fung-Shuen Sit
LABOUR RELATIONS AND LABOUR CONDITIONS IN HONG KONG

Guy Standing
UNEMPLOYMENT AND FEMALE LABOUR

Wouter van Ginneken and Christopher Baron (*editors*)
APPROPRIATE PRODUCTS, EMPLOYMENT AND TECHNOLOGY

Susumu Watanabe (*editor*)
MICROELECTRONICS AND THIRD-WORLD INDUSTRIES

A. B. Zahlan
ACQUIRING TECHNOLOGICAL CAPACITY

The ILO's World Employment Programme (WEP) aims to assist and encourage member States to adopt and implement active policies and projects designed to promote full, productive and freely chosen employment and to reduce poverty. Through its action-oriented research, technical advisory services, national projects and the work of its four regional employment teams in Africa, Asia and Latin America, the WEP pays special attention to the longer-term development problems of rural areas where the vast majority of poor and under-employed people still live, and to the rapidly growing urban informal sector.

At the same time, in response to the economic crises and the growth in open unemployment of the 1980s, the WEP has entered into an ongoing dialogue with the social partners and other international agencies on the social dimensions of adjustment, and is devoting a major part of its policy analysis and advice to achieving greater equity in structural adjustment programmes. Employment and poverty monitoring, direct employment creation and income generation for vulnerable groups, linkages between macro-economic and micro-economic interventions, technological change and labour market problems and policies are among the areas covered.

Through these overall activities, the ILO has been able to help national decision-makers to reshape their policies and plans with the aim of eradicating mass poverty and promoting productive employment.

This publication is the outcome of a WEP project.

Africa Misunderstood

or Whatever Happened to the Rural-Urban Gap?

Vali Jamal
Senior Economist
International Labour Office, Geneva

and

John Weeks
Director of the Centre for Development Studies
School of Oriental and African Studies
University of London

A study prepared for the
International Labour Office
within the framework of the
World Employment Programme

M

First published 1993 by
THE MACMILLAN PRESS LTD
Houndmills, Basingstoke, Hampshire RG21 2XS
and London
Companies and representatives
throughout the world

ISBN 0–333–58890–8

A catalogue record for this book is available
from the British Library.

Printed in Great Britain by
Ipswich Book Co Ltd
Ipswich, Suffolk

Contents

List of Tables

List of Figures

Foreword

There is general consensus, two decades into what is commonly called the African crisis, on two propositions: the imperative to resume growth and the need to restructure the sub-Saharan economies. However, consensus is far from being reached on the appropriate policies to achieve growth or the sort of restructuring best suited for African countries. In particular, although the contrary is sometimes asserted, there is no consensus on the efficacy of the standard stabilisation programmes undertaken by most African countries. These programmes implicitly blame 'mismanagement' and distortionary policies for the African crisis, and by the same token, advocate a package of policies to correct the alleged distortions. Devaluation, wage freeze and higher agricultural prices figure prominently in this package, an important part of the diagnosis being that African economies suffer from 'urban bias', and that these policies should correct such a bias.

This book, written under an ongoing programme of research in the Policies and Programmes for Development Branch of the ILO,[1] shows that distortions may well have been exaggerated in the past, that in the last decade of the crisis most of these distortions have largely disappeared, and that external factors (declining terms of trade and the debt burden) have contributed also to the crisis. Starting from the mid-1970s, most African governments refrained from protecting their urban wage-earners, and in the 1980s began raising agricultural prices. Massive changes in rural-urban terms of trade resulted, precisely the sort of thing attempted under structural adjustment programmes, but with little of the anticipated beneficial impacts. The authors explain this anomaly in terms of the changes in survival strategies that occurred because of collapsing urban wages. They argue that these changes are so vast that indeed a new paradigm is required to provide a framework for the study of the African economies. For the fact is most African families now undertake a myriad of activities – in the formal as well as the informal sectors, in the urban as well the rural areas – to ensure livelihood. In that sort of situation even such basic tools of analysis as 'rural-urban terms of trade' lose some of their bite, given that most families undertake some farming – or have members in the rural areas – in conjunction with urban activities. The intersectoral shifts predicated on changes in the terms of trade that are so much a part of the structural adjustment remedy, fail to materialise; more to the point, the authors do not see a decline in rural-urban migration, let alone reverse migration. On the employment front the drastic fall in wages, the one unambiguous outcome of adjustment programmes, has not created greater employment since at the macro level employment is demand-constrained.

Many of the authors' major findings, first reported in 1987, have already entered into subsequent analyses of African economies. No doubt there may also be criticism from different quarters, but one way or the other, as Professor Singer points out in his introductory remarks, this book will be difficult to ignore. I am pleased to have been associated with it.

SAMIR RADWAN
Chief
Policies and Programmes for Development Branch
Employment and Development Department
International Labour Office

Introductory Remarks

There will be no disputing the crucial importance of a proper understanding of African problems. Sub-Saharan Africa today is the Achilles heel of the world economy and in danger of becoming a marginalised economic underworld. If the authors of this volume are right – as I believe they are – in maintaining that the conventional wisdom now applied to Africa is wrong and based on an incorrect or outmoded paradigm, this is clearly a matter of great importance. All those concerned with policy making in Africa have a moral responsibility to study this volume carefully and consider what changes in approach it would suggest.

In one sense the authors are pushing at an open door: it is now generally recognised that in Africa, as also elsewhere in the Third World, the focus of poverty has been shifting from rural to urban areas, i.e., that poverty has become more urbanised. The wage-earning class has practically disappeared as a distinct entity and there has been an astonishing 'informalisation' of the urban labour markets. The authors can claim justifiable credit for these ideas, with their much quoted article in 1988. Rural-urban migration and recent drastic changes in the internal terms of trade, discussed extensively in this volume, have been responsible for this. But the authors also remind us that the past and present extent of the rural-urban income gap (in the sense of farmers versus urban wage earners) may have been greatly exaggerated, or even misinterpreted in direction. It is clearly essential for an effective policy of poverty reduction to get this matter cleared up. It is equally important for effective structural adjustment policies. Although this publication can be read as a criticism of current approaches to structural adjustment on the part of multilateral financial institutions and others, the authors in their preface remind us that the thinking behind this publication goes back to 1976 – well into the era of debt-led growth and before structural adjustment came to dominate the scene. Having been associated with the 1972 Kenya ILO Employment Mission ('Employment, Incomes and Inequality') I would be tempted to take this back even further to 1972. That Report already devoted much attention to urban poverty, the urban informal sector and the problems of the 'working poor' in Nairobi and other urban areas.

I trust the argument of this book will not be misinterpreted as saying that urban poverty is 'more important' than rural poverty. Such a statement – like the opposite statement governing the conventional wisdom which this book criticises – has very little meaning. Recent developments in Africa have increasingly blunted the distinction between rural and urban income sources, as applied to extended families and divided households. In any case, rural and urban poverty feed upon each other. Even if rural poverty should be statistically more important, its root cause may still lie in the poverty and resulting lack of effective demand in the urban sector; the reverse may also apply. Any policy of poverty reduction worth its name would have to attack both locations of poverty simultaneously. I believe that is the real lesson of this book.

A particularly valuable feature of the book is that it is so carefully documented and underpinned by ten case studies. One would wish that these case studies could be extended to include also the Francophone countries. One can only hope that it will be read with an open mind and a willingness to abandon even well-ingrained and cherished paradigms. Not the least service rendered by this book would be to broaden attention away from exclusive emphasis on domestic distortions towards more symmetrical attention being given to international distortions, such as the deteriorating international terms of trade for African countries and the resulting import strangulation which leads to excess capacity, under-employment and low efficiency in the urban sector.

H.W. SINGER
Institute of Development Studies
University of Sussex

Preface

Yet another book on the African crisis requires some justification for being read, if not for its very existence. At the risk of immodesty, we contend that this is rather a special book on the African crisis, examining as it does in great detail a particular model of the African economies – that they suffer from 'urban bias' – that has long been the staple of their analysis and that in recent years has provided the main diagnosis of the crisis afflicting the African countries and a basis for its cure. Through careful, retrospective calculations it is shown that the gap between farmers and wage earners, allegedly the main manifestation of urban bias in Africa, was never as great as made out and that in the last 15 years this gap has practically disappeared, and, by any proper reckoning, even turned in favour of the farmers. The argument thus goes to the heart of the structural adjustment remedy which attempts to provide the cure for the African crisis by removing the urban bias.

Our thesis has been around quite some time now – a fact that is worth documenting, not only to establish our claim to originality but also to divulge the basis of our association and its evolution. In 1985 John Weeks was asked by the International Labour Organisation to write a report on the impact of economic policy on vulnerable groups in sub-Saharan Africa. It quickly transpired that an extraordinarily large number of studies addressing this question had been done within the ILO itself, and by a single author, Vali Jamal, between 1976 and 1984, during his tenure as Senior Economist at ILO's African regional team, Jobs and Skills Programme for Africa. The results of this empirical work, published in a series of working papers entitled *Rural-urban gap and income distribution* (Jamal 1982) and also as unattributed chapters in several high-level employment missions in which Jamal participated, were quite striking, very much at variance with the prevailing orthodoxy. Thus it was natural for Weeks to approach Jamal suggesting the possibility of joint collaboration on a work that would present these findings in a clear and concise form. The initial output of this collaboration appeared as an ILO working paper (Jamal and Weeks 1987), then as a major chapter in ILO's *World Labour Report* of 1987 (ILO 1987a); and finally as an article in the *International Labour Review* (Jamal and Weeks 1988).

While we anticipated critical reaction to our study, we could hardly have hoped for the overwhelming response it elicited from experts in the field.[1] Buoyed by this and the immodest belief that we might have something useful to contribute to understanding the functioning of African economies, past and present, and, by extension multilateral structural adjustment programmes, we embarked upon an elaboration of the study. A first draft was completed in 1988 and circulated among ILO colleagues and leading economists, and presented at several conferences and seminars. Again the reaction was very favourable; in fact the manuscript became by some accounts the most quoted unpublished manuscript in ILO history. An opportunity for making the final revisions did not occur till June 1991. At that time care was taken to incorporate comments made by readers and update most of the data (some of our calculations are deliberately historical and therefore 'old'), and advance the discussion on the African crisis and structural adjustment programmes by taking account of new UN and academic publications. The result is what follows.

We received extensive written comments on the first draft from Manfred Bienefeld, Frank Ellis, Ajit Ghose, Martin Greeley, Reginald H. Green, Rolph van der Hoeven, Samir Radwan, Peter Richards, Douglas Rimmer, Hans Singer and Richard Strickland. Professor Singer in fact was one of the official referees of the manuscript. The manuscript was presented in its various forms at academic seminars at Bergen, Cambridge, Glasgow, London, Middlebury, and Sussex, and at several United Nations conferences. On those occasions we received more than the usual amount of comments from Adebayo Adedeji, Firimooni Banugire, Christopher Colclough, Terry Byers, Vremudia Diejomaoh, Keith Griffin, Kjell Havnevik, Michael Hodd, Goran Hyden, Tetteh Kofi, John Loxley, Thandika Mkandawire, Bade Onimode, Sadig Rasheed, Derek Robinson, Ashwani Saith, John Sender, Timothy Shaw, Ajit Singh, Lawrence Smith, Arne Tostensen, Ben Turok and Mark Wuyts.

A veritable 'who's who' of Africanists has thus read all or parts of our book and benefited us with their written or oral comments. We have tried in subsequent drafts to accommodate as many of these as we could. These saved us from many embarrassing errors and contributed to a better presentation of substantive points. We most gratefully acknowledge this help from friends and colleagues; however in the time-honoured formula, we also absolve them of responsibility for any remaining errors. Neither should the ILO be held liable for views expressed here. Special thanks are also in order to Cheryl Wright and Rosa del Rosario of the ILO who ploughed through interminable drafts with fortitude and good cheer and to Sue-Anne Mayne, Assistant Director, Centre for Development Studies, School of Oriental and African Studies, for her encouragement and support.

Despite the evident acceptance of our central contention that a significant income gap in favour of urban areas no longer characterises the sub-Saharan region, many of the positions we question continue to provide the justifications for IMF-World Bank adjustment programmes. For example, in its 1989 policy document on sub-Saharan Africa the World Bank after conceding that real wages had fallen, quoting 'ILO studies', still felt impelled to argue that 'high wage costs' helped to explain the uncompetitiveness of African exports; and that in any case because of the alleged distortions, the wage declines represented 'a brutal but necessary adjustment' (World Bank 1989b, p. 29).

Thus four years after the appearance of our *ILR* article, the myth of the rural-urban gap still persists. We conclude that the publication of this book is of more than historical interest; that the fallacies of fact and analysis that guided adjustment programmes in the 1980s continue to do so in the early 1990s. Like generals who are always fighting the last war, adjustment programmes to a great extent target 'distortions' that no longer exist and perhaps never did to any significant extent in most of the sub-Saharan countries.

VALI JAMAL
JOHN WEEKS

1 Introduction

For sub-Saharan Africa the 1960s will be remembered as the best of times – the enthusiasm of independence, the expectation of building upon a base of infrastructure and educational progress laid down during the colonial era, a relatively favourable world economic environment, and an international development community tolerant of eclectic paths to economic modernisation. Thirty years on these must be the worst of times. The post-independence enthusiasm is gone, replaced in many countries by cynicism that so much seemed possible but so little was achieved. The external economic environment facing African governments and citizens today has deteriorated to the point of being the most unfavourable to developing country growth since the end of the Second World War. Equally dramatically, the international development community, particularly the bilateral and multilateral lenders in the West, have returned to a pre-Keynesian fundamentalist faith in the efficacy of unregulated markets and outward orientation. This shift in economic ideology has narrowed the options of governments – all the more so in the context of the debt crisis which has resulted in a closing of the ranks of international lenders, official and commercial.[1]

These changes in the development context – the emotional (evaporation of enthusiasm and hope), the economic (international trends), and the ideological (faith in free markets) – are closely related to the central purpose of this study, which is to consider a particular aspect of the underdeveloped nature of the sub-Saharan African countries, namely the division of income, wealth, and access to livelihood among rural and urban families, and to draw out its implications for standard adjustment programmes. Once utilised to typify the African country experience in the immediate post-independence era, rural-urban income differentials have changed dramatically in the last 15 years, as have the enthusiasm and the environment for economic growth. The economic baggage that goes with the old perceptions has, however, yet to catch up with the changed environment of the 1980s, and diagnosis and prescriptions still abound based on past models.

At least since the mid-1960s the concept of rural-urban inequality or 'urban bias' played a major role in the conceptualisation of African development.[2] As a result of the extremely influential book by Michael Lipton (1977), the term 'urban bias' achieved the status of an epitomising cliché applicable to the developing world as a whole. It presented a 'master hypothesis' (Byres 1979), a global explanation of the poverty of nations, as implied by the title of Lipton's book – *Why poor people stay poor*. Lipton stated the urban bias hypothesis as a situation prevailing in all developing countries, in which policy focused upon urban-based development, and resources were overwhelmingly allocated to urban areas, with the result that the rural population, where one found most of the poor, benefited little. Associated with this policy focus was a process of surplus transfer, so the urban bias not only manifested itself in the allocation of resources at the margin, but also the redistribution of resources, income, and wealth. The reason for the bias was the concentration of political power in the hands of 'townsmen' (ibid., p. 269).

As an all-encompassing explanation of Third World underdevelopment and poverty, the urban-bias hypothesis came under severe attack, both at the analytical and empirical level. Particularly damaging was the critique of Byres (1979), where it was shown that the hypothesis failed to take account of either urban or rural social structures, substituting for them an over-simplified urban-rural social dichotomy.[3] As a balanced judgement, one could say that while the urban bias hypothesis raised provocative issues and served to crystallise debate, it failed to survive analytical and empirical critique in the academic literature.

However, in a vaguer and less intellectually coherent form it did resurface in the 1980s as a 'common sense' explanation of the complex inequalities and economic and social imbalances in African countries, especially in the policy reports of the multilateral and bilateral development agencies. In their case, there was none of Lipton's theoretical contribution, but rather an emphasis on selected (and frequently dubious) measures of urban and rural welfare: access to social services, infrastructure, and, most of all, incomes. Ignoring the analytical critique of the urban bias hypothesis, development practitioners stressed the purely empirical manifestations of urban-rural differences. This approach we refer to as the 'accepted orthodoxy'. Once propounded, it acquired a life of its own. Development practitioners treated it not only as a simplified way of understanding the African context, but the very synthesis of that context. The essential ingredient of that view was the belief that sub-Saharan African societies were characterised by large and widening inequalities between town and country, that these inequalities were caused by governmental interference in markets, and that these inequalities overwhelmed all others, with implications not only for income and wealth distribution but also for resource allocation and productive efficiency. The particular aspect of rural-urban inequality that received the most attention – and that became for many the quintessential description and explanation of African economies – was the inequality between the urban wage earners and the farmers. It was asserted that this inequality was huge, and widening dangerously, to the detriment of agriculture, as also of urban unemployment. Our concern throughout this study will be with this aspect of rural-urban inequality. We shall demonstrate that this characterisation of African countries is no longer valid and further that even at its height the rural-urban inequality properly measured was much smaller than one was led to believe.

Clearly our definition of 'urban bias' and 'rural-urban inequality' is quite restricted. We shall direct our critique to the standard of living of farmer and wage earner households as measured by monetary income and the imputed value of non-marketed consumption; that is, we shall be primarily interested in the trend in the rural-urban gap in terms of household welfare and the implications of that for household behaviour. At points we consider other aspects of the rural-urban differential, such as social services. But the argument does not address itself specifically to the broad issue of the quality of life in town and countryside, nor to whether a government's development priorities on balance favour rural or urban areas. These broader issues are indeed alluded to in the country studies and we shall return to them specifically in the concluding chapters but for the sake of comparative analysis we shall exclude them from our formal presentation. This restriction far from being considered a drawback is actually incumbent upon us since most past analyses of African countries have indeed focused on the farm-wage gap. Most policy questions, particularly with regard to migration, employment and structural adjustment programmes also relate to the rural-urban gap as we define it. Thus, by placing limits on our analysis we have not restricted the relevance of our study, but focused it more clearly on an aspect of African economies considered crucial in past analyses as well as the current policy debate.

ORGANISATION OF THE PRESENTATION

In Chapter 2 we lay the background for our study by analysing the impact of the economic crisis of the last decade in the sub-Saharan countries. This survey of macroeconomic trends anticipates our later arguments that the severe economic shocks of the 1970s have radically altered the relationship between rural and urban areas in most countries. But contrary to what the accepted orthodoxy would hold, along with this alteration of rural-urban income differentials has gone a worsening of the distribution of income, in some cases to an astonishing degree. So drastic in particular has been the change in the relationship between rural and urban populations that a new conceptualisation of the African context is required – a new stereotype, as it were. Real wages have fallen sharply, employment in the formal sector has declined, living standards of urban workers and peasants have drawn closer together, and in some countries urban poverty now rivals rural poverty in intensity and extent. The falling wages in urban areas have engendered profound changes in urban economic structures. No longer is the urban wage sufficient to support an average-size family in towns – something that colonial administrations consciously tried to achieve in the immediate pre-independence period and African governments had tried to nurture in the decade following. In most countries the wage earning class has ceased to exist as an independent entity as urban families have been forced into seeking basic survival from informal activities and backyard gardening. These developments will be duly documented and their implications for the functioning of African economies brought out. But right at the outset we must record that there is no evidence that these dramatic changes represent equilibrating adjustments which have eliminated or even reduced the various problems which rural-urban inequality was alleged to cause. Falling real wages have not stimulated employment; a declining wage/peasant income gap has not stemmed migration; and if in the past wage earner gains were at the cost of peasant losses, the reverse does not hold.

Having treated the macroeconomic trends of the last 15 years and anticipated our main arguments, we then provide a critical survey of the 'urban bias' view in Chapter 3, drawing on relevant literature. Our central argument here is that even to the extent that the rural-urban and wage-farm bias characterisation of sub-Saharan countries was correct, the approach tended to overlook major aspects of the distributional dynamics of the societies so characterised. The much-lamented gap between the wage earners and farmers was much smaller, even in the immediate post-independence period, than most suggested.

These points are made in some detail with particular reference to ten case studies – Ghana, Kenya, Lesotho, Liberia, Nigeria, Sierra Leone, Somalia, the United Republic of Tanzania, Uganda and Zambia. The ten studies are grouped into four chapters according to common economic structures. Three east African countries (Uganda, Kenya, and Tanzania) are covered in Chapter 4, the mineral-exporting countries of Zambia and Liberia in Chapter 5, two remittance-dependent economies (Somalia and Lesotho) in Chapter 6, and three West African countries (Ghana, Sierra Leone and Nigeria) in Chapter 7. In all the case studies emphasis is placed upon both the impact of internal economic policies on income distribution as well as on the consequences of the particular economic structure of the country. Care is taken to measure the extent of the wage earner-farmer gap as well as the trend in these incomes. The discussion is left in a free form to capture nuances of the countries studied. The major lessons are summarised at the end of each case study.

The general conclusions drawn from the case studies relate back to the analysis of macroeconomic trends in Chapter 2, and are developed in a broader context in Chapter 8. Here region-wide tendencies are summarised and their associated dynamics elaborated. Major policy implications of the shift in the nature of rural-urban inequality are taken up in Chapter 9. Three policy issues are stressed. First, we consider the relationship between the oft-recommended measure of devaluation on rural-urban differentials. Second, it is argued that the fall in urban wages relatively to peasant incomes has not succeeded in 'clearing' labour markets. This should not be surprising, for despite the simple parables of neoclassical labour market theory, there was always sufficient reason to doubt that falling real wages would clear markets. Certainly in the context of sub-Saharan countries, the traditional labour market model is singularly inappropriate. Closely related to this, it is argued that the behaviour of both the urban as well as the rural labour markets in the sSA countries should be understood in terms of what we call 'survival strategies' in the face of drastically reduced real incomes. Third, it is reiterated that the dynamics of income distribution in the sub-Saharan countries are now not primarily rural-urban. The simplistic idea that freer play of market forces would reduce rural-urban inequality and thereby improve both income distribution and efficiency of resource allocation does not serve to capture the present distributional dynamics of African countries. In sum, our conclusion is that issues of equity and poverty remain high on the agenda of governments of sSA countries and multilateral agencies; these issues are not subsumed within nor adequately addressed by market-oriented internal reforms and 'outward-looking' trade policies, though both types of measures may be forced upon governments by pressure of circumstances.

CHARACTERISTICS OF SAMPLE COUNTRIES

Although we look in detail at only ten countries, their economies are so diverse and their total population so vast that we may be justified in concluding that similar trends are happening all over sub-Saharan Africa. In Chapter 8 we shall make amends by bringing in evidence from other African countries. The following list summarises the salient characteristics of the sample countries:

Ghana	Once collapsed economy
Kenya	Dualistic agriculture
Lesotho	South African dependency economy
Nigeria	Oil economy; rural exodus
Sierra Leone	Severe class-related income inequalities
Somalia	Predominantly pastoral; remittance economy
Tanzania	Socialist development
Uganda	Once collapsed economy
Zambia	Urbanised mineral-based economy

The diversity of the sample clearly has an influence on the analysis of the rural-urban gap and its trend. At one extreme there is Nigeria with her tremendous oil wealth, and, at the other, Somalia with a relatively unmonetised rural sector based on nomadic pastoralism. Tanzania has a fairly egalitarian agricultural sector and Kenya and Liberia a dualistic structure, in Kenya inherited as a legacy from colonial days and maintained more or less intact after independence, and in Liberia the consequence of concessions granted to foreign-owned estates. Uganda and Ghana are extreme examples of economic collapse in the 1970s, while Somalia and Lesotho may be characterised as 'remittance economies', Somalia in terms of remittances received from migrant workers in the Gulf States and Lesotho in terms of remittances from migrants in South Africa. Sierra Leone perhaps typifies best an economy where governmental interference in the market was very selective – not at all in setting wages and food prices, but considerable in setting export crop prices. Zambia offers another form of diversity by its high level of urbanisation and dependence on copper rather than agriculture, both of which provide new insights into the genesis of the rural-urban gap and the African crisis. The combined population of the ten countries covered comprises nearly one-half of the total population of sub-Saharan Africa, and their total income amounts to two-thirds of the total GNP of sSA countries. The most glaring omission in terms of types of economies covered are the francophone countries, which have their currencies tied to the French franc. Again some partial amend will be made in the concluding chapters by bringing in the evidence on real wages in these countries.

Within diversity there is uniformity, reflecting the real commonalities of most sub-Saharan countries. By and large these are rural-oriented economies (with regard to the majority of the population, if

TABLE 1.1: *Sample countries: Economic characteristics, c. 1990*

	Population, mid-1990 (million)	GNP p.c., 1990 (US$)	Share of agriculture in			Urban population as per cent of total, 1990
			Labour force, 1986–89 (av.)	GNP, 1990	Exports, 1990	
Ghana	14.9	390	59	48	64	33
Kenya	24.2	370	81	28	70	24
Lesotho	1.8	530	23[a]	24	–	20
Liberia	2.6	450[b]	74	37[b]	34	46
Nigeria	115.5	290	45	36	2	35
Sierra Leone	4.1	240	70	32	32	32
Somalia	7.8	120	76	65	94	36
Tanzania	24.5	110	86	59	84	33
Uganda	16.3	220	86	67	97	10
Zambia	8.1	420	38	17	3[c]	50
Total sSA	495.2	340	68	32	29	29

NOTE: [a] Labour force figure for Lesotho is reported to be 23, down from 92 in 1965. Definitional changes must be involved because of the migration factor. World Bank 1989, table 34 reports 86 per cent agricultural employment for 1980.

[b] From World Bank 1989b, tables 1 and 3 respectively and relates to 1987.

[c] From World Bank 1991b, table 16 and relates to 1989.

SOURCE: World Bank 1992, tables 1, 3, 16 and 31, UN 1992, table 16, for column 3, and World Bank 1989b and 1991b for Liberia and Zambia as noted.

not production), typically with 70–80 per cent of their labour force in agriculture – with the notable exceptions of Zambia and Nigeria, Lesotho being a special case of a migration economy – and around one-third of their GDP arising in that sector (see Table 1.1).

Again with the exception of oil-rich Nigeria and copper-based Zambia and possibly Liberia, agriculture in the sample countries dominates the productive sectors and contributes over two-thirds of total exports. A final indication of the rural orientation of these economies is provided by the urbanisation ratio. The sample countries – even including Nigeria – are overwhelmingly rural, with on average less than one-quarter of the population in towns (the exception provided by Zambia should be noted, however). Typically for the ten sample countries, as for most others in Africa, the largest city holds half of the urban population, with the rest spread over innumerable small towns. Germane to our theme of the rural-urban gap, rural-urban ties are strong in most of the sample countries, in the form of rural to urban food flows and urban to rural cash remittances. The former strenghtened in the 1980s, while the latter weakened because of the breakdown of urban incomes during the crisis.

Table 1.2 shows indicators of human resource development for the sampled countries. The figures are all on the low side; thus compared to industrial countries, the gap in life expectancy for sSA as a whole

TABLE 1.2: *Sample countries: Human development indicators, 1960–90*

	Life expectancy at birth (yrs.)		Under-5 mortality rate (per 1,000 live births)		Population with access to safe water (%)		Adult literacy rate (%)	
	1960	1990	1960	1990	1975–80	1988–90	1970	1990
Ghana	45.0	55.0	224	140	35	57	31	60
Kenya	44.7	59.7	208	108	17	30	32	69
Lesotho	41.6	57.3	208	129	17	48	62	73
Liberia	41.2	54.2	310	205	–	–	18	40
Nigeria	39.5	51.5	316	167	–	–	25	51
Sierra Leone	31.5	42.0	385	257	14	42	13	21
Somalia	36.0	46.1	294	215	38	37	3	24
Tanzania	40.5	54.0	249	170	39	56	–	–
Uganda	43.0	52.0	223	164	35	20	41	48
Zambia	41.6	54.4	228	122	42	59	52	73
Total sSA	40.0	51.8	284	175	27	40	27	45

SOURCE: UNDP 1992, table 4, except adult literacy rate in Lesotho which is up from UNDP 1991, table 4 and the last year relates to 1985.

was 30 points, for under-5 mortality rate 84 points, and so on across such other indicators (not shown on the table) as food supply, medical personnel, school enrolment ratios, etc. (UNDP 1992, Tables 6 and 7). The individual country figures are equally low, with Sierra Leone and Somalia standing out particularly. However one thing remarkable is that in all countries the trends were positive despite the pervading crisis. For sSA as a whole life expectancy increased by 12 years, for a gain of 30 per cent; infant mortality declined by 38 per cent; population with access to safe drinking water increased from 27 to 40 per cent, while adult literacy increased from 27 per cent to 45 per cent. As these indicators embody long-term trends, perhaps it was to be expected that they should not exhibit a downturn yet.[4] What is undoubtedly true is that there has been an erosion in social services and the impact of this may well show up in the future.

Technological data on agriculture in sub-Saharan Africa and three other developing regions are given in Table 1.3, another piece of background information for our study. The data are for 1978–80, but still provide a representative picture for the present. If anything, the difference between sSA countries and the other regions has widened, since one of the central problems of African agriculture is that it has not exhibited substantial technical change over the last decade.[5] All

TABLE 1.3: *Africa and other developing regions: Agricultural characteristics, 1978–80*

	% of economically active population in agriculture	Cultivated area (ha) per person economically active in agriculture	% of cultivated area irrigated	Tractors per 1,000 ha of cultivated area	Fertiliser consumption (kg) per ha of cultivated area	Cereal yield (kg/ha), 1975–77
Africa	69.8	1.5	1.7	1.4	8.2	850
Far East	62.8	1.0	24.8	2.0	35.1	1 700
Near East	54.0	2.5	21.4	6.6	33.0	–
Latin America	34.7	4.2	8.6	5.4	42.2	1 600

NOTE: In the first five columns, as per FAO usage, Africa includes all African countries except South Africa, and Egypt, the Libyan Arab Jamahiriya and the Sudan which are classified as Near East. In the last column the figures for Africa are for sSA only, while the figure for Far East is that reported for 'Asia' in the source. These latter figures have been read approximately from a chart.
SOURCE: FAO 1984, tables 1, 3, 7, 9 and 11, except last column which is from USDA 1981, figure 5.

indicators suggest a technologically rudimentary method of cultivation. With regard to land–labour ratios, African agriculture is much more labour-intensive compared to Latin America and the Near East, but certainly not compared to the Far East. Other indicators are strikingly low: the proportion of area irrigated (1.7 per cent, compared to over 20 per cent for the Far and Near East); tractors per 1,000 hectares of land (1.4, compared to 2 in the Far East, the next lowest figure); and fertiliser (8.2 kilogrammes per hectare, with all other regions over 30). The consequence is that yields are low – for cereals (basic staples) around 850 kilogrammes per hectare, compared to twice as much in Latin America and Asia. Even for roots and tubers yields lag behind Asian countries. Moreover, for both these types of crops, as well as pulses, yields in African countries have been stagnating whereas in Asia they have increased perceptibly.

The implications of the technological state of African agriculture for incomes are obviously quite important. With acreage and yields limited, most African farmers have to expend the bulk of on-farm effort to procuring sufficient food for the household. It is the otherwise unused resources that are devoted to growing export crops – which in Africa are not domestically consumed – such as cotton, coffee, cocoa, tea, etc. Food crops and export crops are typically grown on the same farms, and often on the same plot of land (which partly explains low yields). The limited degree of specialisation is in great part a survival strategy of the small farmer, who tries to ensure that at least some crops reach maturity. If and when a surplus arises – of food crops as well as export crops – farm households bring it to the market, the size of the surplus being more a function of the weather than product prices. Cash income generated from sale of food is relatively minor in the aggregate income of farmers compared to export-crop income, and both together are a small part of farmers' total 'income' including 'auto-consumption'. Obviously, it is cash income which determines the rural household's demand for urban commodities – sugar, salt, tea and spices, as well as luxuries such as beer and cigarettes. But at the low level of yield and income characterising African agriculture, any proper accounting of total income would find the highest proportion to comprise non-marketed own-farm consumption ('subsistence production').[6] This part of farm income remains immune from inflation and goes far in explaining the survival of African rural households despite the ravages of the current depression, a point pursued in the case studies and more generally in Chapter 8.

2 Economic Crisis in Africa

The dramatic shifts in income distribution in sub-Saharan countries which are documented and analysed in this book have not occurred by accident. They are the direct consequence of a profound and in some cases catastrophic economic depression. This economic depression, we would argue, has been largely the result of changes in world commodity and financial markets beyond the control of the governments of sub-Saharan countries. Since they play their part throughout our discussion, we begin our analysis by briefly considering the economic trends of the last decade and their sharp contrast to the decade before. Here, as throughout this volume, our objective will be to scrutinise the stereotypic explanation of the African crisis.

The thrust of the conventional wisdom about the crisis is that development strategies followed in the decade after independence were misguided and resulted in huge 'factor price distortions' (e.g. subsidised interest rates, overpriced labour, underpriced crops, overvalued exchange rates), and a debilitating deadweight of inefficiency.[1] The economic difficulties suffered in the last decade are explained as these misguided policies coming home to roost.[2] In this accounting, the successful growth in the halcyon days of the 1960s is seen to be spurious, for it carried the seeds of self-destruction and was based upon gross inefficiencies. In our view the successes of the development effort during the 1960s, particularly in comparison to subsequent years, should not be dismissed so lightly.[3]

Table 2.1 brings out the sharp decline in the rate of growth of sub-Saharan African countries after the first oil shock of 1973–74.[4] For purposes of comparison, it also includes the average rates for all less developed countries and for Asia and Latin America. The African growth record is particularly poor compared to all other low income countries (i.e. excluding African countries). However, a substantial part of the difference in growth rates is attributable to the rapid growth of China, which accounts for almost half the population of non-African low-income countries.

In the years preceding the oil price boom, sSA countries performed quite satisfactorily, achieving between 1965 and 1973 an increase in per capita income of around 25 per cent. All this gain however was

TABLE 2.1: *sSa and others: Rate of growth of GNP per capita, 1965–89* (per cent per annum)

	1965–73	1973–80	1980–86	1987	1988	1989
Sub-Saharan Africa	3.0	0.1	–2.8	–4.4	–0.3	0.5
All LDCs	4.0	2.6	1.5	2.7	3.4	1.2
Low-Income LDCs	3.6	2.4	4.0	3.9	6.8	1.8
East Asia	5.4	4.4	6.6	8.0	8.7	3.1
South Asia	1.0	2.0	3.2	0.9	6.1	2.3
Latin America and the Caribbean	4.1	2.4	–1.6	1.5	–0.8	0.8

SOURCE: World Bank 1990c, table A.2, p. 160.

wiped out in the next 16 years – and the prospects are no brighter.[5] In the meantime South Asian incomes grew almost continuously between 1965 and 1988, by around two-thirds, while East Asian incomes more than tripled. Latin America and the Caribbean region, despite faltering growth in the early 1980s, still managed to register an increase in income of 50 per cent.

The main difference between growth during 1965–73 and subsequently was in the performance of manufacturing in sSA countries. In the 1960s and early 1970s, the industrial sector grew much faster than agriculture or services. Both before (1965–73) and after (1973–80) the oil shock, the agricultural sector grew at slightly over 2 per cent per annum, while the industrial sector expanded at 8 per cent in the earlier period but barely over 1 per cent in the latter. Since 1980, the industrial sector has actually contracted, while agriculture and services grew at slightly over 1 per cent annually.[6] In consequence, the share of industry in sub-Saharan African GNP fell from a high of 19 per cent in 1973 to 16 per cent in 1984.[7] Thus, the stagnation and decline of industry in Africa has been on going for a sufficiently long time to qualify it as a medium-term tendency verging on the long-term.

The persistent and extended decline in industrial growth is pointed out to let events cast their shadow before them. Later in the book we shall consider 'stabilisation' and 'structural adjustment' programmes prescribed for several countries by the International Monetary Fund and the World Bank, designed to shift fundamental sectoral priorities, primarily from industry to agriculture. Such a shift has in fact already occurred – with disastrous consequences for the urban population. The sSA countries have been de-industrialising for the last decade and more, and while it is debatable whether this has brought about a more efficient allocation of resources, it certainly has not generated growth; on the contrary, it has been a symptom of the general decline undergone by African countries.

With per capita income falling, it is not surprising that savings and investment have fallen as a proportion of GNP and that consumption has risen (Table 2.2). Interpretation of the table, however, shows the degree to which economics is an inexact science, for one can come away from these figures with two diametrically opposite conclusions. If one is influenced by the Keynesian tradition, the story is straightforward: assuming the short-run consumption function to have an income elasticity of less than unity, one would expect the share of consumption to rise as per capita income fell. Indeed, many economists would interpret Table 2.2 as verifying by and large an empirical law of macroeconomics which holds generally, regardless of the level of economic development. The corollary of the law is that in the short run the consumption share will fall and savings share rise as growth begins to accelerate. In contrast, the observer viewing the table through classical spectacles would come to quite a different conclusion: the savings effort has deteriorated in recent years and steps must be taken to stimulate it if growth is to recommence.[8]

In our view the pre-Keynesian prescription that the savings rate must be raised to stimulate growth (and the implicit diagnosis that slow growth is partly caused by a low savings ratio) is singularly inappropriate for the sub-Saharan African countries, which are primarily agricultural and almost exclusively smallholder-oriented. Investment is largely a function of household income, and as long as incomes remain depressed – in 1989 around 20 per cent below the level of 1973 – it is unrealistic to expect that government policies could be deployed to increase savings and investment, for this would have to be at the expense of further depressing consumption levels.

TABLE 2.2: *sSA: Consumption, investment and savings as percentage of GDP, 1965–88* (selected years)

	1965	1973	1980	1985	1986	1987	1988
Consumption	84.0	79.1	78.6	87.8	89.0	85.5	85.0
Investment	14.3	18.3	20.5	12.2	14.6	15.4	15.4
Savings	13.8	16.9	18.2	8.8	6.7	8.1	8.3

SOURCE: World Bank 1990c, table A.7, p. 163. The figures relate to all sub-Saharan countries, low- and middle-income.

Of course, the more important point is that most of the sSA countries are driven not by investment ratios but by the world demand for primary products.[9] As Table 2.3 shows, export performance has deteriorated sharply over the last 15 years. In the eight years prior to that (1965–73), primary product exports grew at the staggering rate of 15.4 per cent per annum in real terms, but then stagnated for the next seven years, followed by eight years of negative growth rates.

The conventional explanation for the alleged poor export performance apportions blame to the policies of sub-Saharan countries, with overvalued exchange rates and monopsonistic marketing boards which set export crop prices coming in for particular criticism.[10] Short of conducting a country-specific general equilibrium simulation analysis, it would be impossible to adjudge the relative impact of internal and external factors on the export performance of sub-Saharan countries (though this has not prevented some from doing so[11]). The fact that Africa's share in world and developing country exports fell (Svedberg 1991) does show that given the same external markets Africa performed worse than other continents, but still this was under conditions of declining terms of trade (Table 2.3). Already between 1965 and 1973 sSA's terms halved, meaning that the sub-Saharan countries had to give up twice as big a bundle of exports to buy the same import basket. Despite some improvement between

TABLE 2.3: *sSA and others: Rate of growth of export volume and terms of trade, 1965–88* (per cent per annum)

	1965–73	1973–80	1980–86	1986	1987	1988
Exports						
sub-Saharan Africa						
Manufactures	7.6	5.6	4.8	2.9	4.3	5.3
Primary products	15.4	0.0	–2.5	–0.4	–2.3	0.8
All products	15.1	0.2	–2.0	–0.1	–1.8	1.2
All LDCs, all product	5.3	3.8	4.8	5.9	7.4	7.3
Terms of trade						
sub-Saharan Africa	–8.5	4.8	–4.0	–21.5	2.9	–4.4
East Asia	–0.6	1.2	–1.3	–6.1	0.5	1.1
South Asia	3.7	–3.4	1.5	3.1	1.2	2.0
Latin America and the Caribbean	3.8	2.3	–3.3	–14.0	–2.3	1.7
All LDCs	0.1	2.5	–2.7	–10.9	2.3	–0.2

SOURCE: World Bank 1990c, tables A.8 and A.9.

1973 and 1980 sSA's terms registered a decline of 60 per cent between 1965 and 1988. As Table 2.3 also shows, no other developing region suffered similarly. The massive decline in the command over imports and the resulting disruption to the development process can only be wondered at. It is equally pertinent to note that the unit value of exports declined in the 1980s, i.e. export prices in nominal terms fell.[12] Given these trends, not blaming the external environment for Africa's problems is something that has to be explained. In a study of changes in the world economy Cline (1983) had come to the conclusion that almost 85 per cent of the total increase in developing country debt during 1973–82 could be attributed to external factors over which governments of non-oil-producing LDCs had no control.[13] In this respect it is once again worth reiterating that the fall in the terms of trade of sub-Saharan countries was considerably more than for developing countries taken together and in particular for low-income Asian countries.[14]

A bit of simple economic theory tells one that it is hardly surprising that export performance should decline with the deterioration of the terms of trade. Falling export prices shift relative returns in favour of production for the domestic market. Those who have tended to blame internal policies for poor export performance in Africa have usually glossed over this imperative facing the African countries.[15] Instead they have put the major part of the blame on the internal (domestic) terms of trade – i.e. what the farmers receive for their produce on the internal market – with the implicit assertion that internal terms fell more than the external, causing a greater fall in exports than would have occurred under free market conditions. Again, how the blame should be apportioned is a matter for country-by-country analysis – something that has generally not been done by proponents of 'African mismanagement'. Instead the remedy is rather swiftly suggested that African countries should devalue to restore the shift in the terms of trade. It is rarely specified whether the prescribed devaluation is to align internal terms of trade to the external terms, or more drastically, to restore internal terms to a level of the past, regardless of trends on the external market.[16]

Any policy recommendations require recognition that there is considerable theoretical ambiguity with regard to the net impact of devaluation upon the relative prices of tradeables and non-tradeables.[17] Given this, one must be careful in diagnosing that the fault for poor growth performance in African countries lies primarily in domestic policies, and that success awaits a greater opening to the world economy.[18] This type of recommendation is particularly problematical viewed against growing protectionism in developed countries. Basic neoclassical trade theory teaches that under certain circumstances welfare gains are obtained by compensatory retaliation to protectionist measures taken by trading partners. On balance the agnostic view taken by Todaro in his influential textbook on development, that macro-economic difficulties of some developing countries may be the result of too much contact with developed countries, should not be dismissed lightly (Todaro 1985, p. 558).

We cannot here resolve the debate over the causes of the deteriorating growth performance of African countries, but do argue that what the statistics show are the symptoms of economic decline and not its cause. Over the last decade and a half (and longer for some countries), the sSA region has been in a profound crisis that has brought fundamental structural and distributional changes. A voluntarist approach in which one presumes that the crisis could have been substantially avoided had appropriate policies been followed is not conducive to a diagnostic analysis of what actually occurred.

Up to this point the survey of the 'underdevelopment period' has been highly aggregative. Table 2.4 takes a more detailed look at the principal economic indicators for the ten sample countries as well as selected others in the sub-Saharan region. Our objectives here are first to verify whether the broad trends summarised in Tables 2.1–3 are confirmed by country-level data; and second, to draw out any correlation with policy regimes followed or the degree of openness of the economies. The overall message is that the poor economic performance summarised in the previous tables was indeed shared uniformly by the individual countries listed, regardless of their policy orientation. Not a single country for which data are available enjoyed a positive balance of payments in the 1980s. Kenya had a relative deficit in the 1980s of the same magnitude as Sierra Leone and Tanzania, although Kenya pursued an import substitution policy, whereas Sierra Leone did not, and Kenya followed more market-oriented policies whereas Tanzania did not. Malawi and Côte d'Ivoire, often held up as even greater paragons of liberalism than Kenya, had even larger balance of payments deficits than some of the more 'shut' economies shown in the table. Indeed, scanning the table, the conclusion emerges strongly that balance of payments pressures befell countries indiscriminately.

Growth performance, too, was depressingly similar. Of the 17

TABLE 2.4: *Sample countries: Principal economic indicators (also selected sSA countries), 1965–88*

	CAB (% GNP)	Rate of growth (per cent per annum)					
		GDP		Agriculture		Industry	
	1980–88	1965–80	1980–90	1965–80	1980–90	1965–80	1980–90
Ghana	−5.1	1.3	3.0	1.6	1.0	1.4	3.3
Kenya	−7.0	6.8	4.2	5.0	3.3	9.7	3.9
Lesotho	n.a.	6.8	3.1	n.a.	−0.7	n.a.	2.9
Liberia	−8.1	3.3	−1.3	5.5	1.2	2.2	−6.0
Nigeria	−1.6	6.0	1.4	1.7	3.3	13.1	−1.2
Sierra Leone	−6.3	2.7	1.5	3.9	2.6	−0.8	−1.5
Somalia	n.a.	3.5	2.4	n.a.	3.3	n.a.	1.0
Tanzania	−8.8	3.9	2.8	1.6	4.1	4.2	0.0
Uganda	n.a.	0.6	2.8	1.2	2.5	−4.3	5.5
Zambia	−14.0	2.0	0.8	2.2	3.7	2.1	0.7
Ethiopia*	−7.1	2.7	1.8	1.2	−0.1	3.5	2.9
Zaire	−9.8	1.9	1.8	n.a.	2.5	n.a.	2.3
Malawi	−11.1	5.5	2.9	4.1	2.0	6.4	3.0
Senegal	−15.8	2.3	3.0	1.4	3.1	5.5	3.5
Côte d'Ivoire	−11.5	6.8	0.5	3.3	1.0	10.4	0.3
Zimbabwe	n.a.	5.0	2.9	n.a.	2.4	n.a.	2.4
Cameroon	−4.7	5.1	2.3	4.2	1.6	7.8	3.1

NOTES: CAB = Balance on the current external account.
* Beginning with Ethiopia, countries are listed in reverse order by per capita income according to World Bank estimates.
SOURCE: World Bank 1990c, tables A.11 for column 1 and World Bank 1992, table 2 for the rest, except Liberia which is from World Bank 1990c, table 2 and 1980–90 refers to 1980–88 only.

countries listed, 14 grew slower during 1980–90 than during 1965–80. Open economies based upon mining exports did particularly poorly – e.g., Nigeria, Sierra Leone, Liberia, Zambia and Zaire. Since the poor growth rate of the Ugandan and Ghanaian economies can be largely attributed to political turmoil, it would be more correct to say that a majority of the low growth rates went to mineral-exporting countries.

For 13 countries, growth rates for agriculture and industry are available for both periods. In eight cases the rate of growth in agriculture was lower during the 1980s than in the earlier period, the exceptions being Nigeria, Tanzania, Uganda, Zambia and Senegal. No policy-related pattern emerges here either; certainly, none exists to suggest that countries with state marketing boards performed worse than those without. As for industrial growth, for ten of the 13 countries growth was slower in the second period, again with no obvious link to the degree of protectionism or flexibility in the exchange rate regime. More instructively, in five of the 17 countries, industrial growth was negative in the second period, or nearly so, whereas there were only two such cases in the earlier period. The overall impression is of a region sunk in a pervasive crisis of stagnation and decline, and whether any particular set of policies proved more effective than others in moderating or accentuating the external factors is an empirical question that could be settled only through country-level investigation. Even then it is doubtful whether any general conclusion could be reached given the ever-present importance of exogenous factors in these types of economies – climate, political unrest, terms of trade.

TABLE 2.5: *Sample countries: Growth of exports, imports, and per capita food production (also selected sSA countries), 1965–90* (percentage per annum)

	Exports			Imports			Per capita food production		
	1965–73	1973–84	1980–90	1965–73	1973–84	1980–90	1976–80	1981–85	1986–89
Ghana	3.5	–4.0	3.8	–3.3	–7.4	–0.1	–5.7	7.1	–4.3
Kenya	3.8	–2.3	1.0	5.9	–1.7	1.6	–3.5	–0.2	1.3
Nigeria	8.8	–6.5	–1.6	8.7	10.1	–15.1	–0.9	0.7	–1.7
Lesotho	–	–	–	–	–	–	1.1	–2.8	–4.3
Liberia	8.9	2.3	–2.7	3.7	–5.1	–2.2	–0.9	0.3	–2.0
Sierra Leone	3.7	–5.5	–1.4	1.0	–6.8	–2.3	–1.3	–1.8	–1.9
Somalia	5.7	–0.7	–3.3	5.1	5.9	–4.3	–2.9	–0.6	0.2
Tanzania	0.9	–4.7	–7.4	7.1	–4.3	–0.5	1.1	–0.7	–1.6
Uganda	0.2	–6.2	–1.9	–2.5	2.2	3.2	–5.1	–2.6	–1.8
Zambia	–0.3	–2.4	–3.2	3.0	–7.9	–4.5	–4.1	–1.8	–0.6
Ethiopia	2.9	0.4	0.3	–0.2	4.6	4.2	0.5	–2.1	0.1
Zaire	6.4	4.1	–11.2	9.4	–4.5	–4.0	–1.8	–0.4	–1.8
Malawi	3.8	2.4	4.3	6.4	–1.5	0.7	0.3	–2.0	–1.0
Senegal	–1.3	–0.8	5.6	5.6	–1.2	4.6	–11.7	4.9	0.6
Côte d'Ivoire	6.9	–2.2	2.7	8.0	–1.7	–1.2	2.3	–0.4	0.6
Zimbabwe	–	–	3.1	–	–	–7.4	–4.7	4.2	–4.1
Cameroon	4.2	2.3	–1.3	6.3	3.9	–3.3	–3.1	–0.5	–0.3

SOURCE: World Bank 1986b, table 9 for columns 1, 2, 4 and 5; and World Bank 19921b, table 14 for columns 3 and 6 (Zambia and Zimbabwe from the corresponding 1991 report, table 14 and relate to 1980–89). Rest of the figures from UN 1990, table IX.17.

To complete our summary of the 'lost development decades', we consider performance in exports, imports and food production in the ten sample countries and seven others (Table 2.5). Several characteristics of the economic crisis in sSA countries come through from this table. First, there was a general decline in export performance. Of the 15 countries for which comparable data are available, real export growth was negative for only two during 1965–73, whereas it was negative for as many as 11 during 1973–84 and remained so for nine during 1980–90. Further, while sub-Saharan countries had a considerably better export performance than all low-income countries in the earlier period they fared considerably worse subsequently.[19] Statistics on food production provide another proof of the lack of correlation between policies and performance.

If one is to stress the wisdom of government policies as an important explanation of relative export performance, then the sub-Saharan governments must have been doing something right during 1965–73 and something drastically wrong subsequently. We find this type of explanation rather tautological, particularly when no one had documented a profound policy shift sweeping the sub-Saharan region during the 1970s. A more compelling explanation is provided by changes in the terms of trade: while the sSA countries enjoyed more or less constant terms of trade during 1965–70, they suffered relatively huge declines in the subsequent years. The fall was much greater than for other less developed countries taken together (refer back to Table 2.3).

Second, during the economic crisis of the last 15 years, governments of sub-Saharan countries have been successful in reducing imports, though this has done little to relieve balance of payments pressures. Indeed, the economies of sSA countries have not been particularly import-intensive for at least two decades. During 1965–73, imports grew in real terms at 4.4 per cent. While this was above the rate for low-income countries, it was below the rate of growth of GNP of sSA countries. Many are the governments of developing countries that would look enviously upon an import elasticity of less than unity. And it is not altogether justified to attribute the decline in imports to government policy. Simple Keynesian open-economy analysis tells one that imports are in part a function of the level of national income, so the import decline might be a symptom of stagnation rather than a consequence of conscious policy. Further, in the African context imports are a function of that part of the national income partly generated by exports. Exports have been falling, so have imports.

These points are consistent with our view that economies of sub-Saharan African countries should be analysed as being buffeted over the last decade by forces largely beyond the control of policy-makers.

To conclude our survey of the lost development decades, we turn to an issue which will loom large in subsequent discussion – rural-urban migration. Rates of growth of urban areas are given in Table 2.6, where we see a slight increase in the regional average rate of urban growth during 1980–90 compared to the previous period. Disaggregating, we find that for six countries the rate of migration increased, while for 11 it declined. Even for those countries where the *rate* of migration declined, the *absolute* number of migrants increased, since migration was occurring from a much larger urban base; least of all was there any question of reverse migration. The continuing urbanisation in the face of a dramatic fall in rural-urban income differentials implies that the relationships between the two was tenuous at most.

TABLE 2.6: *Sample countries: Rate of growth of urban population (also selected sSA countries), 1965–80 and 1980–90* (percentage per annum)

	1965–80	1980–90	Direction of change
Ghana	3.2	4.2	+
Kenya	8.1	7.9	–
Lesotho	7.5	7.0	–
Liberia	6.2	6.1	–
Nigeria	5.7	6.0	+
Sierra Leone	5.2	5.3	+
Somalia	5.4	5.6	+
Tanzania	11.3	10.5	–
Uganda	4.8	4.4	–
Zambia	6.6	6.2	–
Ethiopia	4.9	5.3	+
Zaire	4.9	4.8	–
Malawi	7.4	6.2	–
Senegal	3.3	4.0	+
Côte d'Ivoire	7.6	4.5	–
Zimbabwe	6.0	5.9	–
Cameroon	7.6	5.9	–
All sSA	5.8	5.9	+
All low-income*	3.7	6.6	+

* Low- and middle-income LDCs.
SOURCE: World Bank 1992, table 31.

The last almost two decades have been difficult ones for the populations of sub-Saharan countries, years of hardship and increasing poverty. It has been suggested in some quarters that the hardship and suffering were primarily the consequence of incorrect policy decisions taken in response to what was euphemistically called 'a rapidly changing world economy' (World Bank 1986b, p. 2). The obverse of this is that pursuing 'correct policies' promises a bright future regardless of developments in the international economy.[20] Five years later, in the *World Development Report, 1991*, a 'new consensus' was proclaimed in favour of a 'market-friendly approach to development', involving openness to international trade.[21] UNDP's *Human Development Report* of the same year joined the consensus, viewing, as Brewster (1991) points out in a review:

> the economic misery of the Third World . . . as almost wholly self-inflicted and thus also amenable to self-correction by raising the percentage of national income devoted to human priority concerns . . . [I]nternational policy has been virtually entirely absolved of any responsibility for the parlous state into which the developing countries have fallen.

The 'correct-policies' hypothesis is attractive, particularly in difficult times when circumstances may make one's best efforts irrelevant.[22] It remains, however, a hypothesis – and moreover a hypothesis at variance with the miserable economic performance of most sub-Saharan countries, many of which by 1993 had undergone nearly a decade of strict market-oriented programmes. We find it less than convincing for two reasons. First, if there exists a set of policies whose unambiguous result would be to generate growth in the face of unfavourable would market conditions, economists do not agree on what it is. The hypothesis that appropriate policies can snatch growth from the jaws of world recession derives from a general equilibrium model in which the world economy is viewed as being self-equilibrating. Whether governments should place the fate of their populations on such models is open to question, particularly when the economics profession is hardly in agreement on their validity. This lack of agreement should be a cue for reticence on the part of economists in passing judgement upon the efforts of governments of developing countries. Certainly, African governments have made policy errors, perhaps major ones. Whether alternative policies would have produced substantially different results is the type of speculation which does not lend itself to definitive conclusions.

Second, while the impact of alternative policy regimes is speculative, the extremely unfavourable international environment faced by sSA governments is a fact. Terms of trade have moved against products exported by African countries;[23] interest rates on world financial markets reached virtually unprecedented levels for a decade starting in the mid-1970s (largely due to fiscal and monetary policies in the United States); and industrial country protectionism has thwarted the development of non-agricultural exports from sub-Saharan Africa. These facts suggest that the cautious path is to avoid judgemental hypotheses and treat the phenomenon of rural-urban income differentials on the presumption that their change reflects in great part a general process of economic stagnation and decline in sub-Saharan Africa, mostly arising from instabilities in the world economy. While the manifestation of these forces has varied in each country, their effect has been to plunge nations into a deep and pervasive crisis. Out of this crisis have emerged profound changes in rural-urban interactions.

3 The Accepted Orthodoxy

As shown in the previous chapter, changes in the international economic environment have had dramatic effects upon the economies of sub-Saharan Africa, particularly since the oil price increases of 1973–74, which coincided with the start of the second decade of independence for most sSA countries. In the immediate post-independence decade a certain characterisation of the region emerged in the literature on development and economic policy. Central to this characterisation was the view that these societies exhibited wide differentials in living standards between town and countryside, and that to a large extent the privileged position of the towns resulted in the impoverishment of the countryside. In this chapter we argue that such a characterisation of sub-Saharan countries was misleadingly simplistic in the past and is now no longer valid. However great the past rural-urban inequality, the last 15 years (and longer in some countries) have caused a dramatic compression of the gap between town and countryside. This compression has a number of important implications for economic policy, particularly with respect to the standard 'structural adjustment programmes' now being applied in Africa.

The hypothesis that the growth of industry and capitalist development in general tends to be at the expense of the peasants and creates an élite of urban dwellers whose privileges are based upon artificial wealth ('hot-house industry') is far from new in the literature of economics. The physiocrats believed this in the eighteenth century, arguing that only agriculture generates a surplus and all secondary and tertiary industries merely transform products without enhancing their value.[1] In the same tradition, Sismondi argued that the growth of industry tended to impoverish society, generating technological unemployment and turning the terms of trade against agriculture.[2] By the middle of the nineteenth century the obvious dynamism of industry had relegated these theories to the realm of romantic criticism of capitalistic development. Whether neo-Sismondism has been relevant for the countries of sub-Saharan Africa during the last two decades is open to question.

THE POST-COLONIAL PATTERN OF DEVELOPMENT

In the 1960s there emerged what we shall call 'the post-colonial pattern of development', which at the risk of some over-simplification can be said to have characterised most of the African countries south of the Sahara. The modifier 'post-colonial' is used not only to refer to a particular historical period, but even more to a specific social phenomenon, decolonialisation. Decolonialisation manifested itself in all aspects of life in African countries, not excluding the economy and economic policy. Many aspects of rural-urban inequality in these countries were and continue to be closely linked to the period of decolonisation.

In only a few African countries was the struggle for independence from colonial masters a violent one in which European rule was ended by insurrection. However, in all countries there was political agitation for independence, based upon a national coalition of regional, ethnic and class diversity. Political differences along economic and social lines were obscured by the dichotomy between Europeans (including settlers in some countries – e.g. Kenya and Zimbabwe) and Africans, with Asians (almost always as traders) assuming an intermediate position in some countries. Correspondingly, divisions in wealth presented themselves as divisions between the privileged Europeans and the impoverished African population. The dichotomy incorporated a stark contrast between the wealth of the cities – particularly cities like Nairobi and Salisbury – and the poverty of the population in the countryside. This rural-urban division was of course only an aspect of foreign domination, not 'urban bias' as such.

With independence there followed a process of 'Africanisation', the replacement of Europeans (and Asians) with Black nationals[3] in the civil service, the universities, and, increasingly, in the private sector. In some countries, e.g. Ghana and Tanzania, colonial salary scales, which had incorporated enormous pay differentials between Europeans, Asians and Africans, were compressed. But everywhere the difference between what an unskilled labourer earned and the salaries of professionals and managers remained great. Further, in the absence of a landed élite in most African countries,[4] persons earning high incomes, comparable to salaries in the former colonial centres, were concentrated in the major cities, often overwhelmingly in the capitals. In essence, the great income differences passed down as a colonial legacy changed appearance from an African/European dichotomy to a rural-urban one.[5] The rural-urban division from this perspective was not the creation of the post-independence period; rather, its ethnic character changed and so did its perception.

Central to this new perception of inequality were the wage earners, concentrated in urban areas in most African countries. Trade unions played a prominent role in pressuring for independence, though few union leaders came to lead governments. Once independence was granted, workers' organisations represented a vocal interest group, particularly in the more urbanised countries, such as Zambia, Ghana and Nigeria. With their prestige high and influence at a peak, trade unions were able to win substantial wage increases, in most cases during the immediate post-independence period.[6] Although the power of unions to influence real wages was exaggerated,[7] it did enhance the perception of a fundamental division in privilege and wealth between town and countryside. Part of this mythology was the belief that wage earners were grossly overpaid both in terms of labour market conditions and compared to earnings in the countryside.[8] In most cases the basic arithmetic to support such assertions had not been done.

The rural-urban division also seemed to be reflected in the development orientation of the post-colonial governments. With rare exceptions, the colonial masters had not encouraged the growth of industry in the territories they occupied. As both an economic strategy and a nationalistic desire to redress arrested development, the new governments embarked upon programmes of import substitution and large-scale public and social works such as roads, schools, hospitals, etc. By their nature, these projects tended either to be located in urban areas or to have their benefits concentrated there. Even public works located in rural areas, such as the Niger Dam in Nigeria, drew their labour force from urban areas for the most part and thus benefited the urban populations.

The particular way in which these development programmes were financed also contributed to the interpretation that the rural-urban division was primary for considering questions of wealth and income distribution, and brought out the neo-Sismondi tendencies in commentators. Most governments derived a large proportion of their revenues from the taxation of agriculture, directly through state marketing boards that held producer prices below world prices, or via export taxes (see Hesp and van der Laan 1985). Similarly for the food crops, too, producer prices were held down through various forms of control. In consequence, it seemed the case that urban industry was being financed at the cost of an undifferentiated rural population.

Since the State dominated the formal employment sector in most African countries and the state wage bill was funded in great part by taxes on agriculture, it could plausibly be inferred that peasants were paying for the perceived privileges of the working class in the public sector. Moreover, it was commonly argued that the dominance of the State in the labour market made it a wage leader throughout the economy, so that one could infer that private sector wage earners, too, benefited at the expense of the peasantry.[9] Interestingly enough, this judgement that wage earners represented a privileged and perhaps parasitic class was endorsed by observers across the political spectrum.[10] For neoclassical economists, it fitted well into their anti-wage-labour bias and their simplistic models which said that if labour markets did not 'clear' then workers were too highly paid. On the left, the failure of African independence movements for the most part to adopt a revolutionary ideology was attributed to the relatively privileged position of the working class – an 'aristocracy of labour'.[11]

This characterisation of sub-Saharan Africa persists to this day. It created in the minds of most academic observers and policy-makers, national and foreign, a certain stylised picture of the typical African country. The inequality between urban and rural areas was the centerpiece of this picture: the typical sSA country was divided starkly between a privileged modern sector (later, 'formal' sector), where urban élites and wage earners enjoyed high living and subsidised services, and a vast, undifferentiated peasantry that lived in poverty and largely produced the wealth to finance urban dwellers' privileges. Between the two, as the 1960s drew to a close, was noticed a growing population of urban squatters, caught in increasingly miserable conditions around cities, drawn by the magnet of 'bright lights' and high wages.[12] This epitomising of capitalist development in sSA countries as profoundly distorted would have been endorsed by the physiocrats and Sismondi.

For the neoclassically minded, the perceived rural-urban inequality was symptomatic and in great part the root cause of a general malaise of development, being contrary to the dictates of the market. The high and increasing real urban wage militated against the dictates of growth according to the famous Lewis model in which the modern sector enters upon the virtuous path of development by drawing down an unlimited supply of labour at a constant subsistence-level wage.[13] To cope with increasing wages modern industries in sub-Saharan Africa had to be protected against cheaper imports by tariffs and quotas; this represented inefficiency *par excellence*. Working with a model of general equilibrium in which implicitly there was no switching of techniques, neoclassical economists had a particular story to tell. Protectionist measures resulted in rendering enterprises profitable which otherwise would not have existed. If one invoked all of the assumptions necessary to apply the Heckscher–Ohlin–Samuelson trade model,[14] it followed that the protected enterprises used excessively capital-intensive techniques. Further, minimum wage laws that held urban wage levels 'artificially' high and legislation that protected workers on the job (e.g. from arbitrary dismissal) tended to foster even greater capital-intensity – so the argument went.[15]

The non-neoclassical observers had a similar story to tell, though from different premises. Here, too, rural-urban inequality played a central role, though unlike neoclassical theory, more emphasis was laid upon the distribution of income between élite and non-élite groups. In an analysis that had considerable affinity to the Latin American 'dependency' literature, it was argued that development in sub-Saharan African countries was 'inappropriate', particularly in terms of the technologies employed in the modern ('formal') sector: technology and factor proportions tended to be specific to products. The poor consumed labour-intensive products while the élites consumed capital-intensive products of Western origin.[16] Because development policy in sSA countries tended to generate a more unequal distribution of income, it necessarily resulted in inappropriate, capital-intensive technologies.[17] Those of the 'inappropriate technology' school thus agreed with the neoclassicists that wrong techniques were being used, but argued that no set of relative factor prices would put the matter right.

Thus, wage earners in sSA countries were seen as occupying a position of privilege within an enclave which was essentially alien to the countries in question. In manufacturing, these wage earners were described as working in modern, high-technology plants, earning far above average rural incomes, and enjoying legislative protection that virtually ensured them employment for life.[18] Referring to Kenya, one writer concluded, '. . . the trend towards the formalisation of employment relationships seems to be an inevitable consequence of having exclusive, relatively affluent enclaves in an otherwise poor agricultural economy.' The social cost of this was 'rising unemployment outside the factory gates' (Henley 1973, p. 589). Despite the lack of empirical studies, most observers concluded that the gap between wage earners and farmers was substantial.[19] Evidence suggesting that the relationship between wage incomes and farm incomes might be less than straightforward had little impact on the evolving orthodoxy.[20] Turner probably summed up the view of a generation of observers of the African scene when he wrote:

> Comparative studies in underdeveloped countries usually show the average real wage for workers outside of agriculture of two to three times [the] family income in the traditional sector. The calculations . . . add an indication that recently this differential between wage earners and traditional cultivators appears to have been widening pretty fast. (Turner 1966, p. 13)

Closely related to the judgement that urban workers were overpaid was the view that high pay provided a powerful 'pull' force to potential migrants. At the same time, these high wages (along with legislation restricting the employers' power to fire workers) induced greater capital-intensity in production that restricted the growth of wage employment. In the 1960s and early 1970s one saw a flood of articles attempting to document rapid modern sector output growth with little increase in employment.[21]

FORMALISING OF THE ORTHODOX VIEW

When the obvious link between urban wages and labour migration was made, virtually all emphasis on rural-urban inequality focused upon one aspect of that inequality – the differential between the living standard of the urban wage earner and the potential rural migrant. At least in the economic literature the stark inequalities within urban areas received little attention. The crucial 'price distortion' in sub-Saharan African countries was the unskilled urban wage. If not the cause of all imbalances in the economy, it came to be viewed as at least the most fundamental distortion. On the production side it induced capital-intensive techniques, which were inefficient in and of themselves and retarded the growth of employment, while on the other side of the labour market, it was the main cause of excessive rural-to-urban migration,[22] which provoked a variety of ills. It drained agriculture of the cream of its labour force, while in the urban areas it forced governments to divert resources into services such as health, sanitation and schooling.

Once this stylisation of the sSA countries became conventional wisdom and the urban unskilled wage was seen as the crucial distortion, the Todaro model of rural-urban migration was indeed an idea whose time had come (Todaro 1969 and 1971). It epitomised and encapsulated the impressions of a generation of development practitioners. The Todaro model itself represented a significant advance upon the Lewis-type labour-surplus models which were in vogue up to then. However, its more sophisticated aspects and insights were lost in a superficial application of the model which bordered on vulgarisation. The anti-wage-labour and anti-urban critique of the post-colonial pattern of development reached its fullest expression in the Todaro model. The flow of migrants from rural to urban areas was determined by the ratio of expected urban income to expected rural income.[23] The latter was in effect assumed to be constant and the former to be determined by the prevailing urban wage and the probability of obtaining employment at that wage. Under appropriate assumptions, the expected urban wage was simply the prevailing wage discounted by 'the rate of unemployment' in urban areas.[24]

It followed that increasing the rate of growth of employment in the modern sector would not necessarily reduce the rate of unemployment, except in the short run. For were employment to expand and unemployment to drop, the probability of obtaining a job would rise (assuming random selection) and call forth further migration. Other things being equal, a given actual differential between urban wage earnings and rural income would be associated with a unique rate of urban unemployment: the rate of urban unemployment equilibrates the model, and employment-expanding policies are self-defeating as long as the degree of rural-urban income inequality does not change. The conclusion of the model was that urban unemployment in Africa can only be reduced by raising rural incomes.

This over-simplified interpretation of the Todaro model captured the attention of academics and policy-makers in less developed countries in much the same way as the equally simple Phillips curve did in advanced market economies. It seemed to explain a complex and massive problem – the explosive growth of cities – in terms of two easily understood variables, a short-cut, as it were, around the difficult analysis of the urban migration phenomenon. It was not without its critics, but our interest is more in the way it encapsulated a certain conventional wisdom rather than its theoretical strengths or weaknesses. Accepting the model as the true explanation of rural-urban migration required considerable 'willing suspension of disbelief', to use Coleridge's phrase referring to the pleasures of literary fiction. This suspension had already become part of the conventional wisdom before Todaro published his article, so acceptance of the model was almost universal and its influence great.

Inspecting the analytical difficulties with the model and their largely uncritical reception indicates much about the prevailing wisdom on African development in the early 1970s. Because the Todaro model seemed to render rigorous and systematic the impressions of most academics and policy-makers, the analytical problems of the model were glossed over. Crucial to the model was the concept of 'unemployment', yet a mass of theoretical and empirical literature showed that this was a developed-country specific concept of little relevance to sub-Saharan Africa.[25] With the burgeoning of the cities and emergence of the 'informal sector', one perceived the birth of a special category of workers, neither 'employed' nor 'unemployed', but 'underemployed'. If urban migrants could not correctly be viewed as unemployed, then one must deal with a three-sector model (agriculture, formal sector and urban informal sector). Once in such a model, migration could no longer be explained in terms of the formal sector wage and probability of employment at that wage.

Further, the model implicitly assumed no transfer of incomes between urban and rural populations as well as individual utility maximisation. Were migration prompted by an attempt to maximise family income, the decision calculus between urban and rural work would be quite different than that suggested in the model (the relevant 'margin' would not be the individual's). In fact, numerous studies had indicated that both rural-urban and urban-rural family income transfers were significant in African countries.[26] The appeal of the Todaro model was that it provided a simple framework in which a variable called the 'rural-urban income differential' was the analytical centerpiece. Such a view of sSA countries had been present in the literature for at least a decade, and the model seemed to give it rigorous expression.

ASSESSING THE ACCEPTED ORTHODOXY

The 'urban-bias' view of African countries persists to this day, with its inherent beliefs that wages are always too high unless labour markets are 'cleared' and that urban workers' gains are at the expense of rural producers. Despite the critical comments in the previous section, we do grant that in many sSA countries a substantial differential existed between average living standards in town and countryside; however, in most cases the differential was exaggerated.

Thus we argue that (1) these differentials were not systematically investigated or measured with any precision except in a few cases,[27] and (2) unwarranted emphasis was placed and continues to be placed upon the rural-urban income gap, with the result that the dynamics of income distribution in sub-Saharan African countries are inadequately addressed. Rather than present our objections in the abstract, it is useful to take an example of the type of analysis we consider to be inappropriate. In the 1983 World Bank report on Kenya (World Bank 1983, p. 23) one reads:

> The [present] policy of wage restraint should probably be maintained for the foreseeable future. First, labour markets are not in equilibrium, as there is a considerable gap between wages earned in the modern or formal sector and those available in [the urban informal sector] for comparable skill levels. Second, in so far as wage restraint moderates increases in domestic prices, this policy has beneficial effects on real rural incomes . . . Thus, this policy effectively redistributes income from urban to rural households.[28]

This recommendation for indefinite wage restraint comes after the report had documented a fall in real urban average earnings of 10 per cent from 1972 to 1980. It embodies a typical judgement passed upon sSA countries and incorporates a number of questionable assumptions. First, there is the argument that labour markets operate in such a way as to 'clear' in the absence of 'arbitrary' limits on money wages, such as minimum wage legislation. This assertion is pursued in some detail in our final chapter. Here it is sufficient to note that such a view of labour markets, that they are self-equilibrating in the absence of institutional constraints, is not generally accepted in the neoclassical literature.[28] It is well recognised that the clearing of labour markets, even in theory, requires a general equilibrium model with a Walrasian auctioneer to prevent 'false trading'[29] or the New Classical Macroeconomics interpretation of the Rational Expectations Hypothesis (see Begg 1982 and Shaw 1984). It is simply not the case that neoclassical economists (much less post-Keynesians, neo-Ricardians, etc.) are in agreement that falling real wages will equilibrate labour markets, even in theory. Therefore, we find it inappropriate to make such a controversial assumption in the context of African countries and to invoke it as the basis of highly political policy decisions.

Second, even were it the case that falling real wages would clear labour markets, there is no reason to presume that the equilibrium wage would be one that approximated the income level in the urban informal sector or in rural areas. If maximising strategies refer to family income, then different types of employment become in part complementary, not substitutes, and agents evaluate these in terms other than individual opportunity cost. Further, a judgement over the appropriateness of urban wage levels relatively to other types of incomes cannot be accurately made without reference to specific groups. For example, the 'raw' ratio of the unskilled wage to average rural earnings is not directly relevant to migration; the relevant comparison would require one to measure the average size of wage-earner and peasant households, opportunities for secondary employment for both types of households (e.g. off-farm income for rural households), differences in rural and urban cost of living, and so on. In the next few chapters precisely these considerations are incorporated into our calculations of the rural-urban income gap. But even this more sophisticated ratio has no clear bearing on migration since the locus of decision does not involve moving the whole family to town, but rather a young male adult of the family. In that case the trade-off would be between the net addition to family income from staying on the farm or relocating to town. In the context of African family ties, this kind of family-oriented calculus has always existed in the decision to migrate. In the new context of falling cash incomes in all sectors the calculus has become further reinforced.

As a final comment for the moment, it is not satisfactory to assert, as is done above, that wage restraint benefits rural producers – 'effectively redistributes income from urban to rural households'. This is a common view for which there is very little theoretical or empirical evidence. The particular mechanism suggested in the World Bank report on Kenya (quoted above) – that slower growth of wages results in slower growth of prices, which benefits rural households as consumers – is hardly credible. First, it is well recognised – indeed it is part of the neoclassical critique on import substitution – that manufacturing for the internal market in sub-Saharan countries deviates substantially from the ideal model of perfect competition. In the absence of strong competitive pressures only naive faith would prompt one to believe that wage restraint would lead to price restraint instead of increased mark-ups and an increased profit share.

Second, even if domestic product markets in sub-Saharan countries were sufficiently competitive to yield the result suggested in the quotation, the significance for income distribution would be doubtful. As we showed before, many authors have argued that manufacturing in sSA countries is to a great extent directed at an élite market and that most rural consumption items are produced in the informal sector. Thus, the redistributive gains for rural households from wage restraint would be minor, but considerable for the urban élites. Certainly, no general conclusion can be reached without a careful empirical study of the structure of manufacturing and of household budgets in a particular country.

The central problem in the analysis of distributional dynamics in the sub-Saharan countries is that much of the literature has been fixated by an accepted orthodoxy based upon a simplistic view of rural-urban relations. This simplistic view encourages generalisations which careful analysts would otherwise avoid.[30] When on top of this it is realised that the simplistic view was never based on careful calculations, or even conceptualisation, one begins to question many of the past diagnoses of African economies. It is our contention that the distributional dynamics of sSA countries are not conducive to broad generalisations, but must emerge from country-specific analysis, moderated by the structure of employment (e.g. import substitution versus export promotion), land tenure, and social stratification, among other factors. In Chapter 8, after looking at individual country case studies, we attempt to assess the forces which affect income distribution in Africa. To the extent that broad generalisations can be made, one may say that the distributional shifts are intimately linked to the economic crisis and collapse of sSA economies over the last 15 years. Singularly inappropriate in this context is an analytical framework which treats income distribution within an automatically adjusting system assumed to be arbitrarily constrained from seeking its natural state of general equilibrium by government intervention in markets.

SUMMARY

During the 1960s and early 1970s a view of sub-Saharan African countries became orthodox. At the heart of this was the judgement that these countries suffered from a severe differential between rural and urban incomes. This view persists to this day; indeed, the 'structural adjustment programmes' being recommended to African governments incorporate it, with their emphasis on the need for a dramatic shift in the 'rural-urban terms of trade'. In so far as the accepted orthodoxy correctly identified a phenomenon, it did so at the cost of obscuring important distributional dynamics in the African countries. The evidence from the next four chapters shows that in any case the turnaround in rural-urban income differentials which structural adjustment programmes seek has in fact already occurred. In a number of countries, the turnaround has gone beyond what one could have imagined possible 15 years ago. Yet, none of the problems (e.g. migration, unemployment) attributed to a wide rural-urban income gap has significantly abated. This leads us to the conclusion that those problems were and are considerably more complex than the accepted orthodoxy supposed. Further, it shall be argued that along with the average shift in rural-urban income have gone major intra-rural and intra-urban redistributions, with the result that the degree of income inequality in sub-Saharan countries today is substantially greater than in the past.

4 The Rural-Urban Gap in East Africa

This chapter begins our case studies with an examination of the three East African countries of Uganda, the United Republic of Tanzania and Kenya. The Uganda case is considered first, as it provides the most dramatic and accelerated example of structural breakdown, by now common in most African countries. In contrast to the West African countries which we consider in a subsequent chapter, the East African countries had distinct rural and urban zones before independence, with the urban areas strictly controlled to enforce 'orderly planning'. As a result, the 'informal sector' was notable by its absence. When it was 'discovered' (by the 1972 ILO mission), it is not surprising that this occurred in Kenya, since the newly-emerging sector provided such a sharp contrast to the 'orderly' manner in which this economy had developed up to then. The mission suggested that even though the sector may not be considered 'orderly' by the government, discrimination against it should be removed to enable it to contribute its full potential. In West Africa, on the other hand, small-scale indigenous activities have always been a feature of the urban areas and thus less likely to be noticed as a contrast. Because of this 'merging' and its widespread presence the informal sector is perhaps less harassed than in East Africa.

UGAÑDA

Of all the countries studied here – and perhaps of all sub-Saharan countries – Uganda must take the dubious honour of being the country that experienced the widest range of misfortunes in the last two decades. As in other African countries there were the negative impacts of the recession in the industrialised countries, the oil price shocks, and crop failures caused by inclement weather. But in addition, Uganda had to adjust to the break up of the East African community, to a war with Tanzania, and to General Idi Amin Dada as the supreme planner and political overlord. During a regime of singular economic mismanagement and political repression, Amin reduced a once-prosperous and promising country to one of the poorest in the world. Amin's most notable foray into the economic field, and one which set off the collapse, was his so-called War of Economic Independence against the Asian community in 1972. This vendetta against Ugandans of Asian origin had its roots in the colonial period. The British rulers pursued a policy of importing workers from the Indian subcontinent for construction of major public works, especially the railway from the coast, rather than paying wages sufficient to attract indigenous labour.[1] This labour policy, along with many conscious acts to keep the Asian and African communities apart, laid the basis for the subsequent ethnic animosities – animosities which were shared for similar reasons throughout East Africa.[2] The confiscation of property and expulsion of Asians from Uganda was but an extreme example of hostilities latent in all three countries.

The collapse of the modern sector after the departure of the Asians triggered off a general economic decline which eventually engulfed the physical infrastructure as well as the export sector, bringing ruin to virtually every segment of the population except for the court of retainers around Amin himself. Figures show that between 1970 and 1980 monetary GDP fell by 25 per cent, implying a decline of as much as 40 per cent in per capita terms (Uganda 1984; Jamal 1985). 'Modern sector' GDP (i.e. monetary GDP less peasant agriculture but including the urban informal sector) was reduced to less than half its 1970 value (a fall of 55 per cent). Export production declined massively, perhaps by 80 per cent.[3] In contrast, the food sector held up surprisingly well,[4] confirming the point made in Chapter 1, that regardless of pricing policies, inflation, or breakdown of the infrastructure, African farmers will strive to produce sufficient food to feed their families. While outside observers may bemoan the rudimentary state of technique in African agriculture, the Ugandan case demonstrates the resiliency of the peasant sector and the efficacy of the survival strategies pursued by rural and urban households.

In terms of living standards, the economic collapse affected urban wage earners most severely. Both in the late colonial and early independence periods Uganda was characterised by a 'high wage' policy, intended to establish a permanent and 'committed' labour force in urban areas.[5] Much of the folklore about privileged workers in Africa represented a generalisation from this experience. The generalisation was invalid: only in a few countries did the colonial masters pursue a 'high-wage' policy. Uganda was one such country, but the

British did not adopt a generous wage policy in any country of West Africa, as we show in Chapter 7.

The colonial government embarked upon the high-wage, labour-stabilisation policy in the late 1950s in Uganda. Minimum wages were raised fourfold after 1957, whereas export crop prices declined by 40 to 60 per cent. These large wage increases completely changed the nature of wage employment and structure of incomes in the country. In 1957 the minimum wage would have bought only three-fifths of the food requirements of an average size family in towns, using as the unit of measurement the most basic staple, *matoke*, or green bananas (see Table 4.1 and Figure 4.1). By 1967 only one-half of the minimum wage would have sufficed for family food requirements. With regard to the farmer-wage earner gap, in 1957 the average farm income (including subsistence income) was three times the minimum wage; ten years later the minimum wage exceeded the average farm income by nearly one-fifth. This structure of incomes collapsed in the 1970s. The minimum

TABLE 4.1: *Uganda: Minimum wage in nominal and real terms, 1957–90, selected years*

	Minimum wage (U.Sh. p.m.)	Price index	Real wage	Percentage of minimum wage to purchase 9,000 *matoke* calories
1957	33	61	29	164
1959	75	62	65	–
1962	138	67	111	–
1964	150	71	114	–
1967	150	75	108	49
1970	185	90	111	–
1972	185	100	100	60
1976	240	368	35	–
1980	400	3 348	6	–
1981	950	6 068	8	–
1984 (Apr.)	6 000	22 000	15	–
1984 (Nov.)	6 000	35 000	9	450
1985	–	55 000	–	–
1987	55 000	495 000	6	–
1989	800 000	4 410 000	10	400
1990	1 000 000	5 580 000	10	350

SOURCE: Jamal 1985 and data collected in Uganda by Jamal in January 1991. Figures are in old shillings (= 0.01 new shillings). Up to 1984 'minimum wage' is the official minimum wage for lowest-grade worker in government.

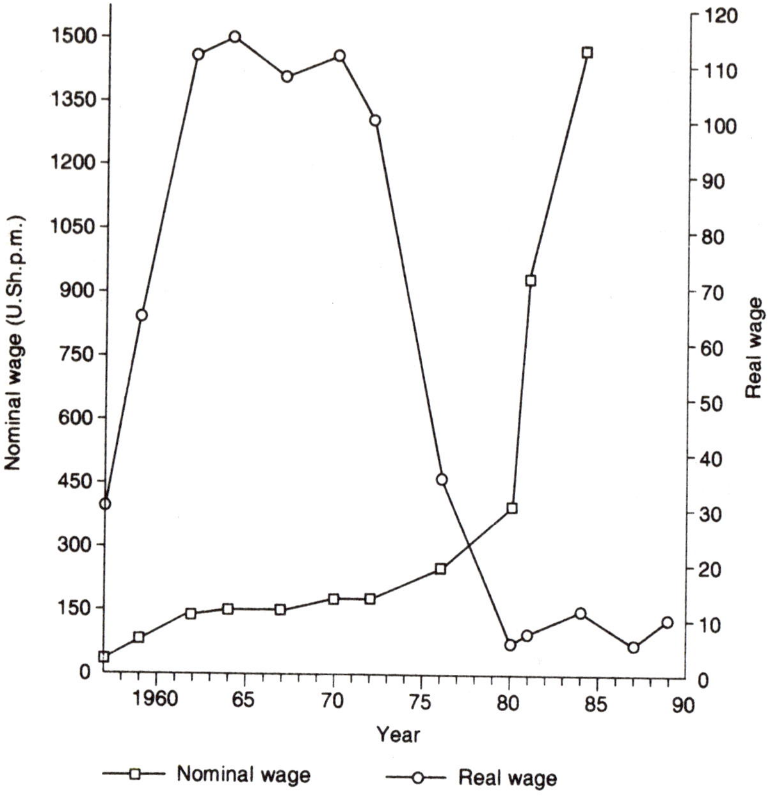

Source: Table 4.1

Figure 4.1 Uganda: Minimum wage in nominal and real terms, 1957–90, selected years

wage fell to 10 to 15 per cent of its 1972 value in the 1980s and the monthly wage would have bought no more than a week's supply of food. Thus, the period during which urban wage earners were a privileged group in Uganda lasted at most 15 years. The trends in the minimum wage were by and large reflected in the trends in the average wage.

Such massive declines in wages induced equally dramatic changes in the lifestyle of the urban wage-earner households. As we shall see in other case studies, similar changes have happened in other African countries; the Ugandan case stands out because the changes occurred so fast and drastically. All ethnic groups had to reduce the consumption of their preferred foods (meat, milk, fruit, etc.), which in the 1960s were absorbing a sizeable and growing proportion of household income. Even within the category of staples, there were shifts in response to scarcity and relative prices, particularly to maize-meal, which became a cheaper source of calories than *matoke*. For the non-Baganda groups this signified a continuation of past trends; for the Baganda it indicated a major departure from traditional dietary patterns.

Alteration of diet still left a large gap between family subsistence needs and income. To compensate, wage-earner households re-established their links with the countryside, reversing the labour force stabilisation process of the 1960s. Trips back to the family farm *(shamba)* became common, and some members of urban households were sent permanently to tend farms. Further, urban households began to grow their own food, something that had always been practised to some degree, but had declined because of increasing rural and urban specialisation and the influx of migrants who had no access to cultivable urban land. With the departure of these migrants, Kampala became a more Baganda city than in decades and increasingly semi-rural in its economy. Before 1972 urban budget surveys showed that Kampala was 20 per cent self-sufficient in calories; in the 1980s that proportion quite likely doubled.

The second structural change that occurred in the urban areas was the break up of the wage-earning class. With the minimum wage down to one-tenth of its 1972 value, a person could no longer support a household on formal sector employment alone. Increasingly, members of wage-earner households turned to trading, an activity which had been opened up by the expulsion of Asians. Compared to pre-1972, one is struck by the increase in street trading in urban areas. A similar phenomenon characterises cities in other sSA countries, but in Uganda the cause was unique. Unlike in other African countries, urban migration actually slowed down or even changed its net flow up to 1985.[6] Yet the informal sector grew, and this growth resulted because a great part of the trade previously done by the Asians passed into the hands of wage earners-turned-petty traders. Thus, the informal sector expanded without migration. In a culmination of these trends, after the mid-1970s the distinct classes that had existed in urban Uganda in the previous decade coalesced into a grand trader-cum-wage-earner-cum-*shamba* class. The final outcome was such that while urban cash incomes fell quite sharply, the total income available to urban groups from trade, wages, and subsistence farming kept households at least above basic food poverty. The structural changes described above and the accompanying changes in the rural-urban gap are shown in Table 4.2.

In 1967 a person earning the minimum wage would have had to spend half of his or her income on food, the other half being available for non-food commodities. Most of these non-food items would be necessities – clothing, rent, fuel, transport – with little income left over for discretionary spending on such things as the cinema and processed drinks. At the same time, farmers had an income at a level of 80 per cent of wage earners. Most of this consisted of the valuation placed on subsistence food production. However, in terms of cash income available for non-food needs, farmers would appear to have had a real consumption level of two-thirds of wage earners. Thus in the late 1960s Ugandan wage earners had only a marginal advantage over farmers – i.e. after six to seven years of the heaviest urban bias. If one were to discount urban incomes for non-discretionary expenditures on rent, fuel, and transport, one is left with very little advantage for wage earners in the income structure created after independence. Certainly, the wage earner's position improved dramatically during the first decade of independence, but it still left him at the level of subsistence consumption.

TABLE 4.2: *Uganda: Wage earner versus farm incomes, 1967 and 1984* (indices, with wage earner income in 1967 = 100)

	1967		1984	
	Wage earner	Farmer	Wage earner	Farmer
Food	50	50	40	55
Non-food	50	33	10	10
Total	100	83	50	65
Gap	1.2		0.8	

Composition of 'wage earner' income in 1984

Wage	10
Own *shamba* food	15
Non-wage income	25
Total	50

SOURCE: Jamal 1985 and explanation in the next.

There is a general point here that appears as an issue of measurement, but is in fact much more fundamental, and which we shall encounter in several case studies, particularly Tanzania. In circumstances in which farmers grow their own food, their cash income is directed to non-food items for the most part. When comparing farmers and wage earners, the relevant categories are total farm income and wage income. Given that farmers at least provide sufficient food for themselves and wage earners, even in their heyday, spent up to one-half of their incomes on food, the maximum gap this suggests is 2:1. Any figure higher than this – and 4:1 has been advanced – would imply starvation for farmer families. This point may seem obvious, but surprisingly enough one searches for it in vain in the literature, finding instead the grossest and crudest calculations of the farmer-wage earner gap. Yet no meaningful comparison of rural and urban incomes is possible (not in Uganda or anywhere else) without a clear specification of cash and in-kind expenditures. It is not too much to say in retrospect that most of the calculations of the rural-urban gap in the heyday of the 'labour aristocracy' were of little analytical value (though of great political and ideological impact).

By 1984 the 'wage earner' family had disappeared as a distinct entity in Uganda. The minimum wage itself was down to 10 per cent of its 1967 level. Food produced on an urban family's shamba contributed more to a family's real living standard than the wage, and non-wage income from petty trading contributed even more. Families changed their diets to inferior food to maintain their calorie intake, as well as to leave cash income free to purchase the most desired non-discretionary non-food needs. Nevertheless urban families suffered a drop of 50 per cent in their living standards, practically all of this consisting of consumption of non-food items. Farmers, on the other hand, maintained their food production and auto-consumption or even increased it somewhat, taking advantage of labour released from export crops. Their cash income from export crops fell catastrophically, but that from food sales quite likely held up in terms of purchasing power because of increasing prices of staples. Even considering sales of food, cash income fell by around 70 per cent. However, since 'food income' – i.e. the valuation given to on-farm food production (and consumption) – was always the greater part of total family income, one can conclude that the total fall in real consumption of farm households was only of the order of 20 per cent, compared to 50 per cent for wage earner households. The rural-urban gap moved strongly in favour of rural livelihoods, though one must distinguish livelihoods from households since the rural-urban distinction became increasingly blurred.

The Uganda discussion enables us to make a generalisation applicable to most sSA countries. This generalisation is based on what the statistics show and what we observe. The statistics show that the real wage fell by 90 per cent in Uganda between 1972 and 1990, and a rough calculation suggests that the 1990 wage would buy only one-quarter of a family's food needs. Yet one does not perceive there to be a massive increase in malnutrition in urban Uganda.[7] There is thus a 'wage puzzle'. This wage puzzle we solved in terms of the huge structural changes undergone by the Ugandan economy – the emergence of informal activities, the increase in subsistence production in towns, and the re-establishment of urban ties with the rural sector.[8] Thus, after the mid-1970s one could no longer talk of a 'wage-earning class' or a 'trader class'; rather, all families had some members in both of these occupational groups in addition to undertaking subsistence farming in urban areas. Finally, all families increased their stake in rural areas. One witnesses in Uganda a regression to a primordial stage of society in which the division of labour begins to break down. Along with that regression disappeared notions of class and explanations of income distribution based on distinct classes.

The Ugandan economy has by now undergone a period of shock therapy at the behest of the IMF.[9] In June 1981 the shilling was floated and immediately plunged from 8 to the dollar to 77. By 1985 the rate had reached Sh. 1,540 and by 1987 Sh. 8,512 (IMF 1991, p. 540). In May of the latter year a new shilling was introduced equal to 100 old shillings; the exchange rate continued to deteriorate, reaching Sh. 510 by November 1990. As a major innovation the Government had allowed conversion of foreign currency without restriction; the open-market rate in November was Sh. 728 to the dollar, or some 43 per cent above the official rate. The interest rate stood at 50 per cent at this time, up from 16 per cent in 1983. The consumer price index, as may be evident from Table 4.1, marched on – at triple digit rates up to the end of 1989, but then slowed down dramatically to within 25 per cent in 1990. The economy recorded an average rate of growth of 5 per cent in 1988 and 1989 but declined to 3 per cent in 1990.

On the employment front the purchasing power of the wage remained depressed at the level of 1980. With the return of security and the restoration of the infrastructure, prices of basic staples rose less than the general consumer price index and hence the command over food increased to 10 days' supply of food. There was some evidence up to the mid-1980s that rural-urban migration had slowed down, with some towns – Jinja and Tororo – even registering declines. This was mostly due to the group insecurity that prevailed in the urban areas during the Amin years and in any case is no longer true, despite the continuing low level of urban wages and the vastly higher 'real' incomes that can be earned in the rural areas, reiterating our point about the lack of correlation between migration and rural-urban differentials.

LESSONS FROM UGANDA

The Ugandan experience is the first and most extreme example of our contention that the rural-urban gap has narrowed in sSA countries, albeit in a context bordering on the pathological. However, it would be a mistake to attribute the dramatic decline in wage-earner real incomes (and urban incomes across the board) to the violence and chaos of the Amin regime alone. From 1972 to the first half of 1984 real wages fell by 85 per cent in Uganda; next door in Tanzania the decline over a somewhat shorter period (1974 to 1983) was in excess of 60 per cent with no Idi Amin to augment the 'natural' forces of the market. In Kenya, without any of the catastrophes visited on the economy by a despot or by 'socialist' ideology, the decline was 40 per cent between 1975 and 1985. And as we shall see in Chapter 7, the wage decline in Ghana over roughly the same period was equal to if not greater than that suffered in Uganda. Certainly Uganda is an extreme and unique case, but the uniqueness lies in the violence and repression suffered during the Amin years, not in the catastrophic changes in the structure of incomes.

At first impression, the dramatic collapse of the Ugandan economy seems to offer few general lessons. But quite the contrary, in the Uganda experience we see foreshadowed (both chronologically and in terms of our order of presentation) events, forms of adaptation, and structural changes repeated in other countries. Sub-Saharan Africa in the 1980s has taken a giant step backward in the process of economic modernisation through the social division of labour. Perhaps the most important point to take from the Uganda experience is that it demonstrates the amazing resilience and courage of human beings in the struggle to survive; it also shows that success in that struggle may involve reversion to forms of household economy which none would voluntarily choose.

THE UNITED REPUBLIC OF TANZANIA

While they share a common border and have a certain ecological similarity, the United Republic of Tanzania and Kenya (which we consider next) are strikingly dissimilar societies; indeed, they are so different, especially in development policies, that the temptation to do comparative studies has produced a small cottage industry among academic Africanists. For the purpose of this book, certain historical differences are crucial. While Tanganyika (the mainland portion of the United Republic) had large European- and Asian-owned estates during the colonial period, the territory never manifested any of the characteristics of a settler state. Further, while both Kenya and Uganda have extraordinarily fertile regions in which great wealth could be accumulated by a powerful oligarchy (indigenous in Uganda), Tanganyika's ecology is much more uniform, and no wealthy African élite of note developed before or during the colonial period. In consequence, mainland Tanzania came to independence with perhaps the lowest degree of inequality in the distribution of income and wealth of any British colonial possession in Africa. The post-independence government reduced whatever inequality existed through the nationalisation of the large foreign-owned estates and industrial enterprises. Therefore, the much-commented upon commitment to broad-based development by the Tanzanian Government should be seen as an attempt to maintain a relatively egalitarian society rather than to create one. Because of this history of relative equality which has characterised the country, the rural-urban gap in Tanzania has always been narrower than in other sSA countries. In recent years Tanzania has suffered severely from the world recession and her virtually unique commitment to spreading the gains from growth and meeting the basic needs of the population has been severely threatened, perhaps to the verge of abandonment.[10] The emphasis on equity was always controversial, with some observers going so far as to attribute the current economic difficulties to domestic policies intended to promote egalitarianism.[11] When considering such arguments it is worth remembering that many other African countries are facing difficulties equal to or worse than those suffered by Tanzania, and few of these countries stand accused of having taken significant steps to improve income or wealth distribution.

As should be evident from the above, allegations about the rural-urban income distribution in Tanzania have to be seen within the context of the country's economic ills and the generally negative judgement passed on the Government's attempts to maintain an equitable distribution of the fruits of growth. As suggested in previous chapters, emphasis upon the rural-urban gap as the key aspect of inequality tends to generate (or reflect) conservative economic policies – reliance upon markets to correct 'distortions' created by governments, a predilection to weaken trade unions because of their 'monopolistic' effects (but rarely to regulate monopolistic firms), and so on. In the case of Tanzania, focusing on the rural-urban gap implies a particularly anti-government bias, for what significant privileges can be obtained in this extremely poor country derive from the state bureaucracy, as there is no formal private sector of great significance. As shall be shown, the rural-urban gap is in fact quite narrow, and virtually zero between urban unskilled workers and peasants.

Tanzania's most pressing problem in the 1980s from a narrow economic viewpoint was the adverse balance of payments. In the early 1980s current imports were double the value of current exports. The large trade deficit was partly the result of a decline in the volume of exports (at about –3 per cent per annum). Domestic policies contributed to the poor export performance, with blame particularly cast upon the villagisation programme (which some view as forced relocation of peasants), the role of the marketing boards, and the nationalisation of sisal estates. However, by any balanced judgement domestic policies can explain only a part of the trade deficit. Tanzania's barter terms of trade have declined sharply, such that in 1980 with the volume of imports the same as in 1973, the value in current prices was three times greater. Had export volume grown at the average rate for all low income countries over the period (about 5 per cent per annum), the trade deficit would still have been large and required external assistance to finance. In 1979 (and periodically since then) the government entered into negotiations with the IMF to reach agreement on high conditionality loan packages. The negotiations were quite contentious. At issue were policy changes demanded by the IMF (e.g. devaluation and the elimination of food subsidies) which would have a detrimental effect upon the poor, particularly the urban poor.[12] As elsewhere in the region, advocates of IMF structural adjustment justified these distributional effects (in as far as they were conceded to exist) by the familiar argument that urbanites were relatively privileged.

Whether or not this is so is an empirical question. But as in the Uganda case study it is not self-evident what measures are the most relevant to test this hypothesis or how a proxy measure should be calculated. Our purpose is apparently simple: to estimate incomes of farmers and wage earners. Three sources are available for this: (1) household budget surveys (HBSs); (2) national accounts; and (3) income imputations. The household budget surveys are not usable in Tanzania: first, because at the time this book was written the latest household budget survey was for 1976–77, whereas our interest is in trends since then; second, because the existing HBSs (as indeed all HBS's) do not give farm incomes as such but farmers' incomes (income from all sources to farm families rather than income from farm work); and third, because they do not give wage earners' incomes at all. Thus, we have to resort to the other two sources for our purposes.

The procedure for using the national accounts to derive incomes of farmers and non-farmers is as follows. We decompose total GDP into its agricultural and non-agricultural components and then attribute them to the respective farm and non-farm populations to obtain average incomes. Two corrections are made for price differences. First, as we now know, the greatest part of farm income consists of subsistence production/consumption. In the national accounts this 'subsistence' output is valued at farm-gate prices, but should be revalued at town prices to make comparisons to town incomes.[13] In the opposite direction we have to adjust farmers' cash income to reflect its purchasing power in the rural areas (i.e. prices for non-agricultural commodities are higher in the countryside).

Income imputations have to be used when GDP data are known to be unreliable. This is often the case with subsistence data – and is particularly the case with Tanzania's subsistence data.[14] The purpose is to give the same value to farmers' food production/consumption basket as it would have in towns. This requires making a critical assumption about the food bundle produced and consumed by the farm family. Below, we discuss this assumption further. With regard to farmers' cash income, agricultural money GDP may be used intact and added to the subsistence imputation.

Table 4.3 shows the derivation of agricultural income at town prices for 1982, compared to urban wages. Agricultural income figures are based on national account estimates of agricultural value added. In converting to town prices, it is assumed that 'town goods' – clothing, matches, utensils, etc. – are 50 per cent more expensive in rural areas compared to urban areas, and that in the opposite direction food crops retail in towns at 55 per cent above producer prices. There is

TABLE 4.3: *Tanzania: Agricultural income (aggregate and average) compared to wages, 1982*

Aggregate income (Sh. m)			
Cash	6,301		
Subsistence	15,488		
Smallholder numbers ('000)	3,234		
Average income (Sh. p.a.)	*Uncorrected*	*Revalued*	*Adjustment factor*
Cash	1,948	1,305	0.67
Subsistence	4,781	7,423	1.55
Total	6,737	8,728	–
Memo item			
Minimum wage		7,200	
Average wage		11,568	
Average non-agricultural wage		14,292	

SOURCE: Tanzania 1982, for aggregate income; smallholder numbers estimated as described in Jamal 1982 (Tanzania). Re-evaluation based on the assumptions that (1) consumer goods prices are 50 per cent higher in the rural areas than towns; and (2) town prices for food are 55 per cent higher than farm-gate prices.

considerable evidence for such price differentials in Tanzania (as in other developing countries), though whether their proportion is as assumed could be disputed. It might be argued, for example, that because of import restrictions on consumer commodities, resulting in a 'goods famine' in Tanzania in recent years, cash incomes in rural areas were worth much less than specified as compared to town-based incomes. There is no practical way of obtaining the 'true' price differentials in the context of quantity rationing. There has always been some form of price control in operation in Tanzania, and controls should have kept price differentials in check. The same applies for prices of staples in towns. Thus, the differentials we have assumed seem of the right order of magnitude. So as not to overload the data, we have also given the uncorrected figures and order-of-magnitude checks at several points.

By our measure, in 1982 average farm income at town prices was Sh. 8,728, compared to a minimum wage of Sh. 7,200, so that the average farmer had a 21 per cent income advantage over the minimum wage earner. Without the price correction, the advantage would go in favour of the minimum wage earner – by 7 per cent (Sh. 6,737 for farm households and Sh. 7,200 for the minimum wage). Our judgement is that the revalued figure is a truer measure, since the existence of a producer price/retail price differential is certain, reflected in the valuation of the national accounts. Since subsistence income constitutes the major part of farm income, putting a price differential on it tilts the advantage in favour of the farmers. The average non-agricultural wage was Sh. 14,192, giving an advantage of 64 per cent for urban workers against farmers. Since 45–50 per cent of the wage earners earn near the minimum wage mark, it is arguable that the relevant comparison is with the minimum wage.

Let us now pursue an alternative measure of farm income as an independent check on the figures in Table 4.3. This alternative set of estimates uses income imputations and is based on the notion that equal baskets should be valued at equal prices in both town and country, but additionally incorporates an assumption about the level of consumption of food crops by farm families. The assumption we shall make is that the typical farm family obtains on an average 2,200 calories per capita per day from its own production. This is the item called 'subsistence production' in the national accounts. We value this assumed basket at its town price level. In 1982 a consumption basket in the proportion 75:25 for cereals to 'other' products would have cost around Sh. 2.75 per day.[15] For a family of five, then, we enter Sh. 5,000 (i.e. 2.75 x 5 x 365) as the value of own produced food.

The critical assumption here is that the average farm family at least gets its requirements of calories from its own farm. FAO statistics show that on average Tanzania does produce sufficient food for her needs from her own farms. Perceptions are also important: does the average Tanzanian farmer produce enough food for self-sufficiency or not? Certainly, the Tanzanian farmer has suffered huge declines in cash income, but no one has argued that food production has declined drastically or that it was below subsistence needs in the recent past. Along with valuing self-produced food, we should also include the valuation of self-provided housing and fuel, but for the moment we simply take note of these qualifications. Family farm income resulting from this method of calculation is Sh. 5,000 worth of food and Sh. 1,305 worth of town-equivalent cash income. As compared to this, the minimum wage was Sh. 7,200, implying a nominal advantage for the minimum wage earner of 14 per cent. When self-provided housing and fuel-wood is included in rural income and charges for non-discretionary items – transport, lighting, water – included on the urban side, we reach the conclusion that in real welfare terms there was very little to choose between the consumption levels of a minimum wage earner family and an urban family in Tanzania in 1982. Even against the average wage earner family the gap was probably no more than a few percentage points.

The relative income position of farmers and wage earners was quite different in the late 1960s and early 1970s from that just described, and the trends began to favour the farmers only after 1974–75. This is shown in Table 4.4, where the farm-household–wage-earner gap is derived for selected years from national accounts figures (as in Table 4.3) and imputed subsistence income. The first set of figures uses agricultural GDP divided by farm population. The second set uses cash marketing figures plus the imputation of subsistence food income. Neither set of figures is corrected for price differentials and nor have we imputed non-food subsistence income; thus the data only reflect trends.

Between 1969 and 1973–75 the farm-wage gap increased, then fell quite sharply up to 1982 (after which it stabilised at this low level). The underlying figures indicate (Jamal 1982, (Tanzania)) that between 1969–70 and 1983–84 farmers' income fell by 24 per cent, whereas the non-agricultural wage fell by 71 per cent. During the period 1974–75 to 1979–80, when the gap changed dramatically in favour of the farmers, farmers' real income increased by 8 per cent, whereas the average non-agricultural wage declined by 23 per cent and the real minimum wage by 36 per cent. These figures might seem startling: that farmers' incomes fell so little (or even rose) and wages fell so catastrophically. The wage fall is well documented, being based on statistics of wages and prices available in the usual government documents. The farm incomes have had to be estimated, but theassumptions used are well within reasonable bounds.[16] As before,

TABLE 4.4: *Tanzania: Wage earner-farmer gap, 1969–82, selected years* (ratios)

	1969	1973–75 (av.)	1980	1982
National accounts	3.41	3.81	2.07	1.96
Cash marketing + subsistence food	2.55	3.70	2.22	1.91

SOURCE: See text. An average for 1973–75 is used to even out the impact of drought on farm income.

the main assumption is that the average farmer's subsistence production/consumption remained constant at 2,200 calories per capita per day. This production bundle is then given a monetary value to reflect its cost in town. If we deflate by the food price index, then the value of this basket remains constant over time. During any given period 'food income' constitutes the major part of a farmer's standard of living – a variant, as we saw before, of Engel's law. Thus, a substantial share of farm family income remains immune from inflation. Between 1969–70 and 1983–84 farmers' cash income declined by 70 per cent in real terms, yet their total income declined by only 24 per cent, precisely because of the cushion provided by subsistence production.

The importance of subsistence production is again worth pausing to underline, as we shall encounter it in various guises throughout the case studies, and as it is not sufficiently credited in terms of trade analyses. As the excellent work of Ellis has shown (1982, 1983, 1984), farmers' price terms of trade fell by 35 per cent between 1969–70 and 1983–84;[17] output of cash crops fell even more, so that the income terms of trade or real cash income fell by 64 per cent. With a 2.5 per cent rate of growth of farm population, a 75 per cent drop in average real cash income would be implied. This percentage is consistent with what we obtained for cash income above (over a shorter period), providing confirmation of our estimates. However, it must be reiterated that terms of trade calculations should not be mistaken for changes in the 'real' income of farmers, as Ellis tended to do in his earlier papers. If real income fell by 75 per cent, we would have to ask how did farmers survive, given that they did not start much above the bare subsistence level? It is true that their cash incomes have fallen catastrophically (75 per cent is the figure here); but even if all of their cash income were to disappear, farmers would still be left with their food production. On the assumption that most farm families produce sufficient food for themselves, falling cash incomes do not result in food poverty.

The same could not be said for the urban wage earners: their wages would not buy a minimum food basket in 1985 (nor at the end of 1991). This is shown in Table 4.5 where a poverty line is derived for an average urban family (five members) based on prices prevailing in March 1984 and December 1985. A most austere basket was chosen, in which maize-meal (sembe) provided 75 per cent of calories, and beans, fats, and sugar the rest. Only the most minimal consumption of non-food goods was included. The results show that in 1984 an average

TABLE 4.5: *Tanzania: Poverty line for an urban family, March 1984 and December 1985* (Sh. p.m.)

	March 1984	December 1985
Food	483	1 325
Maize-meal (75%)	173	950
Beans (15%)	154	176
Fats (5%)	98	132
Sugar (5%)	48	67
Non-food	455	540
Clothing	125	150
Rent	130	150
Fuel and water	100	120
Transport	100	120
Total	938	1 865
Memo items		
Minimum wage (Sh. p.m.)	600	810
Maize-meal price (Sh./kg.)	2.50	13.75
Oct. 1991 Minimum wage (Sh. p.m.)	3 500	
Maize-meal price (Sh./kg)	50	

SOURCE: Estimated as explained in the text.

wage earner would have to spend 88 per cent of his or her income to buy the poverty-line consumption basket; the minimum wage earner would exhaust practically 80 per cent of his or her wage on food alone. By the end of 1985 the situation was completely untenable, with the postulated expenditure on maize-meal alone exhausting the minimum wage. Thus it is not surprising that the Government for a long time balked at the IMF conditionality requiring that the price of maize-meal be raised significantly (to Sh. 17 in 1982). This condition was eventually met in large part, with the complete abolition of the *sembe* subsidy (Jamal 1986a and 1988d). In just two years, the price of *sembe* went from Sh. 2.50 to Sh. 13.75. In the meantime the minimum wage increased by a fraction of the price rise, from Sh.600 to Sh. 810. The purchasing power of the minimum wage dropped from eight kilograms of *sembe* per day to just two. By 1988 there was further erosion, with the *sembe*-equivalent wage at only 1.3 kg. per day. And at the end of 1991 the situation was only slightly better.[18] Maize had now to be bought in the unprocessed form – at Sh. 3,500 for a 100 kg bag – and taken for grinding at Sh. 50 per bag. Assuming an 80 per cent out-turn ratio for maize to maize-meal this amounts to a maize-meal price of Sh. 50 per kg, as entered at the bottom of Table 4.5. The minimum wage stood at Sh. 3,500 per month. Thus its purchasing power was now 2.3 kg per day. This is a slight improvement on the 1985 situation – 2 kg per day – but still it means the minimum wage being able to buy nothing apart from *sembe*. The ensuing survival strategies of urban wage earners have been well documented by Maliyamkono and Bagachwa (1990, p. 42):

> Some urban residents discovered new productive ways of becoming truly self-reliant by getting involved in sideline activities (for example, food vending, operating small kiosks, repair and maintenance services, furniture making, shanty eating places, tailoring, shoe-making and repair, local beer brewing, hair braiding, urban farming). . . . Typically when wage earning members of the family return from their regular jobs they get involved in one or more of the above mentioned activities. Those who remain at home are usually engaged in urban farming or food vending, besides performing their routine domestic tasks. Some children even sell buns and peanuts after school hours.

Aili Mari Tripp (1989) provides corroborative evidence. Her survey of the informal sector in Dar es Salaam during 1987–88 showed that over three-fourths of the enterprises were started during the crisis years of 1980–87, most by women to supplement their husband's wages. Many professional women (teachers, nurses, accountants) dropped out of the formal economy, as did children out of school, since formal sector jobs no longer guaranteed an adequate living.

We have shown that there was no 'rural-urban gap' in favour of wage earners in after the late 1970s. Indeed, to make a stronger point *à propos* 'privileged workers', it is doubtful if a large gap ever existed, although comments to this effect abound. In 1974 the minimum wage was at its highest level in real terms for any time between 1963 and 1986 (Table 4.6). This probably represented a 50 per cent advantage for wage earners compared to farmers, which could easily be wiped out if non-discretionary expenditures were included in the urbanites' budget. In absolute terms, the 1974 minimum wage represented the ability to purchase just two food baskets of the type in Table 4.5. Given that farmers could always 'buy' such a basket (in that they produced it for themselves) and had some cash income left over, the

TABLE 4.6: *Tanzania: Wages in current and real terms, 1957–91, selected years*

	Current terms (Sh. p.m.)		Real (1969 terms, Sh. p.m.)		
	Minimum wage	Non-agricultural sector wage	Minimum wage	Non-agricultural sector wage	Consumer price index
1957	82 (Apr.)	–	100	103	80.0
1963	150 (Jan.)	210	186	261	80.5
1964	"	224	182	272	82.6
1965	"	302	170	343	88.0
1967	"	347	160	370	93.8
1968	"	359	153	366	98.1
1969	170 (July)	381	170	381	100.0
1972	240 (July)	416	206	356	116.7
1973	"	432	186	335	128.9
1974	340 (July)	686	221	445	154.1
1975	380 (May)	659	174	339	194.3
1976	"	672	183	324	207.6
1977	"	708	164	305	231.8
1978	"	710	146	273	260.0
1979	"	967	129	329	293.0
1980	480 (May)	1 036	126	271	382.0
1981	600 (May)	1 105	131	230	480.1
1982	"	1 191	97	192	619.5
1983	"	1 060	76	135	787.0
1984	810 (June)	–	65	–	1 070.9
1985	810	–	57	–	1 428.8
1986	1 035 (June)	–	47	–	1 892.8
1987	1 230 (July)	–	39	–	2 460.3
1988			38		
1989	2 075		37		
1991	3 500				

SOURCE: Jamal 1982 (Tanzania) and ILO 1988, supplemented by ILO 1967 and 1975 and ILO/JASPA 1991, p. 40 (real minimum wage in 1988 and 1989), and personal communication, Mr. Hassan Raha, OTTU, for minimum wage in 1991. Deflation of the minimum wage is based on effective minimum wage for the whole year.

advantage of the minimum wage earner must have been considerably less than 40 per cent. Compared to the situation before and after, the 1974 position was favourable for wage earners, but certainly did not justify the 'aristocrat' label.

Urban wages in Tanzania fell dramatically and continuously after 1974, as shown in Table 4.6. Three comparisons tell the story: (i) in just 12 years from 1974 the minimum wage lost 85 per cent of its purchasing power; (ii) in 1974 half the monthly minimum wage would have sufficed to meet food needs, whereas by 1986 the minimum wage would have bought just ten days' supply of food; and (iii) in 1974 the minimum wage represented a 50 per cent advantage against farm incomes, whereas by 1986 the average farmer's income was at least three times the average wage earner's income.

The Tanzanian case mirrors in many ways the Ugandan one, not only in terms of the catastrophic wage decline suffered in the recent period but also the development of the urban wage-earning class. Dar es Salaam attracted migrants from quite early on, but mostly young adult males. It was only after 1957 when the basis of fixing the minimum wage changed to a family support wage that the population of Dar es Salaam began to stabilise and its male:female sex ratio to narrow – from 1.41:1 in 1948 to 1.31 in 1957 and 1.15 in 1978 (Bryceson 1985, p. 513). As Bryceson (1990, Table 12.3) has also shown, the real value of the unskilled wage rate crept up gradually from 1943 to 1962 but then shot up in the next year to stabilise at the higher level till 1974. After that came the catastrophic decline in wages. One point she makes is important in understanding rural-urban differentials and interactions in Africa:

> In a period of depressed rural income, like the 1970s, the nuclear family unit based in the urban areas received innumerable obligatory requests, if not dictates, from its up-country extended family . . . Very often these demands entailed the urban household's absorption of up-country relatives who had either come as dependents in need of urban social services . . . or who had come in search of urban job opportunities . . . Others came to render service, since the urban-rural exchange within Tanzanian extended families was by no means one-sided. (Bryceson 1985, p. 515)

This is also a point made by Iliffe (1987). Intra-family exchanges help to equalise rural-urban differentials – and to explain how major changes in factor prices could occur, in particular the increases in wages in the 1960s and the decline after the mid-1970s. If wage earners were gaining at the expense of their rural counterparts they were still part of the extended family and could always be counted on to redistribute some of their gains. Conversely in the 1980s the rural half of the family could be tapped to supply foodstuffs. We shall take up this point further in the concluding chapter.

LESSONS FROM TANZANIA

In summary, the evidence indicates that in Tanzania there has been a dramatic shift in income from urban to rural areas, contradicting the view of a universal and permanent 'bias' towards urban development in African countries. We are not alone in making this point: Ellis challenged the allegation that there was ever an 'urban bias' in Tanzania's development policy in the sense of a division between rural and urban interests as two distinct categories of pressure groups (Ellis 1982). Rather, he argued that the conflict was between a portion of the urban élite and the peasantry, and the surplus appropriation associated with this conflict merely (and necessarily) took the form of emphasis upon urban development. In this process, urban wage earners were secondary and transitory beneficiaries, their gains quickly dissipated by rising prices.

Investigation of the Tanzanian case raises a number of related methodological issues, the most fundamental being the role of subsistence production for African farmers. Both in this case and for Uganda, we 'assumed' that farm households produced enough food for their needs. However, this is not an assumption in the usual sense of the term, but a simplification of a more complex reality involving inter-family allocations, inter-family barter, and shifting of labour and land resources under the threat of food poverty. It is likely that at some point the process of agricultural commercialisation in Africa will result in specialisation and landlessness so that our simplifying treatment of subsistence production will no longer be valid. But that stage has yet to arrive in most sub-Saharan countries. Any consideration of rural-urban differentials which does not incorporate the notion that farmers have for generations been food self-sufficient is fundamentally flawed. At the present juncture the inability of farmers to be food self-sufficient is primarily a result of natural disasters, not market fluctuations. For urban wage earners, however, it is the market that rules their ability to support themselves. The extreme real wage declines in Uganda and Tanzania drove them, too, back to their rural subsistence links for survival, and even created a new subsistence mode in the urban areas, as urban families took to backyard farming.

KENYA

Kenya's economy, similar to two others we treat (Liberia and

Zambia), has a dual structure with three aspects. Two of these are common to other African countries. First, there is the duality between the urban and the rural sectors, exhibited in terms of income levels as well as other factors such as technology. The 15 per cent of the population living in towns in 1983 earned nearly two-fifths of the national income, implying a gap between average rural and urban incomes of the order of one to four. The second duality occurs within the urban areas: the gap between wage earners and informal sector operators on the one hand and the formal sector entrepreneurs on the other. To give a preliminary indication, this gap was of the order of one to 20 in the mid-1970s. The duality that sets Kenya apart from the typical African country manifests itself as a sharp dichotomy within the rural sector. A very small number of large-scale farmers (around 2,000) control nearly one-half of the agricultural cash income. Over time, large farms and estates (formerly European-owned) have been subdivided, but the disparity in numbers remains high – about 2,000 or so large farmers versus 1.5 million smallholders. The income gap between the two groups is correspondingly enormous, of the order of 1:50.

The consequence of these dualities is that Kenya in the mid-1970s was thought to have one of the highest degrees of inequality among countries listed in a joint publication of the World Bank and the ILO (van Ginneken and Park 1984). Thus, Kenya's Gini coefficient for 1977 was found to be 0.590, which is extraordinarily high even compared to estimates for some notably inequalitarian countries such as Brazil (0.544), Peru (0.516), and Côte d'Ivoire (0.456) (Vandemoortele 1984a). One can dispute all these figures, and Jamal 1982 (Kenya) expressed reservations about similar estimates for Kenya based on the celebrated Integrated Rural Survey (see also Jamal 1977a). Disaggregating GDP data and applying proxies for distributions within the subcomponents of income categories, he calculated a Gini coefficient of 0.52 for 1976 which is still quite high (Jamal 1982 (Kenya), p. 24).[19]

The inequalities observed in Kenya are a direct consequence of the settler-state nature of British colonial rule, rather than of urban bias as such. Large European estates and firms dominated both the rural and urban sectors in the pre-independence period. The estates were worked by Africans who had been coerced into wage labour through dispossession from their lands or imposition of 'head' taxes. After independence many Europeans sold their lands, some of which came into the hands of the post-colonial State and were redistributed. Other large estates were acquired by Kenyan nationals and subdivided privately. However, large estates remain. In 1975, there were 2,148 farms of over 100 hectares and at least 443 over 1,000 hectares, and the numbers were virtually the same in 1983 – 2,200 and 440 (Kenya 1984, pp. 199 and 103). Perhaps more significantly, the proportion of marketed production arising from small farms, after being stable in the first half of the 1970s, fell from 55 percent in 1975 to 51 per cent in 1983. These percentages indicate that inequality worsened in the countryside between 1975 and 1983, continuing a trend. During this eight-year period, agricultural output grew at a substantially lower rate than previously, and the growth rate of exports was negative in real terms.

In the urban areas, too, the pattern of development in the colonial period implied huge privileges for Europeans – and peripherally for the Asians. Exports and imports passed through European hands, as did most internal commerce. Africans were restricted to petty trade in basic commodities – cigarettes, matches, oil, soap, etc. – and because of strict zoning laws confined to outskirts of the cities. This dominance by non-Africans in the modern sector continued after independence, and quite likely even increased. Newly-established industries remained in Asian and multinational hands, as did wholesale trade. The post-independence government reversed some discriminatory regulations, for example barring Asians from certain towns and trades; but the overall impact on non-African economic dominance has been limited. As the 1972 ILO Employment Mission report noted:

> Since independence economic growth has largely continued on the lines set by the earlier colonial structure. Kenyanisation has radically changed the racial composition of the group of people in the centre of power and many of its policies, but has had only a limited effect on the mechanisms which maintain its dominance – the pattern of government income and expenditure, the freedom of foreign firms to locate their offices and plants in Nairobi, and the narrow stratum of expenditure by a high-income élite superimposed on a base of limited mass consumption. (ILO 1972, p. 11)

The importance of class stratification and inequalities indicates that the term 'rural-urban gap' is misleading in Kenya: first, because there is great dispersion around average rural and urban incomes (and not normally distributed); second, because this dispersion is becoming more skewed; and, third, because the relevant distributional dynamics are not primarily between town and country, but between large farmers and small farmers, and between wage earners and informal sector operators and entrepreneurs. To emphasise the nature of inequality in Kenya, Table 4.7 shows some measures of the rural-urban gap for three selected periods.

TABLE 4.7: *Kenya: Measures of urban and rural incomes, 1969, 1976 and 1983* (K£ [= K.Sh. 20] p.a., unless otherwise indicated)

	1969	1976	1983
Wages[a]			
(1) All urban (nominal)	365	624	1 127
(price deflated)	690	624	432
	(110)	(100)	(69)
(2) All rural (nominal)	155	286	574
(price deflated)	(102)	(100)	(77)
(3) Minimum wage (nominal)	90	180	288
(price deflated)	170	180	110
	(94)	(100)	(61)
Incomes per capita[b]			
(4) Rural (nominal)	29.3	60.5	152.7
(5) Smallholder	–	(38.2)	–
(6) Urban (nominal)	217.6	326.5	626.0
Ratios[c]			
Urban wage/rural wage (1/2)	2.3	2.2	2.0
Urban income/rural income (6/4)	7.4	5.4	4.1
Urban wage[d]/rural income (1/4)	3.1	2.6	1.8
Min. wage[d]/rural income (3/4)	0.8	0.7	0.5
Min. wage[d]/smallholder income (3/5)	–	1.2	–

NOTES:
a First two series are average wage (i.e. wage bill – wage earners). All wage series have been deflated by low income cost-of-living index for urban areas.
b 1969 and 1976 from Jamal 1982 (Kenya); 1983 estimate is by the authors based on national accounts. It should be noted that because of changes in the national income accounts (redefinition of non-monetary income) it is not possible to have a direct comparison with Jamal's monetary/non-monetary division of rural incomes.
c A number greater than one indicates that urban incomes are higher. Last three ratios measured in per capita terms.
d To obtain this ratio it is assumed that wages are shared by a four-member family.
SOURCE: Kenya 1978 and 1984; and Jamal 1982 (Kenya).

All indications from the table are that rural-urban inequality at the aggregate level declined, and quite considerably. But one should not jump to the conclusion that overall inequality declined. Such a conclusion was reached in a government document by comparing the ILO Employment Mission Report (1972) and the Crawford and Thorbecke (1978) study which, taken together, indicated a decrease in inequality.[20] The ILO study found a Gini coefficient of 0.64, whereas the Crawford and Thorbecke calculated it at 0.48. The latter ratio was relatively close to a 1980 estimate by Jamal of 0.52. On the face of it, these calculations indicate an improvement in income distribution between 1969 and 1976 (the data years for the ILO and Crawford-Thorbecke studies). Serious difficulties arise in comparing two Gini ratios, however. Apart from the fact that the studies used different methodologies, captured different proportions of the national income, and omitted certain groups, there is the more important consideration that what one should compare are shares of different groups in terms of real income, whereas income distribution studies normally give shares in terms of current income. If prices facing different income groups move at different rates, a comparison of money incomes would not reveal the true trend in distribution.

When components of real GDP are inspected, one finds that inequality worsened in the 1970s, with a deterioration in both the rural and urban areas (Jamal 1982 (Kenya)). Inflation, which had been partly responsible for the fall in the rural-urban gap, primarily benefited large farmers because of their strategic position in the rural economy. In the urban sector too, inequality worsened: the incomes of informal-sector operators declined as a result of continuing migration, and real wages increased less than the profits of formal sector entrepreneurs. In the light of these trends in intra-sectoral inequality, the measured improvement in the rural-urban gap only implied that rich farmers gained compared to average urban incomes or, more likely, compared to the urban poor. Even the smaller improvement in the position of smallholders compared to minimum wage earners and informal sector operators did not improve distribution, since the latter two groups had either the same or lower incomes than smallholders.

Vandemoortele (1984b), after reporting that the rural-urban gap closed somewhat, also concludes that overall inequality worsened, and his data take one beyond the period covered by Jamal. The share of GDP accruing to the self-employed group (i.e. those in the informal sector and agriculture) fell from 30 per cent in 1964 to 23 per cent in 1983 (ibid., appendix table, p. 26). At the same time the share of wage employees fell from 45 per cent to 40 per cent (dropping as low as 36 per cent in 1977). In contrast, the share of gross operating surplus (a proxy measure of the profit share) rose from 25 per cent to 37 per cent. Vandemoortele concluded:

> Even after taking into account the increases in profit taxes and the higher depreciation allowances (the economy being about 40 per cent more capital-intensive in 1983 compared to 1964), it still seems that the capital earners have been able to protect their incomes better against inflation than the self-employed or the wage earners. (Vandemoortele 1984b, p. 14)

This discussion demonstrates that one should not make a fetish of the rural-urban gap in any country, especially in countries where vast intra-sectoral inequalities are known to be present. In such cases there is no alternative but to look at all trends carefully in order to judge changes in relative living standards.

Be that as it may, the rural-urban gap has been very much at the heart of the analysis of labour markets in Kenya. No less a contributing factor was the ILO report of 1972. Among the imbalances the ILO highlighted were those between rural and urban areas and formal and informal sectors. In practice this boiled down to an imbalance in returns from wage employment, farming, and informal sector activities. The ensuing income gaps caused migration and hence unemployment and underemployment in the urban areas. The response on the part of the Government was the issuance of the first Wages and Incomes Guidelines, in August 1973, in the form of a Sessional Paper on Employment. The guidelines required wages to be set in relation to earnings in the informal and agricultural sectors, with the proviso that workers' share should be related to productivity and 'should not be consumed by price increases'.

The next set of guidelines, in 1975, however severed the link between wage increases and productivity and between wages and cost of living. Henceforward the guidelines became a tool for combatting inflation and unemployment. In the same vein Sessional Paper No. 4 of 1975 on Economic Prospects and Policies, to which IMF/Bank lending was linked, put forward a strategy of price and wage restraint for coping with imported inflation and the balance of payments.

The seeds of change sown by the wage guidelines and the Sessional Paper No. 4 of 1975 bore fruit in the 1980s under the impact of structural adjustment programmes. The Fourth Development Plan,

1979–83, although its theme was poverty alleviation (in response to the 1972 ILO report), and the subsequent 1980 Sessional Paper effectively set aside equity objectives in favour of a strategy for achieving greater efficiency in resource use. This involved emphasising the more productive sectors – agriculture rather than industry, export processing rather than import substitution, directly productive activities rather than services and infrastructure.

Thus after at least the first oil-price shock, Kenya government's policies were guided by the need to balance the external and internal accounts, more and more in response to conditionalities agreed with the World Bank and the IMF as part of structural adjustment programmes. In 1975 Kenya had become one of the first developing countries to qualify for the IMF's Extended Fund Facility and several agreements were concluded with the Fund after that. Sessional Paper No. 1 of 1986 and the 1988–93 Development Plan generally espoused adjustment-type policies and met with approval from the World Bank and the IMF. In consequence of these policies rural-urban factor prices changed drastically.

As in the other East African countries, in the decade preceding independence and the one following, wages had increased substantially. Thus between 1954 and 1964 African real wages doubled, while between 1964 and 1973 they increased by a further 23 per cent. The objective as elsewhere in East Africa was to create a stable working class in the urban areas and thus obviate the need for workers to oscillate between rural and urban areas in search of income supplements.

After 1973, under the Wages and Incomes Guidelines real wages fell, in some cases dramatically (Table 4.8 and Figure 4.2). The minimum wage fell almost continuously after 1966, but most pertinently after 1975. By 1988 the minimum wage had declined to 57 per cent of its level in 1975. Similarly the real earning per worker in public administration fell by 36 per cent between 1976 and 1985. After that there was some upturn, with the real wage increasing by 13 per cent up to 1989, but even then a decline of almost one-quarter is recorded compared to 1976. In private manufacturing the real wage fell as a trend from 1971 right up to the late 1980s, for a total decline of 42 per cent.

While wages were falling agricultural prices held up quite satisfactorily, especially for domestic crops (Table 4.9 and Figure 4.3). Disaggregating by sub-periods shows up even more clearly the contrasting performance of agricultural prices and wages. Thus

TABLE 4.8: *Kenya: Trends in real wages and informal sector incomes, 1964–89* (1976 = 100)

	Nairobi minimum wage	Public administration	Private manufacturing wage	Total private wage	Informal sector
1964	106.7			83.4	
1965	101.7			83.1	
1966	114.0			90.6	
1967	112.2			95.5	
1968	111.5			101.7	
1969	111.9			101.8	
1970	109.8			103.8	
1971	105.8		121.9	103.5	
1972	99.6		121.4	100.7	
1973	91.1		117.7	94.9	
1974	106.1	92.6	106.8	92.2	58.9
1975	111.4	94.1	102.9	91.8	80.6
1976	100.0	100.0	100.0	100.0	100.0
1977	87.1	96.6	97.3	97.3	102.1
1978	86.9	92.5	86.9	90.4	132.6
1979	80.4	84.7	83.7	92.1	167.2
1980	92.1	77.9	84.8	98.6	152.6
1981	82.4	87.1	85.3	98.1	135.4
1982	72.0	72.9	80.0	90.0	112.7
1983	64.6	66.6	78.6	86.7	–
1984	58.6	62.3	76.8	88.8	93.9
1985	62.2	63.7	71.3	87.5	
1986		67.9	67.7	89.0	
1987		66.3	70.8	92.3	
1988	63.5	76.0	73.0	94.8	
1989		76.9	70.7	95.9	

SOURCE: Kenya, *Statistical Abstracts*, various issues, and data collected by Jamal in Kenya in 1990.

between 1964 and 1974 there was a trend decline in domestic crop prices while at this time minimum wage was more or less constant. Between 1975 and 1980 domestic crop prices held stable, while the minimum wage declined by 17 per cent. After this, while the minimum wage took a major fall, domestic crop prices increased. For example, between 1980 and 1985 the minimum wage fell by 32 per cent, while domestic crop prices (this time proxied by cereal prices) increased by 4 per cent. There has thus been a turn-around in the fortunes of farmers and wage earners. To bring this point home dramatically, in 1970 a

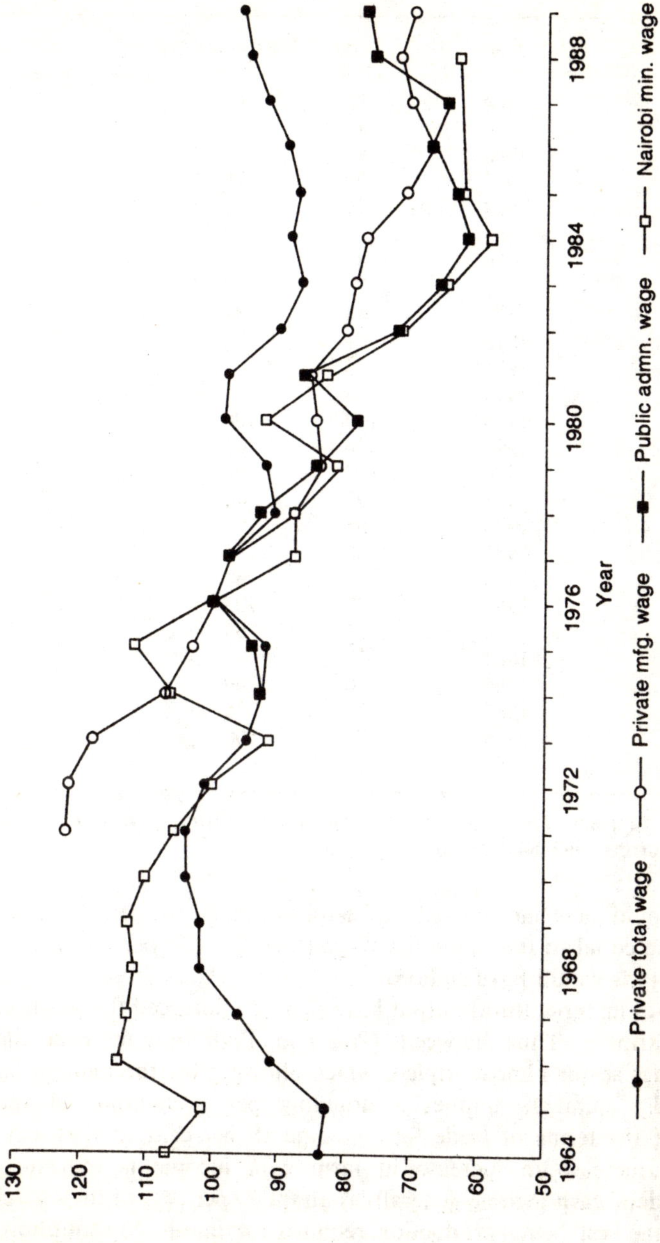

Source: Table 4.8

Figure 4.2 Kenya: Trends in real wages, 1964–89 (1976 = 100)

TABLE 4.9: *Kenya: Terms of trade of agricultural crops, 1964–89* (1976 = 100)

Year	Total	Domestic crops
1964	88	103
1965	81	97
1966	81	93
1967	78	89
1968	77	89
1969	78	89
1970	83	88
1971	76	87
1972	83	84
1973	79	76
1974	75	77
1975	73	95
1976	100	100
1977	126	102
1978	102	98
1979	93	90
1980	83	91
1981	80	84
1982	77	88
1983	78	103
1984	75	93
1985	72	97
1986	76	100
1987	72	99
1988	76	100
1989	75	

SOURCE: Sharpley 1986 and Kenya, *Statistical Abstract*, various years. Domestic crops 1982–84 refer to cereals only.

farmer would have had to produce 7.8 tons of maize per year to attain an income equal to the minimum wage (then Sh. 175 per month); in 1988 3.4 tons would have sufficed.

Increases in agricultural output have further reinforced the position of the farmers. Thus between 1964 and 1988 output from the smallholder sector almost tripled, which allowing for the increase in smallholder numbers implies a doubling per household. In the meantime the terms of trade fell by some 18 per cent so that a 60 per cent increase in increase in farm *cash* income is indicated. Smallholders' cash income generally is about 40 per cent of their total income, the rest being production retained for family consumption.

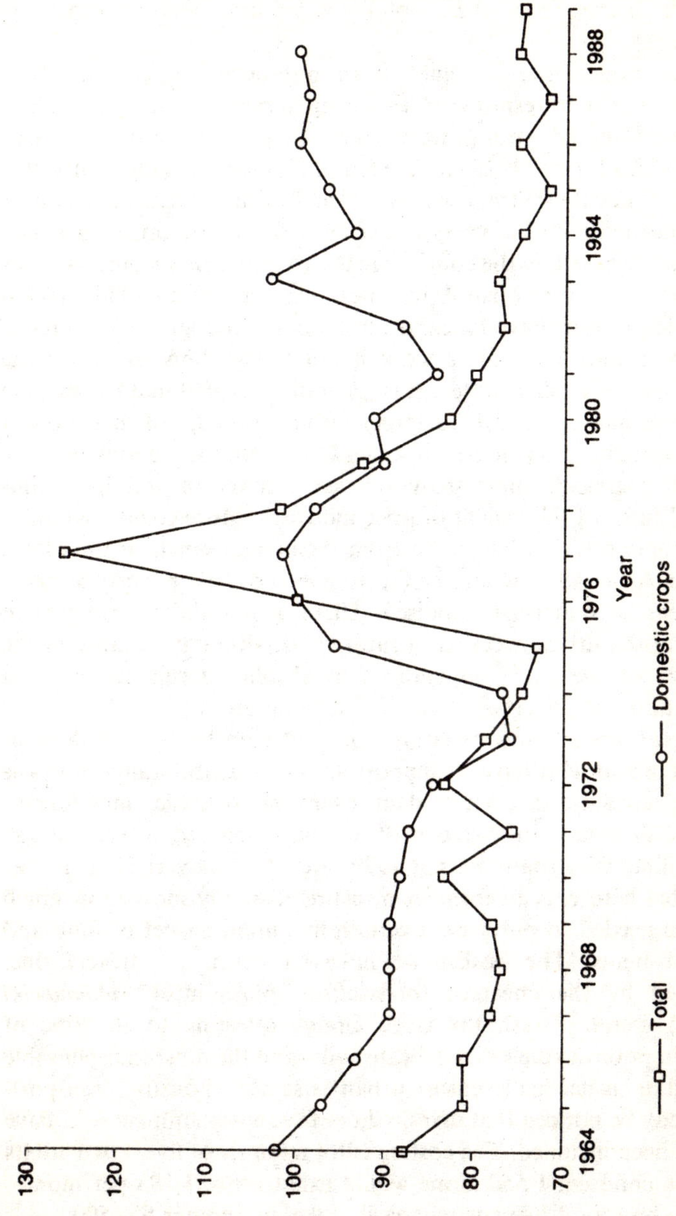

Source: Table 4.9

Figure 4.3 Kenya: Terms of trade of agricultural crops, 1964–89 (1976 = 100)

This part of farmers' income has remained constant, so that on the whole the 60 per cent increase in farmers' cash income has meant a 25 per cent increase in their total agricultural income (cash + subsistence).

At the same time, incomes from non-farm sources too have increased, partly in response to the rising agricultural incomes. These incomes are shared among the extended families in rural areas. Two surveys – IRS I in 1974–75 and the Rural Household Budget survey of 1981–82 – indicate that household incomes in rural areas increased by 37 per cent between the years in question. There are no further data available but based on the continuing increase in farm incomes we may conclude that overall rural incomes have increased. This means poverty levels must have fallen in rural areas, although a more precise statement cannot be made since it is not known how gains in rural incomes have been distributed. It is generally accepted that increases in farm prices mostly benefit the larger farmers because of their greater involvement in cash marketing; however, the smallholders have gradually increased their share of cash marketing and have thus captured some of the benefit of price increases. More consolidation of their income position has come from their involvement in non-farm activities. All in all, it would be fair to conclude that poverty levels in rural areas have at least stabilised. There is now the same extent of poverty in the urban areas as in rural areas, although because of the sheer size of the rural population, in absolute terms the greatest concentration of poverty remains in the rural areas.

Wage earners are now certainly worse off than before and those at the bottom end who have to support an average size family in towns must be considered poorer than even the average smallholder. Towards this end, in Table 4.10 we have derived a very rough 'poverty line' for urban areas at 1990 prices.[21] A poverty line, as has been stated before, is a subjective measure; it simply shows how much income is needed to purchase a certain minimum basket of food and non-food items. The basket we have chosen is an austere one, dominated by the cheapest foodstuffs – maize-meal, *sukumawiki* (spinach; literally 'push the week along', attesting to the role of spinach in poor people's diets), beans, oil – and the most indispensable non-food items needed to ensure urban existence – housing, transport, fuel. It may be noticed that taxes, school fees, entertainment, etc. have not even been included. The costing is for a family of five – two adults and three children. Food alone would exhaust Sh. 1,183 per month, while the non-food items would easily take up another Sh. 500.

TABLE 4.10: *Kenya: Costing of a minimum-needs basket in urban areas, 1990* (per 5-member family)

	Calories (%)	Price (Sh/kg)	Calories/kg	Price/1,000 calories (Sh)	Cost per day (Sh)
Maize flour	50	5.00	3 200	1.56	8.58
Beans	20	11.88	3 200	3.71	8.16
Sukumawiki	15	4.85	500	9.70	16.00
Oil	15	30.40	7 500	4.05	6.69
	100 = 1,000 calories				Sh. 39.43
				Non-food	
				Fuel	2.00
				2 bus trips	7.00
				Rent	9.00
					Sh. 18.00
					Total Sh. 57.43

SOURCE: Estimated by Jamal based on data collected in Kenya in 1990.

Compared to this, background data show that 30 per cent of the urban wage earners had incomes below the food poverty line and one-half below the full poverty line. The situation in 1973 was quite different. On the same basis as in the table the food poverty line would be around Sh. 200. Average wage then was Sh. 540 per month – i.e. 2.7 times the food basket. In 1988 the average wage was only 1.9 time the food basket. In 1973 only 7 per cent of the urban wage earners could be counted as falling under food poverty compared to the 30 per cent in 1988. Indeed urban poverty which once was considered rare[22] has become common, and given the stabilisation of rural poverty due to rising incomes, has come to rival the situation in the rural areas.

The conclusion is reinforced when we look at the situation in the informal sector (column 5 of Table 4.8). Between 1974 and 1979 incomes there increased quite substantially, helping to counteract the fall in wages. The coffee boom and its attendant import boom were responsible for this. After 1978, with the onset of the recession, informal sector incomes began to fall, in sympathy with urban wages. In this respect we have to recall the close relationship between the wage sector and the informal sector. Wage earners are almost certainly the main customers of informal sector goods and services. The drastic decline in wages, along with the decline in the commodity prices, has finally caused the decline in informal sector incomes.

The wage fall in Kenya mirrors the experience of other African countries. However, the situation was not as dire as in the neighbouring countries of Uganda and Tanzania, where the monthly minimum wage at mid-1980s would not even have bought two weeks' supply of basic food for an urban family. In Kenya the minimum wage at this time still purchased the minimum food needs of an average family. Thus, while poverty increased in urban Kenya, it was still of a different degree from that in Uganda and Tanzania; in particular one can not yet talk of the break-up of the wage-earning class in Kenya as has happened in the neighbouring countries.

LESSONS FROM KENYA

Of all English-speaking sub-Saharan African countries, perhaps Kenya had the strongest reputation for embodying a large rural-urban gap and of suffering from a virulent case of 'urban bias'. On close inspection one discovers that the most important aspects of inequality in Kenya have never been based upon the rural-urban dichotomy. Indeed, so great are intra-rural and intra-urban inequalities that it is extraordinary that anyone should have stressed the rural-urban distinction as primary. This characteristic of Kenya, that the rural-urban distinction obfuscates inequalities rather than revealing them, applies to all sSA countries. It obscures for two reasons: first, consideration of class and income stratification within groups is largely ignored and; second, the historical and country-specific nature of the interaction between town and countryside is lost within an arid, static and essentially judgemental framework.

5 Mineral-Exporting Countries: Liberia and Zambia

In this chapter we consider the mineral-dependent economies of Liberia and Zambia together. Shifting the emphasis from the previous chapter, we shall be particularly interested in the mechanisms of macroeconomic adjustment in the two countries and their broader implications for policy orientation. In terms of labour market conditions, Liberia could well be included with the West African countries (low-wage syndrome) and Zambia with the East African countries (high-wage syndrome), where they in any case geographically belong. However, the peculiarities of mineral-based economies are best brought out by treating the two together and separately from the agriculture-oriented countries.

LIBERIA

Liberia made famous the expression 'growth without development',[1] now commonly used to summarise the marginalisation of the poorer groups and regions during the process of economic growth. The country's economy expanded at almost a record rate in the 1940s and 1950s on the basis of iron ore and rubber exports, but because of their modes of organisation and the nature of the Liberian society the benefits of growth remained confined to a small minority. The production of iron ore by definition has few linkages with the rest of the economy, and the same is true for rubber.[2] Thus, in the absence of significant processing of iron ore and rubber within the country, these sectors remained enclaves, with minimal spillover effects. Equally important for distribution, Liberia up to the 1960s was a colonial-type economy ruled by the descendants of freed slaves who regarded the 'natives' – as did colonial administrators everywhere in Africa – as a mere reserve of labour for the mines, plantations and urban industries. Remuneration was never set at a level to induce farmers to take up wage work, and government and employers regularly resorted to forced recruitment.

Thus, inequality was a built-in feature of the Liberian economy, but it did not consist of the simple 'rural-urban inequality', let alone farmer-wage earner inequality. Rather, inequality was of the type we encountered in the Kenya case, albeit in an even more extreme form. Clower *et al.* in the mid-1960s concluded that 'fewer than 5 per cent of the total number of income units in the economy receive more than 90 per cent of total domestic income in money and kind' (Clower *et al.* 1966, p. 65). If that observation is accurate, it would imply a Gini coefficient in the region of 0.8. Another group of 'visiting economists' estimated the Gini coefficient at 0.63 in 1970.[3] Next to these figures Kenya's inequality (0.59) assumes a much milder complexion. Indeed the dualism present in Kenya's agricultural sector is nothing compared to that found in Liberia. In Kenya smallholders claim at least a 50 per cent share in marketed crops, whereas in Liberia the figure for export crops must be less than 10 per cent and for food crops under 25 per cent. Most smallholders remain subsistence farmers growing rice and cassava for on-farm consumption. It is the smallholders who are generally referred to as 'rural' in Liberian literature, with all others – including wage earners working on plantations (called 'concessions') – put under the category of 'urban'. When one disaggregates this rather arbitrary definition, more relevant rural-urban gaps begin to disappear.

We start with the income distribution derived by the 1975 'visitors' – the World Bank mission, based on data for 1970 (Table 5.1). Rural-urban income was distributed in inverse proportion to the population: rural population comprised nearly three-quarters of the total, but had one-quarter of the total income; whereas the quarter of the population which was urban had three-quarters of total income. This yields a rural-urban gap of the order of 1:8.6. However, most of this gap was created by the income accruing to the top group of managers, professionals, etc. – 60 per cent of income for 4 per cent of the population, a figure not too dissimilar from that derived earlier by Clower and his associates. Between farmers and the unskilled group as a whole – i.e. the 'no job' category (presumably equivalent to 'informal sector' workers) and the 'job' subgroups – the gap was only of the order of 1:1.6, which would decline further (perhaps even disappear) were account taken of the higher cost of living in the urban areas.

A significant farm-wage gap is not a feature of the Liberian economy, and never has been. Two special characteristics of Liberian

TABLE 5.1: *Liberia: Income distribution, 1970*

	Population (%)	Income (%)	Income per capita (US dollars)
Rural	73.7	24.6	70
Urban			
Unskilled – no job[a]	3.4	1.2	75
Concessions	7.2	3.4	100
Unskilled – job[b]	3.4	2.4	150
Skilled	8.4	8.0	200
Managerial, professional and other	3.9	60.4	3 272
Total	100.0 (= 1.523 million)	100.0	210
Gini = 0.63			

NOTES:
a Defined as lack of formal employment.
b Formal employment.
SOURCE: World Bank 1975b, p. 16.

society account for this: (1) the development of the economy through concessions granted to foreign corporations; and (2) the colonisation of the country (by former slaves). The concessions (plantations) had no incentive to pay high wages and were abetted in this policy by the officially sanctioned practice of 'labour recruitment', which involved the forced induction of rural workers into the wage labour force.[4] The purchasing power of the minimum wage has never been at a level to support even the most rudimentary standard of living for a family (see Table 5.2).

The figures in the table show how much uncooked rice could be purchased with the minimum wage. But no one eats raw rice nor rice only. Adding fuel costs and vegetables would reduce the value of the minimum wage to a level sufficient to support only 1.5 persons. When other non-discretionary goods are added – transport, clothing, rent, etc. – the minimum wage in 1962 hardly supported a single adult person in town. This conclusion becomes firmer when we take account of the fact that an adult person requires about 2,700 calories per day, compared to 2,200 calories for the 'average' person assumed in the above table. The same situation applied with respect to the minimum

TABLE 5.2: *Liberia: Unskilled wage compared to rice price, 1962–85*

	1962	1974	1980	1985
Unskilled wage (c/day)	40	120	216	216
Rice price (c/lb)	10	25	–	–
(Food CLI)	(100)	(200)	(307)	(335)
lb of rice	4	5	–	–
Equivalent calories	6 360	7 640	–	–
Sufficient for (persons)	2.9	3.5	–	–

SOURCE: 1962 figures extracted from Clower *et al.* 1966: unskilled wage, p. 208; rice price, p. 60, with the assumption that retail prices are one-third above farm-gate prices. Figures in the second column are from World Bank 1975b: unskilled wage, p. 15; rice price, p. 27. Food CLI (cost-of-living index) from World Bank 1982, p. 89 and ILO 1987b. CLI figure against 1962 is that for 1964.

wage in 1974. In 1980 the minimum wage was doubled, a fact much lamented by a 1982 World Bank mission, which blamed the doubling of wages for urban unemployment and a labour shortage on the farms (World Bank 1982, p. 12). The increase could hardly be considered extravagant, however; compared to 1974 it represented a net gain of only 17 per cent in real terms. By 1985 this gain had all but disappeared, for the official minimum wage remained fixed. The World Bank's own figures of the minimum wage compared to agricultural value added per worker for the years 1980–87 show the precariousness of the Liberian wage earner (Table 5.3). Only in the 'collapsed economies' of Ghana and Uganda do we find ratios such as these.[5]

A peculiarity of the Liberian labour force should be noted at this point. A majority of Liberian workers find employment in the rural sector with the rubber and mining concessions. Thus, they are never far from their farmlands and families. Most only take up temporary

TABLE 5.3: *Liberia: Ratio of minimum wage compared to agricultural value added per worker, 1980–86*

	1980	1981	1982	1983	1984	1985	1986
Minimum wage divided by agricultural value added per worker	0.82	0.96	1.14	0.96	0.91	0.90	0.91

SOURCE: World Bank 1987a.

wage employment during the slack seasons and return to the farms for the harvest. The rural-urban fusion that we find increasing in the other African countries has always been a feature of the Liberian economy. Even in the urban areas proper a permanent and distinct labour force has never existed; indeed, it could hardly have when the urban wage has never been sufficient to support more than an individual worker. The typical pattern has been for adult males to migrate to urban areas and make periodic trips back to their farms to maintain their agricultural links. When families come to towns, they have to take up secondary jobs in the informal sector to augment total family income.

The Liberian case is particularly instructive for understanding the current African crisis and assessing the remedies suggested for its cure. The Liberian economy, like Zambia's, is a classic example of transmitted recession. Three particular factors account for this – the small size of the economy, its openness, and export concentration. In a country of 2.4 million inhabitants (mid-1988) and total GDP of 1 billion dollars (against about 6 billion for Kenya and Tanzania) an undiversified export package generated up to 75 per cent of the national income between 1970 and 1981. Thus, Liberia's money economy goes as her exports go – and since about 60 per cent of exports consist of iron ore, we may say that the Liberian economy goes as iron ore exports go. Table 5.4 shows some statistics for Liberia's terms of trade and their apparent impact on growth performance. Between 1970 and 1983 Liberia's terms of trade fell by almost 50 percent. With the quantum of exports fluctuating around an index of 90, the command over imports declined to half its value. Further, the decline in Liberia's terms of trade has been of a long-term nature, extending back at least to 1960–62. UNCTAD data show that in 1960–62 the terms of trade index was 318 (1980 = 100). However, between 1960 and 1970 Liberia's export volume

TABLE 5.4: *Liberia: Annual percentage change in terms of trade, purchasing power of exports and growth, 1960–83*

Period	Price terms of trade	Purchasing power of exports	Rate of growth of GDP
1960–70	–	–	4.7
1970–75	-5.3	-3.4	-0.3
1975–83	-4.2	-6.8	-4.3

SOURCE: World Bank 1982, 1986b and 1987b.

was increasing and hence her income terms of trade more than doubled. These trends were reflected in the per capita growth performance. Between 1960 and 1970 the country had one of the highest rates of growth of GDP per capita in sub-Saharan Africa, 4.7 per cent per annum (equal to that of Kenya). Stagnating export volumes and declining terms of trade put paid to all that, especially between 1975–83, when GDP per capita fell by 30 per cent.

Thus Liberia's export experience has important lessons for the genesis of the African crisis and for structural adjustment. As we saw earlier, there is a tendency to blame government 'mismanagement' for the crisis affecting African countries, the essence of the criticism being that by interfering with the markets governments have failed to pass on to the producers the signals from international trade; specifically, that exporters did not receive the full benefit of international prices. The lesson of the Liberian case for the 'mismanagement' criticism should not be missed: Liberia's currency is the United States dollar; iron ore exports are transacted in dollars, and the resulting export prices are the prices received by the mining companies. There can be no question of interference with the market or an 'over-valued exchange rate', arguments which have been used to berate African governments and cajole them into accepting structural adjustment programmes. When exchange rates cannot be adjusted, as in this case, increased competitiveness requires lower wages; yet wages in Liberia are and have always been abysmally low.

LESSONS FROM LIBERIA

The 'urban bias' model of African countries, so much a part of the folklore of the development community, created a particular stereotype of the African wage employee: he was highly paid compared to his countrymen, integrated into a Westernised urban culture, and the beneficiary of protective legislation and trade union organisation inappropriate to the poverty and underdevelopment of his nation. While once in the dim past African workers had been under-paid, over-worked, and subject to physical abuse at the workplace, such was no longer the case by the 1960s. This sanguine view, with its implicit suggestion that workers have, after all, gone too far in redressing old injustices, is wrong, more so in the late 1980s than ever. Most African workers never enjoyed substantial respite from low pay, long hours, and arbitrary authority. And in Liberia the moderating and legalising of the wage labour relationship along lines found in 45 years of ILO resolutions and guidelines has hardly begun. African workers in other countries, particularly those in countries where significant advances in wages and working conditions were made, have lost much of what they gained; all over sub-Saharan Africa the condition of urban workers more and more approximates the rock-bottom poverty and powerlessness of Liberian wage-earners.

ZAMBIA

In many ways, Zambia is quite atypical of African countries. With one-half of its population in urban areas in 1990, the land-locked southern African country is one of the most urbanised in the sSA region. Second, a large percentage of its labour force is in wage employment – about 30 percent compared to less than a third as much in most other African countries. Third, wage earners have become quite thoroughly urbanised, which is not the case in other sSA countries. These unique features of the Zambian economy have conditioned the evolution of the rural-urban gap, and more recently the governmental and popular response to the standard adjustment programmes. In other respects, Zambia is similar to its neighbours. As in Kenya, the rural sector is divided between commercial farmers and smallholders, with the former dominating the marketing of food. In the urban areas inequalities are rampant, again as in Kenya. But the 'engine of growth', as in Liberia, is mining, rather than agriculture. Thus, the 'rural-urban gap' has a special meaning here, as do the standard adjustment remedies. Yet this has not prevented analysts from lamenting 'the gap', or funding agencies from imposing reforms deriving from models of agriculture-oriented economies.

The ILO/JASPA had identified Zambia as a high-wage economy during two separate employment advisory missions, spanning a period of five years (ILO/JASPA 1977 and 1981c). By the time of the second mission in 1980, wages had been falling as a trend for at least half a decade. But in 1980 no one spoke of declining urban wages in Africa. The JASPA team thus emphasised widening rural-urban differentials, just as it had done five years earlier, when it pointedly entitled its report *Narrowing the gaps*. This emphasis was not new: two 'Turner Reports' on wages policy in Zambia (ILO 1969 and 1978) both wrote of large and widening rural-urban gaps, quite likely influencing the JASPA missions. In the light of these policy reports, we now consider in some detail the specification of the rural-urban gap in Zambia and the characterisation of that country as a high-wage economy. From this consideration we shall draw lessons for other African countries, especially the East African ones with which Zambia shares some common colonial and post-colonial experiences.

In Zambia after independence, as in other East African countries, money wages sky-rocketed. Thus, Turner in his first report (ILO 1969) noticed that wages increased at double-digit rates in each of the five years preceding his mission, at almost 20 per cent annually, registering a total growth of almost 150 per cent. Translated into real terms, the increase was around two-thirds. As nothing like this could be discerned for farmers, the conclusion was inevitable that 'a very wide gap has developed between the standard of life of the urban Zambian employees and that of the Zambian villagers' (ILO 1969, p. 10). Later this was referred to as a 'dangerous gap' (p. 14). Farmers' incomes were shown to have increased by 3 per cent between 1964 and 1968, while those of wage earners increased by 40 per cent or more. By 1968 the gap between farmers and non-mine wage earners was shown to be of the order of 1:4.4, and between farmers and mineworkers 1:9.

These gaps were quite illusory, resting on very shaky data and quite devoid of any conceptual content, for the increase in wages, as in other East African countries, merely enabled a wage earner to support his family in town. Thus the categorisation of Zambia as a 'high-wage' country came entirely from the judgement that money wages increased 'too fast' in the immediate post-independence years, not from any hard evidence showing a relatively high standard of living. Further, the rapid post-independence increase in wages must be analysed in light of the fact that the colonial wage structure in the mines was essentially racialist, only cosmetically different from the wage structure that exists in the mines of South Africa today. It indicated considerable historical insensitivity to judge the increases in isolation from the decades of colonial domination which generated the need for them.

The wage increases experienced in Zambia were of the same order as occurred in the other East African countries and for the same reasons: (i) to stabilise the urban wage-earning class; (ii) to distribute some of the fruits of independence to the indigenous population; and (iii) to 'localise' (i.e. Africanise) the labour force. The last two factors had a racial element and could be called 'equity' – or 'discrimination', depending on one's bias. Wages were raised, and because of the racial mix of these economies it appeared that the non-African employers – the majority of those employing wage earners – were paying for it. Be that as it may, in the meantime Africans were also taking over non-African jobs and wages. The proportion of expatriates in the labour force declined from 12 percent in 1964 to 8 per cent in 1968 (ILO 1969, p. 8). However, since total wage employment was expanding – by about a third – the decline in the absolute number of expatriates was slight. Most of the decline occurred in the civil service, as did most of the increase in jobs. As in other sSA countries, the salary structure established during the colonial period was taken over by the independent government. A large part of the increase in wages and salaries occurred in one 'wage round' in 1961, which started in the Copperbelt when a pay increase of about 20 per cent was obtained. The motivating factor was the gap between the wages of Africans and expatriates. Within a short time a similar raise was obtained for the civil service, and this rate soon percolated down to the whole economy. In closing one gap (the African/non-African), another was created (the farmer/wage earner).

Table 5.5 provides two measures of the extent of this gap, which we now dissect. The first estimate is Turner's, and it shows average income per wage earner divided by total peasant family income. For the comparison to be valid, an implicit assumption has to be made that the average wage earner supported the same size family as the average farmer. We have no quarrel with this. But let us examine the figure for farm income, K145 per household per annum. As Turner indicated, this number was very much in the realm of an estimate (drawn from

TABLE 5.5: *Zambia: Measures of the rural-urban gap, two selected years, 1968 and 1970*

	Year and source	Ratio	Incomes:		Basis
			Wage earners	Farmers	
1. Wage earner/ peasant	1968 Turner	4.9	713	145	Wage compared to peasant family income
2. Minimum wage/ agricultural value added per worker	1970 World Bank	3.5	400	114	Wage compared to output per agric. worker

SOURCE: (1) from ILO 1969, p. 11.
(2) from World Bank 1987a.

the national income accounts); unfortunately the estimate is completely of the wrong order of magnitude. One reason for the misestimate is that peasants' income calculated from the national accounts is measured at producer prices. Because of the rural-urban price differential it is not valid to compare urban wages with farm income measured at farm-gate prices, for this would assume both groups buy and sell at the same prices.

The second inaccuracy arises from an obvious underestimation of agricultural income, particularly subsistence income, common enough in national accounts in Africa, as we saw in the previous chapter. To calculate the extent of the measurement error, we invoke the 'rule' used in the Tanzanian case study: equal baskets in rural and urban areas should be assigned the same monetary value. We postulate that the average farmer in Zambia produced at least sufficient calories for the family. This food basket should be given its value at town prices (so it has the same value wherever it is consumed). For 1974 the first JASPA mission estimated the cost of food for an urban family (4.6 members) at K 360, and at prices of 1968 (the year for the first measure in Table 5.5) for an average rural family of 4.9 members the cost would be K 275. Now, if we assume that food comprised 75 per cent of rural family income, then average farm income would be K 366 per annum, well over double Turner's measure. The gap falls to 1:1.9, a far cry from the ratio of 1:4.9 that so offended Turner. A 4.9 gap should indeed alarm, but the fact is, it simply could not exist, for given that the average wage earner did not at most times enjoy an aristocratic living standard, a gap of 4.9 – or average farm income at only 20 per cent of the average wage – would mean physical starvation for the farmer. Further, the gap we have laboured to correct is not directly relevant to migration, an issue which so concerned the Turner Reports. When considering migration, as previously argued, one should compare farm income with the wage of an unskilled worker; and one should discount for non-discretionary expenditures in urban areas. We have as yet included neither of these refinements; if we did, then the gap would seem quite modest. Finally, the accuracy of our farm income measure compared to Turner's is indicated by the fact that the 1968 national income accounts estimate of subsistence income implies a calorie intake of less than 50 per cent of the normal requirement. This is clearly an understimate for if correct it would mean widespread starvation in the Zambian rural sector.

Having considered Turner's dubious calculations, we turn to a later measure of the wage earner-farmer gap by the World Bank. The incomes compared were the minimum wage and agricultural value added per worker. This is again a wrong comparison, comparing what an urban worker produced at the margin with what a farmer produced on average. It certainly is not directly relevant to migration, income distribution, or any other economic phenomenon. A correct comparison for welfare levels would be between family incomes. Using K 400 as family income for wage earners, let us assume equal family sizes in rural and urban areas for simplicity. Whatever is the relevant farm family income it is not K 114, since this is the average output of one worker. For a family of five, one would expect there to be at least two and perhaps three workers per family. On the assumption of 2.5 adult equivalent workers, the income gap drops to 1:1.4. As we see below, other evidence suggests that this modest ratio is of the right order of magnitude.

Thus, the 'gap' that alarmed most analysts proves to have been quite likely illusory and based on faulty data. Worse, it was based on poor institutional analysis and poor theory. For most wage earners three-quarters of their incomes had to be spent on food. If we accept this proposition, then a wage earner-farmer gap of 3 to 5 would imply *starvation* for rural households. But few if any observers pursued such implications of Turner-like calculations for rural households, accepting the assertion of a 'labour aristocracy' in Zambia. The only empirical support provided was the fact that that wages increased rapidly in the first decade of independence. Wages did increase, but as in the other East African countries the increase merely brought the unskilled wage earner to a level sufficient to maintain a family in town. Perhaps the 'average wage earner' did earn an 'aristocratic' wage of a sort, but in Zambia, more than elsewhere, the typical wage earner did not receive the average wage, but far below it because of the wide dispersion of wages caused by the mining sector.[6] For at least 40 to 50 per cent of the non-agricultural labour force the relevant wage was the government minimum wage, and it would be hard to put the label of 'aristocratic' on this wage.

Table 5.6 and Figure 5.1 show the progression of the minimum wage between 1960 and 1985 and its relationship to a minimum needs basket, the latter a 1974 base line measure by the JASPA mission and widely accepted as accurate (ILO/JASPA 1977, p. 61).[7] In the diagram, the minimum needs consumption basket is represented as a straight line, on the assumption that the cost of this basket varied according to the cost-of-living index (i.e. by definition its cost remains constant in real terms). Since the basket was derived for an average size family of five

TABLE 5.6: *Zambia: Trends in real official minimum wage, 1960–85* (1974 = 100)

1960	56	1977	87
1965	77	1978	74
1968	102	1979	88
1970	128	1980	112
1971	121	1981	97
1972	115	1982	103
1973	108	1983	97
1974	100 (=K 400)	1984	90
		1985	83
1975	124		
1976	104		

SOURCE: 1960–68 from ILO 1969 and 1978 (Turner Reports) and ILO/JASPA 1981c; 1970–85 from World Bank 1987a.

members, its comparison with the wage involves an implicit assumption that the average wage earner supported an average size family.

The diagram shows that at the time of independence the minimum wage was woefully insufficient to maintain a family in town, and only by about 1970 was this critical wage level attained. We also see that the 1970 position was transitory, and regained only briefly when wages

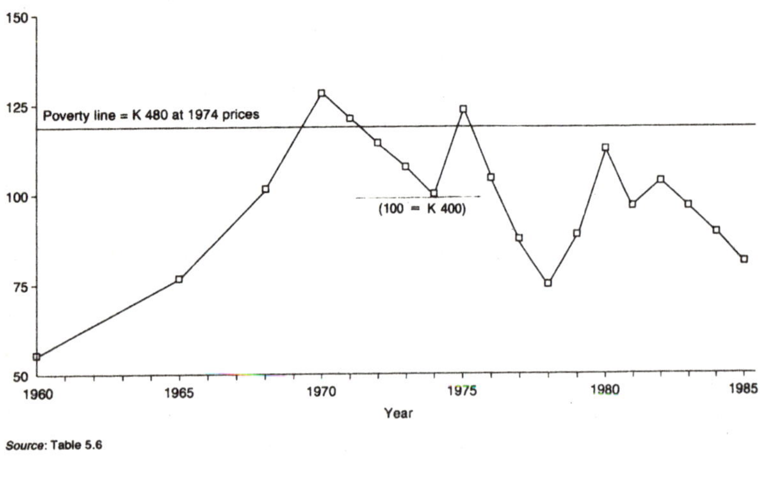

Figure 5.1 Zambia: Trends in real official minimum wage, 1960–85 (1974 = 100)

rose sharply in 1974 and 1975. Ten years later the minimum wage bought only two-thirds of a family's basic needs.

As in other African countries, wages have fallen in Zambia; but there is a difference in this case. In most other African countries the wage decline has been continuous since the mid-1970s, while in Zambia wage earners managed to stave off decline until about 1980. Judgements about trends are made difficult because of the irregular time path in the diagram. Turner, noticing the zig-zag, had hypothesised a three-year wage and salary cycle in Zambia in his 1977 report. Such a cycle of course has no basis in theory – and of course does not exist; and in the second half of the 1980s wages have continued to fall.

In our detailed discussion of measurement, it should not be lost that the Zambian experience indicates important differences arising from the character of its wage labour force. Zambia's economy is much more urbanised, with a much higher proportion of the labour force in wage employment than in other sSA countries. Equally important, Zambia's labour force being concentrated in the copper belt has much more clout in influencing policy than the typical African labour force concentrated on producing export crops on individual plots. Being much more proletarianised than elsewhere, higher food prices automatically translate themselves into higher cost of living – and are resented, as the 1987 food riots in the Copperbelt showed. In other African countries, especially with the recent trend to urban farming, higher food prices do not imply the same catastrophe, as shown when the huge increase in the price of maize-meal in Tanzania in 1985 occurred without organised protest. This point is discussed further below in the context of Zambian negotiations with the IMF.

Loxley (1990) has looked further into the question of living standards of wage earners. He shows the costing of a minimal food basket for a family of six at three periods – August 1980, June 1986 and June 1988 (Table 5.7). Between 1980 and 1986, while the cost of the food basket almost quadrupled average formal sector earnings only doubled. As a percentage of the monthly wage of an ordinary labourer (44 hours per week) the cost of the basket rose from 64 to 88 per cent. It may be noted that the consumer price index rose much more than the cost of the food basket – to 883 in June 1988 compared to 657 for the food basket, so that the drop recorded above is deliberately kept on the low side. Secondly, the roller mill price is the subsidised price; without the subsidy the 1988 basket would exhaust five weeks' wages. Already by 1984 it was estimated that two-fifths of the urban families earned less than the minimum needs basket (Loxley

TABLE 5.7: *Zambia: A simple monthly food budget to meet nutritional requirements of a family of six, 1980, 1986 and 1988* (kwachas)

	Amounts	August 1980	June 1986	June 1988
Roller meal	90 kg	17.28	53.46	53.46
Milk	4 cartons	0.72	3.04	9.20
Green vegetables	7.5 kg	2.40	9.00	32.78
Cooking oil	2.5 litres	4.21	15.78	24.75
Dried kapenta (fish)	2 kg	6.05	33.42	48.66
Dried beans	2 kg	3.15	8.56	26.28
Salt	1 kg	0.24	3.05	2.18
Tomatoes	4 kg	3.40	11.12	29.04
Onions	4 kg	2.00	9.44	32.80
Total		39.45	146.87	259.15
As % of unskilled wage		64	73	88
Index		100.00	372.30	656.90

SOURCE: Loxley 1990, table 3.2 based on ILO/JASPA 1981c, data provided by Central Statistical Office, and Loxley's own calculations.
NOTE: Budget excludes groundnuts and dried fish for which 1986 and 1988 data were unavailable.

1990, p. 58, citing Clark and Keen 1988, p. 28). Apart from the survival strategies already noted in the other case studies – resort to secondary incomes – Loxley points to reduced food intake as a forced coping mechanism, underlining a disturbing finding of Muntemba (1989).

Having dealt with wages and wage earners, we turn to the rural-urban terms of trade, another issue of contention. The JASPA team in 1981 realised that wages had declined, but gave much more weight to the fall in the rural-urban terms of trade. The relevant figures are shown in Table 5.8.

The JASPA mission chose to base its analysis on the period 1965–77 when real wages increased by 43 per cent. Compared to that, farmers' income terms of trade fell by almost an equal proportion, ergo the rural-urban gap increased. But this conclusion is erroneous even for this period (for 1971–77 when wages fell sharply it simply would not stand), reflecting, as we have shown before, a 'money illusion'. The JASPA calculations in effect valued all agricultural production at market prices, a fundamental measurement mistake with which the reader should now be only too familiar. The JASPA argument went as follow because of lower prices off-setting increased output, farm

TABLE 5.8: *Zambia: Real wages versus agricultural production, 1965–79, selected years*

	Real wages	Agricultural production per capita	Barter terms of trade	Income terms of trade
1965	100	100	100	100
1971	171	132	46	61
1977	143	167	36	61
1979	–	121	36	43

SOURCE: ILO/JASPA 1981c, vol. 2, p. 35. 'Real wage' refers to average wage, not minimum wage as in table 6.6.

income in 1971 was below the level of 1965 and urban prices were up, implying a fall in farm purchasing power of about 40 per cent. This method of calculation is quite inappropriate, for to the extent that farmers consumed their own produce prices were irrelevant to welfare; indeed they had a larger output to consume. Of course, Zambian farmers sell some of their staples and purchase other food (mostly non-staples) on the market; terms of trade calculations are relevant for this part of farmers' incomes but this is only a small part of their total 'real' income. If farmers' real income had fallen by 51 per cent between 1965 and 1979 – or, even more dramatic, by 50 per cent in just two years, between 1967 and 1969 (for that is what the figures showed: ILO/JASPA 1981c, Vol. 2, p. 35), a visible increase in suffering should manifest itself, especially when we remember that at any given time most farmers barely rise above minimum self-sufficiency. One would expect such a deterioration to manifest itself in farmer unrest, since the declines shown in Table 5.8 are entirely due to farmers' barter terms of trade falling, which could be blamed on government policy. Given what is known about social and economic conditions in the countryside during the 1970s, the inferences drawn by the JASPA mission about rural incomes are not credible.

Finally, we must examine developments in Zambia's external sector, for as in the case of Liberia they are important in understanding the 'African crisis' and 'structural adjustment' programmes. As we have seen before, the standard adjustment programmes in Africa – and in most African countries a very standard package is offered – are predicated on a stereotypic model of an African country. In this model the country exports certain primary products. Government intervention in the price mechanism causes producers' terms of trade to fall, leading to a fall in output. A devaluation should be effected to restore a more efficient price structure; this will stimulate exports and thus pull the country out of crisis. We have argued that this stereotype about African economies is incorrect. Particularly with respect to export performance it is invalid to apportion all blame to governments for an unfavourable shift between internal and external prices. If farmers' terms of trade have fallen, they have frequently done so parallel to external trends. We shall argue that in some cases – Somalia, in particular – even the most basic elements of the model do not apply, yet most of the ingredients of the standard adjustment package are espoused with equal enthusiasm. Zambia too falls in this category.

The Zambian economy depends almost totally on copper for foreign exchange. In most recent years copper accounted for over 90 per cent of the value of exports, and the contribution of copper to GDP and government revenue is overwhelming. Thus, if Zambia's economy is in the doldrums we have to look no further than the copper sector and the world copper price for an explanation. Table 5.9 and Figure 5.2 show Zambia's terms of trade, which for practical purposes are Zambia's copper terms of trade, and these figures tell us much about the 'mismanagement' stories. Between the two terminal dates in the table, 1970 and 1988, Zambia's terms of trade exactly halved. To put it graphically, in 1970 one ton of copper would have sufficed to buy one unit of imports, whereas in 1988 two tons would have been needed. While the terms of trade fell, Zambia more or less kept up its production of copper output up to 1982 (quite surprising since the market mechanism was signalling otherwise). But with the terms of trade down, total exports in 1982 could only buy one-third the amount of imports as 12 years previously. Here there is no question of a marketing board intervening in the price mechanism nor of the exchange rate being out of equilibrium, since copper exports were transacted in dollar prices and these prices were fully reflected in the signals to producers.[8] Thus, one cannot argue that the downward spiral in the economy started because producer prices were discriminatory as a result of government intervention. The downward spiral started because external prices declined catastrophically. The remedy does not lie in tinkering with internal prices through devaluation (even for non-mineral exporting countries we question this prescription). The swings in Zambia's fortunes depend strictly on the international market. It is little wonder that Zambia decided to back out of agreements with the IMF.[9]

TABLE 5.9: *Zambia: Terms of trade estimates, 1970–1988 (1980 = 100)*

	'70	'71	'72	'73	'74	'75	'76	'77	'78	'79	'80	'81	'82	'83	'84	'85	'86	'87	'88
Exports																			
Value	77	52	58	88	108	62	80	69	67	106	100	83	79	64	50	42	31	67	91
Unit value	68	50	49	81	103	61	68	63	65	92	100	82	71	76	67	69	67	84	120
Volume	114	105	118	109	106	102	118	109	103	115	100	100	111	84	75	61	47	80	76
Imports																			
Value	43	50	51	48	71	84	59	60	57	68	100	96	90	62	55	62	54	67	76
Unit value	29	28	30	41	47	57	52	63	70	86	100	96	94	90	89	90	92	99	103
Volume	166	181	168	117	151	147	114	96	80	79	100	94	96	70	61	70	59	67	73
Terms of trade	232	179	164	196	219	108	132	100	93	107	100	86	76	84	75	76	73	85	116
Buying power of exports	263	188	194	214	231	110	155	110	95	123	100	86	84	90	57	47	34	68	88

SOURCE: UNCTAD 1989a, table 7.2 for all except 1971, 1972, 1774 and 1796 which are from UNCTAD 1984, table 7.2.

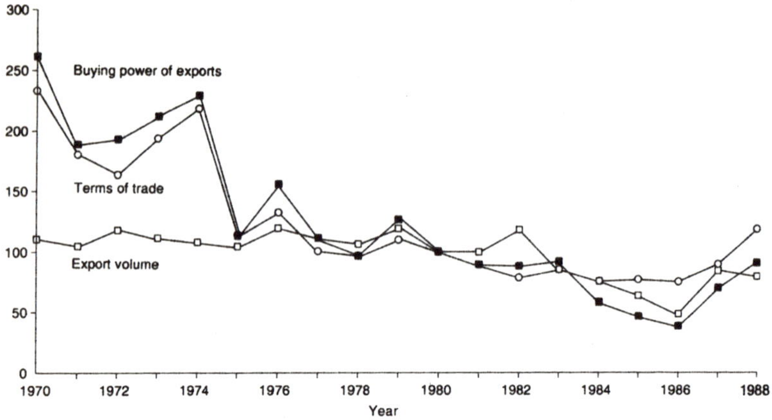

Source: Table 5.9

Figure 5.2 Terms of trade estimates, 1970–88 (1980 = 100)

A contributing factor to this rupture is related to the proletarianisation of the country's labour force, mentioned above. In common with other African countries Zambia was asked by the IMF to rescind subsidies on food products. Tanzania, as we saw, finally accepted this conditionality in 1985 and raised the price of the staple food dramatically. But with regard to popular outrage, nothing happened. In Zambia the mere announcement of impending price increases set off riots. The difference in popular response reflects the much greater proletarianisation of the Zambian labour force, a labour force made up of households which are overwhelmingly net food purchasers. Any price increase signifies a 'real' drop in 'real wages', whereas in the general African case urban subsistence production has served as part of the survival strategy of wage earning households. This option is not available to most Zambian workers.

LESSONS FROM ZAMBIA

In every country of sub-Saharan Africa the relationship between rural and urban areas is the consequence of historical developments. The 'urban bias' view which explains the complexity of rural-urban interactions in terms of arbitrary government policy and crude economistic deductions from apparent material gains is myopic, ahistoric and unscientific. Its myopic character is reflected in treating all sSA countries as if they were essentially similar, capable of being analysed in terms of a single concept that epitomises their social and political nature. The approach is ahistorical in its implicit presumption that while sSA countries may have a history of their own, knowledge of this history is unnecessary for treating questions of income distribution, migration, etc. The lack of precision essential to scientific investigation is evidenced by the inappropriate and misleading attempts at empirical verification.

Zambia perhaps more than any other country studied in this book supports the above judgement. For decades blacks and whites worked side by side in the mines, the former paid miserably, the latter enjoying a standard of living beyond their dreams in their mother countries. That the pent-up frustrations of decades would result in a few years of rapid wage increases after independence is hardly surprising. What is surprising is that it should have received such moral condemnation in the guise of economic science. These wage increases did not create an aristocracy of labour in Zambia. Indeed, Zambia is the case of the purest form of the labour aristocracy myth, demonstrating how little evidence is necessary to create an all-pervasive illusion.

6 Remittance Economies: Somalia and Lesotho

Somalia and Lesotho are countries whose major export is workers. Able-bodied Somalis and Basothos toil abroad and send back remittances which are dominant factors in the domestic cash economy of their countries. The importance of remittances for Lesotho is widely recognised; less well understood is their overwhelming importance in Somalia. One of our central tasks in this chapter is to investigate the impact of remittances on the rural-urban gap.

SOMALIA

In most case studies considered in this volume it is possible to use a common set of concepts and conventional theoretical formulations to 'tell stories' of a familiar type (though they may be controversial stories). The Somali economy is so 'unconventional' that attempts to tell variations on the conventional theme are misleading if not downright erroneous, although this has not prevented many from doing so. The importance of pastoralism in Somali society is only one aspect of the difficulty.[1] The other is to sort out the ramifications of remittances. What is required is an analytical method analogous to the peeling of an onion: layers must be discarded before one begins to approach the core of the economy. Unfortunately (for some) the layers that have to be discarded include the national accounts and stories based on them – in other words the whole gamut of analysis using GDP per capita and GDP growth rates – because of the overwhelming importance of remittances which go mostly unrecorded (see Jamal 1981, 1983b, 1987 and 1988e).[2] Attempts to measure the Somali economy with standard categories not only do not tell the full story; they tell the wrong story. For example, all national accounts and trade statistics show the economy to be in long-term decline, indeed in a state of severe crisis. Yet the impression one got in urban areas (prior to the culmination of the civil war, of course) was of boom conditions. Virtually all studies of poverty suggest widespread deprivation in both rural and urban areas, yet perceptions belie this. The numbers show that in the mid-1980s the urban wage is down to 5 per cent of its level 16 years before, yet one fails to perceive increasing impoverishment – quite the contrary. The choice is either to write up a story based on national accounts or to dig into the Somali economy to explain why in a supposedly declining economy one sees signs of robust consumption expenditure. The answer to the apparent contradiction is that the Somali economy was driven after the mid-1970s by remittances from workers in the Gulf countries.

Both the number of workers abroad and the amount they remit are a matter of guesswork. This implies that both the total national income accruing to Somalis and the foreign exchange accounts of the country remain in considerable doubt. That remittances are of crucial importance in the cash economy is beyond doubt. It has been estimated by one of the authors that 165,000 Somalis worked in the Gulf States in the early 1980s (i.e. more than the total number of wage employees in the country), earning 30–40 times the highest government salary. On the assumption that workers abroad remitted one-third of their income (and some guesses go much higher), $338 million worth of remittances are implied (Jamal 1988e, p. 239; see also ILO/JASPA 1989b, technical paper 3 for a consolidated estimate), equal to 1.5 times the total non-agricultural GDP as measured in the national accounts. This did not include remittances from long-standing migration to nearby African countries; Somali traders and workers in other countries (mainly East African) were estimated to remit about $90 million a year over the last decade (Green and Jamal 1987).

It is not just the amount of remittances that gave the Somali economy its unconventional nature (this it shares with Lesotho and other countries), but equally the way these remittances reached Somalia. During the 1970s and early 1980s a system called the *franco valuta* was in operation. Although discontinued in its pure form in the mid-1980s, its essential features persisted at least till the civil war that erupted in 1990; such is the enterprising nature of the Somali people that at least for basic necessities the system probably survived the ravages of the civil war. Under this system Somalis working in the Gulf States exchanged the currency in which they were paid for Somali shillings through private transactors, who then remitted the shillings to the relatives of the workers.[3] The intermediaries used the foreign exchange so obtained to purchase commodities to export to Somalia. Thus, a virtually unregulated market reigned in foreign exchange through the 1980s. Livestock sales, the largest measured source of foreign exchange, were also transacted under this system. In other African countries markets of this type – foreign exchange transactions out of sight of the authorities – have existed, but in general these are peripheral 'black markets', laden with connotations of clandestinity and illegality. In Somalia unregulated and unmeasured exchanges formed the major and relatively overt market for foreign exchange. The transactions conducted in this market help explain the country's large measured balance of payments deficit. Since the greater proportion of livestock exports are transacted within the unregulated market, the officially measured foreign exchange flows appear to generate a tremendous deficit. In the conventional model the adverse balance is attributed to an overvalued exchange rate and the cure is devaluation. In Somalia the resort to devaluation is largely irrelevant, for the effective exchange rate is not the official rate, and the official rate is marginal with respect to private sector imports. Even for government foreign exchange transactions, the official rate is little more than an accounting rate, since public sector imports are virtually in their entirety based on tied aid.

The Somali economy is unconventional in its rural sector, too, combining nomadic pastoralism with permanent cultivation of food crops. In the case of nomads, the socio-economic life of the pastoral population makes the application of neoclassical parables inappropriate to the point of absurd. Cash exchanges have always been quite important in the sub-sector, for the pastoralists sell a substantial proportion of their animals on the national and international markets (called 'the off-take rate'). Rational decision-making in livestock marketing involves a survival strategy centuries old, which results in behavior that standard economic theory would judge as 'perverse'. Credibility-straining estimates of the degree of rural poverty in Somalia are largely the result of misunderstanding the nature of pastoralism and the relationship between marketed and non-marketed production.[4] Crucial is accounting properly for auto-consumption, a task particularly difficult since pastoralists and cultivators consume different types of foods, and the analysis appropriate for the former is inappropriate for the latter. Putting a monetary value on non-marketed production (and consumption) tends to show nomads to be better off than farmers, even when both groups in the rural population may be consuming equal amounts of calories.[5] Even the rural-urban gap could be measured in favour of nomads by imputation at prevailing market prices. The imputation problem arises because the nomadic diet is made up of milk and meat, high-priced sources of calories compared to the grains consumed by farmers and townsmen.

On the basis of the usual measure of the urban-rural gap, there would appear to have been a sharp fall. As Table 6.1 shows, from 1970 to 1986 real urban wages declined by some 80 per cent.[6] Minimum wages fell even more – by 95 per cent. Most of the fall occurred after 1978 due to mounting inflation combined with stagnating money wages. By 1986 the average monthly wage would have bought only 12 days' supply of food and the minimum wage less than 5 days' supply. Such a catastrophic fall in real wages was possible without a collapse in urban society because of the dramatic increase in remittances in the 1970s which not only supplemented but came to dominate urban incomes.

Two other factors that explain the lack of impoverishment despite falling wages are rural-urban links and multi-occupational families. The first is rather straightforward and occurs, as we have by now seen, to varying extent in other African countries – urban families receive food from rural relatives (particularly maize). The second, multi-occupational families, operates to a greater extent in Somalia than

TABLE 6.1: *Somalia: Average wage, cost of living index, and real wage, 1970–86* (selected years)

	1970	1974	1977	1978	1980	1984	1986
Average wage (So. Sh/p.a.)							
Industry[a]	3 900	4 800	6 168	7 272	8 000	20 000	30 000
Government[b]	5 160	6 000	5 640	6 600	7 300	14 000	18 000
Average[c]	4 284	5 160	6 000	7 068	7 790	18 200	26 400
Cost of living index[d]	100	122	184	202	399	1 854	3 470
Real wage (1970 prices)	4 284	4 229	3 261	3 499	1 952	982	761
Minimum food basket income (So. Sh./p.a.)[e]	2 170	3 200	4 830	4 290	6 220	48 000	65 030

NOTES:
a Includes industries run by autonomous agencies and private firms in industry and commerce.
b Based on data provided by Ministry of Finance, civil service lists.
c Established by giving a weight of 0.7 to industry group.
d Based on national sources, with splicing.
e Estimated from the 1984–85 figure by applying the food price index.
SOURCE: 1970–80 from Jamal 1981, table 17; 1984 and 1986, authors' estimates, with government wages based on trends in civil service pay; cost-of-living index from official sources.

elsewhere in Africa. In other parts of Africa the diversification of household income sources was declining until the economic crisis devastated the purchasing power of wages. In Somalia households with diverse sources of livelihood have been the norm, with trading particularly pervasive. Diversification of income sources arises not only from the different occupations to which labour is allocated, but also because of the broad boundaries of kinship. Indeed, so tenacious is the kinship system that extended families serve as a vehicle for distribution and redistribution of income and goods.

The persistence of kinship distributive mechanisms partly explains how such a drastic fall in wages could occur without starvation or riots. Since urban income rose as real wages fell, the result was a redistribution of wages to profits of commerce via inflation. Because most Somali kinship groups extend over the gamut of economic activities – wage earning, trading, cultivating, nomadism and emigration – the impoverishing effect of the redistribution was slight. While it would be a mistake to romanticise Somalia as a society in which kinship serves to save all from poverty and to equalise wealth holding (there are certainly inequalities) the fact that the kinship system provides a safety net for most Somalis cannot be ignored.

Having highlighted the important characteristics of the Somali economy, we can develop a schematic model of its operation during the last fifteen years (since the boom in the Gulf States). Domestically, the economy was divided into three sectors: basic grains production, nomadic pastoralism, and the urban sector (overwhelmingly a trade and service sector). Crop and livestock production were primarily determined by weather conditions, which establish the acreage that could be planted and the carrying capacity of rangeland. From this characterisation it follows that marketed quantities of grains and livestock reflect the excess of production over subsistence needs, with prices determining money incomes, not output. Urban income, on the other hand, was determined by the external sector, imports and remittances. Remittances determined the real quantity of private sector imports, while the parallel market exchange rate determined urban money income (and indirectly the money supply).

The remaining elements of urban activity – and rural to a small degree – were set by official development assistance (including considerable food aid). During the 1970s and the 1980s the economy of Somalia expanded – it did not stagnate – with little relationship to government policy. With agricultural output primarily a function of weather, pricing policy affected little but the money incomes of grain producers. Since the government had no significant control over foreign trade, exchange rate adjustment, tariffs and quotas were largely formalistic exercises. Monetary policy was of no practical consequence, since the money supply adjusted endogenously to match the remittances migrants sought to convert to shillings. Finally, having lost control of foreign trade, the Somali government lost fiscal control, being unable to tax the bulk of imports and exports.

In the context of this explanatory model, we can consider the structural adjustment programme implemented in Somalia in the mid-1980s with the encouragement of the International Monetary Fund. This programme – in Somalia as elsewhere in Africa – was based on the 'urban-bias' view in which government interference in markets caused distortions in the economy, discouraging agricultural production and exports and sustaining a rentier working class. As we had argued in the earlier chapters, such a model no longer applies in most African countries. For Somalia it was singularly inappropriate because of the unconventional nature of the economy. Devaluation and liberalisation, the major ingredients of the adjustment remedy, were relevant for only a small portion of the Somali economy. Devaluation could not be expected to cure the adverse balance of trade, which consisted for the most part of unrecorded exports and imports, transacted at the *de facto* unregulated exchange rate.

It might be thought that market liberalisation would at least have a dramatic effect on the crop sector. Certainly the World Bank and the IMF thought so, beyond the dreams of believers in highly price-elastic supply curves (ILO/JASPA 1989b). During the 1970s and early 1980s a state marketing board purchased a large proportion of marketed production of maize and sorghum. If one divides the official producer price of each of these crops by the urban cost of living, one finds that the latter rose relatively to the former. From this calculation, the World Bank and the IMF concluded that the 'terms of trade' moved against farmers; and that the measured relative price shift was the fault of the government, in the sense that an unregulated market outcome would have been more favourable to farmers.[7] This line of argument, common as it may be, is analytically unsound and hopelessly confused. Earlier we had criticised the simplistic manner in which terms of trade analyses are usually interpreted. Here we question even the usual calculations of the 'terms of trade'.

The ratio of producer prices and the urban cost of living index does not measure farmers' terms of trade. These terms should be measured by the ratio of prices farmers receive to prices they pay as consumers and producers. As consumers, farmers purchase a collection of commodities quite different from the urbanites – the inclusion of rent, bus fares, many items of clothing, food which farmers produce themselves, etc., is inappropriate. As producers, farmers purchase items which the urbanites do not buy at all – fertilizer, seeds, veterinary services, etc. There is no reason to think that the urban consumer price index bears any necessary relationship to a farmers' price index, even during a period of rapid inflation, as in Somalia in the 1980s. This point holds true for the measurement of the terms of trade in all countries, not just Somalia. Thus as compared to our earlier criticism of the standard interpretation of the Tanzanian and Zambian 'terms of trade' calculations, what we are now arguing is that such measures are analytically worthless, without empirical justification or theoretical validity. They fail even as 'proxy' measures, for with slight effort the urban price index typically used could be rendered more appropriate to the measure of prices paid by farmers (but rarely, if ever, is).

Even were the urban consumer price index by chance an accurate analogue for prices paid by farmers, a fall in the ratio of government fixed producer prices to this index does not necessarily imply state bias against agriculture. That is to say, nowhere is there an economic law which says constant or rising terms of trade for agriculture are optimal, efficient, desirable, or just. The movement of the ratio implies nothing in itself, but requires a relevant comparison. The relevant comparison is between the movement in the terms of trade associated with government intervention and the outcome which would result under conditions of no state intervention. If we take the current wage and assume that unregulated domestic prices would approximate 'border' prices, then the unregulated outcome can be appropriated by the ratio of the world prices of relevant crops to the world 'urban price index'. Recall that this exercise is for purposes of argument only, for the ratio, either domestic to Somalia or internationally, is meaningless. When this calculation is made, one discovers that during the years when state marketing in Somalia was effective, the world market measure of the terms of trade moved against Somali farmers more than the government-affected terms of trade.[8] In other words, by the World Bank's own (unsound) measure, the Somali government's grain pricing policy showed rural bias compared to the unregulated market outcome (see further the argument in ILO/JASPA 1989b).

We conclude the discussion of the Somalia case by reiterating two points: (1) to the extent that the Somali state intervened in the economy during the 1970s and early 1980s, it did so under rural bias (real wages fell and cultivating rural households were protected against declining terms of trade); and (2) the social structure of Somalia society was such as to make the 'urban-rural gap' an irrelevant welfare concept in any case. In the light of these points, the mid-1980s economic reforms fostered by the World Bank and the IMF did little to alter relative prices in the economy or encourage productive investment. The announced measures simply replicated the *de facto* situation. While the reforms may not have harmed the economy directly, there is a danger that they did so indirectly by creating the illusion that far-reaching action was being implemented to set the economy on the path of development. Actually, devaluation and liberalisation were marginal factors in the vast network of relations in the Somali economy. They did little to solve the fundamental problems affecting it, while detracting from the enormous tasks that still await to be tackled. These tasks remain: (1) discovering the manner to direct remittances to productive investments; (2) reforming state expenditure and taxation to fund adequately a minimal level of urban and rural social services; and (3) raising wages to return morale to the civil service and stimulate productivity growth in commodity-producing enterprises. Adding a postscript in 1993, one could provide a list of 101 tasks that remain to be fulfilled in Somalia!

LESSONS FROM SOMALIA

While sSA countries have certain common features, each has its particular history, and the economic structure of each is the consequence in part of historical developments. Somalis are a people with a long history of migration, long-distance trade, and avoiding regulatory attempts by authorities. The present unconventional nature of the Somali economy is not the result of government mismanagement, but the continuation of economic relations centuries old. More than any other of our case studies, Somalia teaches the lesson that each country must be investigated in terms of its specific social and institutional structure if we are to make sense out of economic phenomena; stylised neoclassical stories that abstract from the manner in which markets and production are organised will not serve.

With respect to the rural-urban gap, Somalia is a land of illusions. Measures we have used in other cases with confidence show a catastrophic collapse in urban incomes in Somalia, yet there is little concrete evidence of urban immiserisation. Certainly there is urban poverty, but little evidence that it intensified as wage income fell so dramatically. The lesson from Somalia is that quantitative measures, even when we have our concepts correct, must be interpreted in light of each institutional and social context. Pressed by the task we set ourselves to compare the rural-urban gap in Somalia to other countries, we conclude as follows: Somalia is a country in which the social differentiation between town and countryside has progressed insufficiently to make the concept of a rural-urban income gap analytically appropriate. In other sSA countries the pressure of crisis and struggle for survival produced in the 1980s a reversion of rural-urban structures to the relatively undifferentiated form characteristic of Somalia.

LESOTHO

Lesotho is another country whose economy cannot be understood without taking account of the migration factor. As in Somalia, numbers emigrating and the savings they repatriate completely swamp the domestic economy. However, certain differences are significant: (i) migration for wage labour has been a feature of the economy for at least a hundred years; (ii) most aspects of migration are known, particularly numbers migrating and remittances; (iii) remittances are transacted at the official exchange rate; and (iv) most migrants leave from the rural sector and most remittances return to rural families. Conditioning these four differences is another: migration from Somalia is to a region with which Somalis share a common religion and a political outlook (membership in the Arab League); migration from Lesotho is to the White-dominated Republic of South Africa. Its strategic importance provides South Africa with political leverage bordering on blackmail, and also plays a central role in the policy of the South African government to maintain labour surplus conditions in the Black 'homelands', keeping wages low and Black workers in a weak bargaining position.[9]

Estimates based on the national census show that in 1976 one-quarter of the total labour force (or one-half of the total male labour force) found employment in South Africa (Table 6.2). The remaining three quarters of the labour force were overwhelmingly agricultural, with 'modern sector employment' quite small absolutely and relatively. Most of the domestic wage earners worked in government service

TABLE 6.2: Lesotho: Labour force and employment, 1976
(all figures in thousands)

		Male	Female	Total
Total 15–64 age group		314	340	654
less:	in school	18	36	54
	disabled/inactive females	10	25	36
equals	labour force	286	279	565
of which:	employed in South Africa	129	24	153
	employed in Lesotho	157	255	412
	wage employment	18	12	30
	self-employment	139	233	392

SOURCE: Lesotho 1976.

(one-third according to the Second Five-Year Development Plan) and in miscellaneous service occupations (one-half), such as trade, transport, banking, etc.

Manufacturing accounted for barely 2,000 workers and construction only slightly more. The informal sector is a bit smaller than the formal sector labour force, and evidence shows that it has grown very little in recent years. This lack of growth is in sharp contrast to most sSA countries where high rates of rural-urban migration, combined with stagnant wage employment, have swelled the ranks of the informal sector. Migration to South Africa has siphoned off Lesotho's potential unemployment problem as well as the potential informal sector labour force.

The domestic labour force has been growing in recent years at 10–12,000 persons annually whereas modern sector employment grew by only 2–3,000 jobs. The absorptive capacity of the agricultural sector, too, is limited and unlikely to accommodate a substantial increase in workers gainfully employed at adequate incomes. In the late 1960s and 1970s, South African mining absorbed a rising proportion of the labour force of Lesotho: between 1967 and 1980 the labour force increased by 110,000 and employment in the mines increased by 68,000, so that while in 1967 20 per cent of Lesotho's labour force worked in RSA, by 1980 the proportion had increased to 27 per cent. The tremendous importance of migration may also be judged from estimates of remittances (Table 6.3). In 1970–71 net factor income from abroad amounted to one-half of gross domestic product at factor cost and just under 30 per cent of the country's national income. By 1975–76 this proportion reached nearly one-half, so that remittances

TABLE 6.3: *Lesotho: GDP and GNP, 1970–71, 1975–76 and 1981–82* (million maloti)

	1970–71	1975–76	1981–82
1. GDP at factor cost	42.5	98.2	272.8
2. GDP at market prices	52.5	111.0	340.0
3. Net factor income from abroad	22.3	101.0	200.0
4. GNP at market prices	74.8	212.0	540.0
5. Agricultural GDP	17.3	31.1	73.3
6. (3)/(4) (%)	29.8	47.6	37.0

SOURCE: For 1970–71 and 1975–76: (2)-(4) from Lesotho 1980, p. 124; (1) and (6) from UN Economic Commission for Africa (UNECA) data files. For 1981–82: (1) and (2) from UNECA data files; (2) and (3) are estimates by Lesotho authorities.

almost equalled total domestic income. At the start of the 1980s there was a relative decline in remittances, although in absolute terms remittances doubled between 1975–76 and 1981–82. These movements reflect a twofold increase in mine wages between 1974 and 1976, after which they increased but not as rapidly as Lesotho's GDP, so the proportion of migrant earnings declined slightly. However, throughout the 1970s migrant incomes exceeded agricultural GDP.

The sharp increase in mining wages between 1974 and 1976 dramatically widened the differentials between incomes that could be earned in Lesotho and South Africa. These differentials are at the core of the country's development problem. Since modern sector employment is so tiny in Lesotho, the employment choice facing a worker is to migrate to South Africa for a job in the mines or to take up domestic agriculture. Because of relative returns, the choice is heavily tilted against farming.

Before investigating the urban-rural gap further, labour migration from Lesotho should be placed in a historical context. Current as well as past data show no obvious link between income differentials and migration. The differential between mine wages and agricultural incomes in 1972–73 was only 1.6, compared to 4.0 in 1979–80, yet the same number of Basotho migrated. To go back considerably further, in 1936 the real wage in the South African mines was *less* than what could be earned in Lesotho agriculture, yet 46,000 Basotho went to work in the mines.[10] Taking the long view, one sees that Basotho workers have gone to the mines regardless of the real wage or the differential between mine wage and farming income. This has been the case because at the margin migration has always been more remunerative than farming; whatever the migrant earns is a net addition to the family's income.[11]

Returning to the more recent period, in Table 6.4 we provide data to compare trends in real incomes. The figures are not deflated, for in this case current prices are sufficient for the task. Our purpose is to demonstrate the returns to different activities facing the rural worker. In 1972–73, the entire labour input of a typical farm family would have yielded an annual income of M97. By contrast, one able bodied male could have received M119 as an unskilled worker in Lesotho (were a job available, of course) or M153 in South Africa. In 1979–80 agricultural GDP amounted to M64.5 million. Shared amongst some 242,000 farm families, this yields an average income of M266 per family.[12] Compared to this, an unskilled labourer could get a minimum wage of M665 in Lesotho towns and M1,060 in South African mines. The differential in the early 1970s was considerably less: in 1972–73 an average farm family produced about four-fifths as much as an urban worker and three-fifths as much as a mineworker. In effect, one worker migrating to South Africa in 1980 earned enough to support four farm families at a level equivalent to the average agricultural output. The widening rural-urban gap as measured by the ratio of the Lesotho unskilled wage to average

TABLE 6.4: *Lesotho: Agricultural income and wage income in Lesotho and South Africa, 1972–73 and 1979–80*

	1972–73	1979–80
Agricultural GDP current (M. million)	21.0	64.5
Cash	7.0	21.5
Subsistence	14.0	43.0
Farm families (000's)	217.5	242.0
Average agricultural GDP	97	267
Wages (M.p.a.)		
Lesotho unskilled	119	665
South Africa mining	153	1 061
Ratios:		
LesW/AgricAv	1.2	2.5
SAm/AgricAv	1.6	4.0

LEGEND: LesW – Lesotho unskilled wage. SAm – Mining wage in South Africa. AgricAv – average agricultural family income.

SOURCE: See table 6.3. Division between cash and subsistence income follows practice in Lesotho's national accounts.

farm income did not arise from 'urban bias' in government policy, but rather from the relatively high earnings that could be obtained in South Africa.

LESSONS FROM LESOTHO

In Lesotho there is a considerable rural-urban gap, but this country is 'the exception that proves the rule', for the gap has nothing to do with 'urban bias', minimum wages, or the power of trade unions. It is the direct result of migration – urban employers in Lesotho, public or private, must peg their wages in terms of the South African market for migrant labour or abandon the hope of attracting any but the most unskilled labour. It must be added, however, that when one includes remittances, rural households in Lesotho enjoy a standard of living considerably higher than households of unskilled workers in urban areas, about on a par with the earnings of the semi-skilled. This remittance-enhanced relative prosperity of rural households does not reflect the healthy state of Lesotho agriculture, rather the contrary, a debilitation of agriculture as a result of workers abandoning rural production activities.

It is much the vogue now to attribute poor economic performance in sSA countries to government mismanagement which creates 'distortions' in economies. The possibility that the market mechanism may generate distortions is ruled out by definition. Lesotho refutes this neo-Smithian ideology. The economy of the country is profoundly distorted in that the prevailing price structure undermines the incentives which would prompt people to make the investments in physical and human capital which in turn would bring long term development and security to the people of Lesotho. The behaviour of the government of South Africa towards its neighbours clearly indicates that those bordering countries must reorient their economies or be permanent clients of the white minority government. The South African government does not even need to intervene to maintain clientage by its neighbours for the market forces perform this task. Relatively high wages in mining draw off the workers who would revitalise and develop Lesotho's agriculture. The low cost of South African food production (based, not incidentally, on cheap black labour) keeps food prices low in Lesotho, further discouraging investment by farm families. Finally, in order that employers in Lesotho keep their employees, domestic wages must be high, producing an internal wage-earner-farmer gap between mining wages and farm income. In Lesotho as in Liberia, Somalia, Zambia – and Kenya – we have a rural-urban differential which disguises the real dynamics of income distribution.

7 The Rural-Urban Gap in West Africa

We return in this chapter to economies of a more familiar character, those of Ghana, Sierra Leone and Nigeria. It could be argued that Nigeria should be separated out and indeed treated in a class by itself because of the oil factor. But despite oil-induced structural changes, the Nigerian economy still shares features with the other two West African countries and greater contrasts with the East African countries. For all three countries the wage-farm differential was never very high, though alarmist statements about the gap started here. Further, the formal/informal dichotomy that became such a staple of the analysis of all African countries in the 1970s never provided such a sharp contrast in West Africa.

GHANA

The notion of the 'rural-urban gap' appeared early in Ghana. In 1958 a proposal was debated for the establishment of a national minimum wage, and W. Arthur Lewis, then an economic adviser to the government, inquired why the 'aristocracy' of Ghana should be favoured when there were other more deserving groups (quoted in Rimmer 1970, p. 33). The particular group he had in mind were farmers, and his contention that a high differential existed between urban wages and rural incomes was taken up by other researchers on West Africa (Kilby 1969). It is quite likely, as with other equally eminent economists following him (e.g. Turner in Zambia), that Lewis was misled about the privileged position of the Ghanaian urban workers by the increases in money wages that had occurred in the 1940s and 1950s. These increases were in response to ongoing inflation, and at no time succeeded in arresting the erosion in wages that had set in since before the Second World War. There is no evidence that the colonial government in the 1930s paid workers more than necessary to induce a single adult male to forsake the rural areas.

During much of the colonial period the Gold Coast (as it was called by the British) had the highest per capita income of all sub-Saharan African countries (Morawetz 1977, p. 77), a highly educated labour force, and a thriving agricultural sector based on the export of cocoa. The country was judged to possess the most favourable conditions for development of any on the continent at the time of independence (Bequele 1983). However, after a respectable growth performance in the 1950s, and even in the 1960s, per capita income declined at an annual average rate of 3.2 per cent between 1970 and 1983. The cumulative decline was 35 per cent, thus rivaling the catastrophic collapse of Uganda. Almost every vital statistic one can think of had a negative sign (World Bank 1985). Agricultural output fell by 0.2 per cent per annum, industry by 4.2 per cent per annum, exports by 6.2 per cent and cocoa output by 6.1 per cent. Externally, the price terms of trade fell by 3.7 per cent per annum for a total decline of nearly 40 per cent. Combined with the 57 per cent drop in export volumes meant that the country's income terms of trade fell by a staggering 73 per cent. The only variables with a positive sign were indicators of difficulties – e.g. the consumer price index increased at 16 per cent per annum while the urban population increased by 13 per cent per annum between 1960 and 1980 (compared to 7 per cent each in Kenya, Uganda, Tanzania and Nigeria).

In the urban areas the Ghana story closely parallels that of Uganda, with a catastrophic fall in wages. This fall wiped out whatever rural-urban gap that had existed (Table 7.1 and Figure 7.1). Between the peak of 1974 and the trough of 1984, the minimum wage fell by 88 per cent. In the next two years there was a doubling, but even then the minimum wage was down to 23 per cent of its peak level and one-third of its 1970 level. In 1984 with the minimum wage fixed at 40 cedis per day, a World Bank mission had estimated the daily cost of a minimum diet for a single person at 168 cedis. Working backwards from this estimate implies that the minimum wage at its peak in 1974 would have been just sufficient to buy the food needs of an average sized urban family, i.e. nothing left over for non-food needs. These calculations indicate a very narrow farmer-wage earner gap indeed, consistent with Knight's estimate for the late 1960s, which concluded that wage earner and farm family incomes were not significantly different (Knight 1972). More recent research yields similar estimates (ILO/JASPA 1982b (Ghana); and Tabatabai 1986), though the different studies are not strictly comparable. The obvious conclusion from virtually all empirical work is that there has never been a substantial gap between the living standards of peasants and wage earners in Ghana.

TABLE 7.1: *Ghana: Real minimum wage, 1970–86* (1970 = 100)

1970	100
1971	92
1972	103
1973	88
1974	149
1975	115
1976	74
1977	51
1978	39
1979	25
1980	22
1981	23
1982	19
1983	18
1984	18
1985	30
1986	34

SOURCE: World Bank 1987a.

However, notwithstanding the near equivalence of rural and urban income levels, migration into urban areas has been an enduring feature of the Ghanaian economy since at least the 1950s. And contrary to the

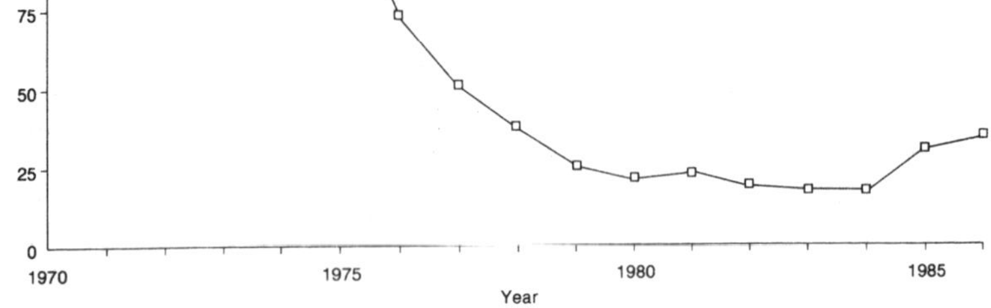

Source: Table 7.1

Figure 7.1 Ghana: Real minimum wage, 1970–86 (1976 = 100)

predictions of simplistic models, migration continued after 1975 though real urban wages fell catastrophically. The rural-urban income gap simply does not explain urban migration in Ghana. With falling wages, unemployment has increased, contrary to the hypothesis that migration serves to equate the expected value of the urban wage with rural income.

One aspect of unemployment in Ghana constitutes an emerging trend in African countries – growing insecurity of formal sector employment. Between 1980 and 1983 wage employment fell from 461,000 to 414,000, and on top of this, the Cocoa Marketing Board alone laid off 41,000 workers in 1985. As a result of such cuts, the share of wage employment in total employment dropped well below 10 per cent in the mid-1980s.

In emphasising the recent decline in wage earner incomes one must not forget that placing stress upon rural-urban inequality was never empirically justified in Ghana. The gap between rural and urban areas was always small, and exaggerating its importance obscured even the most blatant inequalities in Ghana. Throughout the colonial and post-colonial period, these inequalities were not rural-urban but intra-rural and intra-urban. At a number of points we have noted that sub-Saharan Africa, unlike Latin America, South Asia, and North Africa and the Middle East, is not characterised by widespread landlessness or a land-poor peasantry. Ghana is an exception to this generalisation. Thirty-one per cent of Ghana's rural population in 1970 depended primarily on wage employment for its livelihood, and perhaps 60 per cent of agricultural holdings were too small to support the households which tilled them (see Bequele 1983). These percentages reflect a rural population divided between a cocoa-growing elite and land-poor peasants who must devote part of their time to working on the farms of the elite in order to support their households.

These structural characteristics of Ghana's rural sector have tremendously important implications for income distribution. Since the early 1970s, food prices have risen much faster than the non-food cost of living index and faster than the GDP deflator (Tabatabai 1986). The relative rise in the price of food almost certainly resulted in impoverishment and greater income inequality. All the urban poor and perhaps half the rural poor were net buyers of food, and food assumes a larger proportion of budgets at low incomes. Here the situation is somewhat similar to that in Zambia, for a substantial proportion of Ghana's urban wage earners have no access to land for subsistence production. Even if they did, they would not gain from higher food prices (they eat food, not the price of food). While we have no direct measures of distribution, a regressive shift on a massive scale probably occurred during the rapid inflation of the 1970s and 1980s.[1]

What is not in doubt is that urban earners have suffered a tremendous fall in real income, continuously over 25 years, from a base which was never high (Rimmer 1984; see also Loxley 1988 and Jonah 1989). Cocoa farmers lost substantial earnings due to inflation, since the domestic producer price of cocoa rose considerably less than the general price level. There is evidence that smuggling through Côte d'Ivoire reduced actual losses. However, the real gainers in rural areas were food crop farmers, whose incomes rose relatively to those of food-deficit households and cocoa producers. It is our guess that the losses of the latter two groups probably offset the gains of the former. At the same time, State revenue declined due to lower world prices for cocoa and lower quantity of exports.[2] If the net change in the position of workers (urban and rural), cocoa farmers, and the State has been negative, then other groups must have seen their incomes improve relatively or even absolutely, even though per capita income was falling. Medium- and high-level civil servants can be excluded from this category, for their salaries too fell sharply. Finally, under the severe demand-constrained conditions of the Ghanaian economy, it is unlikely that informal-sector operators enjoyed anything but a decline in effective demand for their commodities and services. It follows, therefore, that the most likely net 'winners' during Ghana's long night of declining per capita income (in addition to food crop farmers) were entrepreneurs and rentiers.

LESSONS FROM GHANA

Our analysis of Ghana confirms several of the trends identified in earlier case studies: falling real wages, narrowing rural-urban gap, worsening income distribution, and increasing instability of wage employment. These trends do not bring urban wage earners down from a lofty perch, since they were never an aristocracy of labour. We made this point before for other countries, but in the case of Ghana it is true with a vengeance. At the peak of prosperity (1974), unskilled workers could just meet the food needs of the average urban family. Thinking back to Liberia and looking ahead to Sierra Leone, that modest peak for unskilled wage earners in Ghana represents a substantial (if brief) achievement.

SIERRA LEONE

Sierra Leone provides the clearest example of an 'anti-agriculture' and perhaps even a 'pro-urban' bias economy, but this bias never benefited the wage earners. As we have shown previously, the urban-bias stories about Africa placed great stress on the farmer-wage earner inequality, arguing that the gains of the wage earners were at the expense of the farmers. Three redistributory mechanisms were stressed: (1) high wage awards create inflation which reduces real purchasing power of farmers; (2) government control of food prices subsidises wage earners and penalises farmers; and (3) export taxes transfer income to urban populations via government expenditure. In Sierra Leone the first two mechanisms never operated, for both wages and food prices were left to unregulated markets. But the third mechanism operated with abandon. Here we have what would seem a strange case to the urban-bias school – a systematic anti-agriculture policy with regard to taxation and government expenditure, combined with a low wage policy. The Sierra Leone case might be called 'elite urban bias' at work, reinforcing our arguments about the complexity of the dynamics of inequality in sSA countries and the need for structural adjustment programmes to account for these properly.[3]

Table 7.2 shows a comparison of farm incomes and urban wages. The figures incorporate an assumption that households do not have secondary sources of income. Thus, it is more precise to identify the calculations as farm income per household and wage income for a household with only one wage earner and no non-wage income. The qualifications do not nullify the conclusions. Urban wage incomes in the table are the annual equivalent of average weekly non-agricultural earnings. Some over-estimate may be involved here, for it has been assumed that the average worker was employed a full 52 weeks. Notwithstanding the data problems, the results are surprising if one is a believer in the myth of the privileged African working class. Immediately after independence, wage incomes rose relatively to farm incomes, beginning 30 per cent lower in 1963–64 and rising to 60 per cent higher in 1970–71. Subsequently there followed a continuous and precipitous decline (as in Ghana, provoked by massive devaluations),[4] such that in 1985–86 wage income was only 28 per cent of farm income (37 per cent on a per capita basis, column 4 of Table 7.2).[5]

Jamal had calculated a poverty line for urban areas for the JASPA mission at Le 620 for 1977–78 (ILO/JASPA 1981a, ch. 4).[6] This poverty line was conservative, both because it was lower than

TABLE 7.2: *Sierra Leone: A comparison of farm incomes, wages, and related magnitudes, 1963–85*

	Farm family income	Average non-agric. wage	Ratio: Wage to farm income		Real incomes (1973 = 100)		Divided by GDP per capita		Cost of living (Free-town)
			Per family	Per cap.	Farm	Wage	Farm incomes per cap.	Wage incomes per cap.	
	1	2	3	4	5	6	7	8	9
1963–64	257	188	0.73	0.97	103	73	0.34	0.33	58
1964–65	264	220	0.83	1.10	95	75	0.31	0.35	62
1965–66	269	237	0.88	1.17	92	95	0.30	0.35	63
1966–67	267	367	1.38	1.82	88	113	0.30	0.54	67
1967–68	263	379	1.44	1.91	83	107	0.30	0.57	68
1968–69	271	353	1.30	1.72	83	110	0.27	0.47	70
1969–70	267	415	1.55	2.06	80	116	0.24	0.50	75
1970–71	274	435	1.59	2.10	77	117	0.26	0.54	73
1971–72	286	441	1.54	2.04	82	114	0.27	0.54	80
1972–73	345	441	1.28	1.69	90	106	0.29	0.50	87
1973–74	413	456	1.10	1.46	100	100	0.29	0.43	100
1974–75	636	486	0.76	1.01	133	92	0.38	0.39	120
1975–76	738	537	0.73	0.96	129	86	0.43	0.41	140
1976–77	931	590	0.63	0.84	140	81	0.45	0.38	152
1977–78	995	601	0.60	0.80	138	76	0.43	0.35	167
1978–79	1 146	627	0.55	0.72	144	73	0.44	0.32	192
1979–80	1 185	702	0.59	0.78	130	78	0.40	0.31	217
1980–81	1 308	926	0.71	0.94	127	77	0.40	0.38	268
1981–82	1 842	940	0.51	0.68	144	67	0.47	0.32	340
1982–83	2 222	1 108	0.50	0.66	137	52	0.49	0.32	572
1983–84	2 889	1 142	0.40	0.52	106	35	0.44	0.23	955
1984–85	5 247	1 430	0.27	0.36	115	26	0.53	0.19	1 685
1985–86	6 833	1 891	0.28	0.37	85	32	0.48	0.18	3 048

NOTES: Columns 1 and 2, farm family incomes and the average non-agricultural wage, are measures in current Leone.
Column 3 is the ratio of column to column 1.
In column 4, farm family incomes and average non-agricultural wage have been divided by the average family size for farm and urban families, then expressed as a ratio.
Column 5 and 6 are columns 1 and 2 divided by the Freetown cost-of-living index (given in column 9), with all indices in the table set 1973 = 100 for consistency.
Columns 7 and 8 are columns 1 and 2, first divided by family size (to give incomes per person in current Leone, rather than 1973 Leone, as in columns 5 and 6), then divided by aggregate per capita income.
Column 9 the same as the cost-of-living index in table 1 with the base year shifted. See discussion in text for details of calculations.
SOURCES: Weeks 1990, table 8.

alternative measures and because it referred to a family of four, while the average urban family over these years was six. The poverty line can be extended back to 1957 and forward to 1988 by adjusting for inflation. For the pre-independence years, 1957–63, the wage was well below poverty level for a family of four by about 25–30 per cent. From 1966 to 1973, the average wage came close to covering this measure of basic needs, but subsequently a family seeking to subsist on the average wage alone would have sunk deeper and deeper into poverty. By 1981, the average wage would barely have covered food expenditure alone, and in 1988 the hypothetical average family would have exhausted its monthly wage income on food alone *within a week*. Urban families have managed to stay above food poverty through survival – or straddling – strategies involving family members in all sectors of the economy, formal as well as informal, rural as well as urban.[7]

The fall in wages does not signify improved income distribution. Columns 4, 7 and 8 provide proof. In 1974–75 the income per family member for both farmers and wage earners was roughly the same. Thereafter wage incomes fell relatively to farm incomes as well as GDP per capita and hence income distribution clearly worsened. This finding contradicts the 1984 World Bank report on Sierra Leone which argued that an increase in farm incomes relatively to wage incomes would ensure that 'the resulting redistribution of income will go in the right direction' (World Bank 1984, p. 31). By the second half of the 1970s any redistribution from wage incomes to farm incomes on average went in the 'wrong' direction. Moreover, evidence shows that concurrent redistributions also produced greater inequality. Thus Weeks (1990, Table 9) has shown that while between 1966 and 1975 producer real wage rose (by 24 per cent),[8] in the next ten years it declined by 43 per cent, implying that in those years the gainers from the drastic fall in the rural-urban gap were the entrepreneurs.

How much of the above change was caused by structural adjustment is difficult to assess, part of the difficulty arising from the problem of defining when structural adjustment began. A falling wage-farm income ratio was already an established trend when Sierra Leone entered into major policy-based lending in 1981. What is clear is that in the 1980s this trend was accelerated by rapid inflation which can at least partially be blamed on devaluation. It would be more prudent to conclude that whatever the effect of adjustment, to the extent that it was predicated on the existence of a rural-urban gap in favour of wager earners its diagnosis was incorrect.[9]

By all accounts Sierra Leone has never been a 'high-wage' economy, partly because the government has intervened very little in the labour market. There was no government-set minimum wage, so wage settlements were left to bargaining between employers and workers. In consequence, the substantial short-run increases in wages that occurred in the East African countries were absent in Sierra Leone. In the first few years after independence wages stayed more or less constant in real terms (Levi 1973), unlike in East Africa where they rose sharply. One is not surprised, therefore, to find that urban workers in Sierra Leone had quite a low standard of living at the time of independence. For example, it was estimated for 1961 that the cost of a minimum food basket for a typical family would be Le 15.5 per month, compared to which the average unskilled wage was about Le 20 per month, so that 80 per cent of average earnings was necessary to cover food needs alone (Jamal 1983c).

But if never high-wage, the Sierra Leone economy was certainly characterised by an anti-agriculture bias, but a bias that did not benefit wage earners as the orthodox stories would maintain. Up to the recent period, the Sierra Leone authorities controlled the exports of agricultural products through a marketing board (as elsewhere in Africa), which taxed farmers directly by duties and also by profits from the differential between the producer and export prices. Measures of the effective rate of taxation of export crops show that between 1968 and 1972, the rate was 29 per cent; between 1973 and 1976, 51 per cent; and between 1977 and 1981, 39 per cent.[10] Translated into the incidence of taxation, for farmers this was estimated at 10 per cent in 1979, but for non-farmers only 6 per cent:[11] non-farmers with average incomes 4 to 5 times the farmers' income paid taxes at only 60 per cent of the rate of farmers. These figures, stark as they are, actually hide wide differences within the non-farm group, both in terms of tax incidence and average incomes. Most personal taxes in Sierra Leone are collected through a withholding system and affect mostly civil servants and wage earners in large establishments. The rest of the urban population – i.e. wage earners in small enterprises, informal sector workers, professionals, and entrepreneurs – practically escape taxes. The omission of the first two groups from direct taxation probably rendered post-tax income distribution more equitable. Exclusion of the last two groups obviously increased inequality.[12]

The anti-agriculture bias of taxation policy was reinforced by the bias in government expenditure. The bulk of government expenditure

– 40 per cent in most years – went into the day-to-day affairs of running the State (general administration, police, defence) and to pay for public debt, pensions and gratuities. Given the concentration of law and order forces in the urban areas it could be argued that such expenditures effectively benefited the urban population. Only agricultural expenditure unambiguously benefited the rural areas but data show that in only two years between 1968 and 1980 did it exceed rural taxation (Jamal 1986c, Table 7). Altogether, the total net outflow amounted to Le 48.7 million.

LESSONS FROM SIERRA LEONE

While confirming many of the trends found in other case studies, analysis of Sierra Leone also provides an important antidote to the idea that urban bias is pro-wage-earner bias. There was certainly an anti-agriculture bias in Sierra Leone, but its benefits did not accrue to the wage earners. As in the other case studies, here again we see that concentration on the wage earner-farmer inequality – and even rural-urban inequality – obscured the more important inequalities in Africa.

NIGERIA

Few economies in Africa changed so dramatically in the last 25 years as Nigeria's, but most of the changes can at best be considered a mixed blessing, at least in the medium term. In 1965 the country was primarily agricultural, with cocoa, ground-nuts and palm products accounting for the bulk of exports. Agriculture had performed quite well during the 1950s and 1960s, notwithstanding allegations that the state monopoly marketing boards (legacies of colonial rule) had discouraged export production.[13] While growth was not spectacular, it was steady and the balance of payments position manageable. Twenty years later, Nigeria was a major oil producer (turning out a particularly high-quality grade), but the consequences for the economy were grave and the political repercussions initially tragic. Few would deny that the sudden prospect of oil wealth prompted the civil war which raged in the south-east for half a decade (beginning in 1967). The possibility that a larger economic 'pie' created by oil might facilitate the long-run conciliation of regional political rivalries seems not to have been realised.

The economic consequences of oil have been equally disturbing. Agricultural exports virtually collapsed and food crop production failed to keep pace with urban population growth, making the country a substantial importer of food.[14] This relative and absolute decline of agriculture is a consequence of immense distortions created by the rapid growth of petroleum revenues. The most obvious of these has been the exchange rate. The IMF in particular is wont to admonish governments for administering 'artificially' overvalued exchange rates, but in Nigeria the forces of the market generated a singularly inappropriate exchange rate during the 1970s. The tremendous increase in oil revenues created a strong naira, and on a purely financial view of the balance of payments, no devaluation was called for. However, the balance of payments is a poor indicator of the relationship between internal and external prices for a mineral-exporting country, as government after government throughout the world has discovered. Buoyed by petroleum exports, the naira stabilised at a level which rendered all non-oil exports uncompetitive on world markets. Later, when balance-of-payments pressure dictated a devaluation, a decade of 'market signals' had discouraged the investments that would have made possible a rejuvenation of traditional exports.

So great have been the negative externalities associated with oil that it has been seriously argued that Nigeria's economic growth since 1970 is largely illusory.[15] Certainly, the fact that Nigeria has the largest debt in sub-Saharan Africa can only be explained by the country's brief oil boom. If the view that oil has been a curse upon Nigerians is too extreme, the view that it has been a mixed blessing would be accepted by many. Among the negative consequences have been increased inequality and absolute impoverishment. Although the overwhelming majority of the net earnings from petroleum never reached rural areas, urban poverty in Nigeria increased substantially during the oil boom, while the degree of rural poverty probably remained unchanged.[16]

The oil boom provoked an acceleration of rural-urban migration, which had been a major phenomenon in Nigeria since independence. The urban wealth generated by oil resulted in a near-astounding growth of a number of cities throughout the country – Lagos, Kano, Kaduna, Port Harcourt and Warri – but even with this, Nigeria remains overwhelmingly rural. And while the country had the largest wage labour force in the region, these workers were still a small part of the economically active population, and the proportion declined relatively to all urban workers in the 1980s because of the rapid migration.[17] As elsewhere in Africa, social services such as education, health and sanitation are more available in urban areas than rural ones, but their benefits went disproportionately to the urban rich.

On a continent characterised by considerable urban blight, the cities of Nigeria probably excel all others in their poor living conditions. This is particularly so for Lagos, whose basic services are inadequate on average and largely non-existent for the poor.[18] Ironically, conditions worsened during the oil boom. The increase in urban migration did not prompt the authorities to use the oil revenues to maintain urban conditions, much less improve them. When considering rural-urban differences in living standards in the Nigerian context, the socialised benefits of town life should probably be considered as negative. Particularly in the south of the country, the net amenities found in large villages and small towns exceed those of Lagos and other large cities when one takes account of pollution, the absence of garbage and waste collection, and grossly inadequate transport facilities. These problems worsened in the last 15 years. To give but one concrete example, much of the expansion of formal sector employment in the booming cities occurred in plants far from the areas where workers live, increasing non-discretionary costs of city life (as well as reducing leisure time).

Table 7.3 provides estimates of agricultural and non-agricultural incomes in Nigeria for selected years between 1970–83. Two points should be noted: first, this measure does not indicate agriculture-non-agriculture differentials as such, since rural incomes include some non-agricultural earnings; and, second, the measure does not reveal the income differential between wage earners and farmers, for all non-agricultural incomes are aggregated. With these qualifications in mind the table shows that the oil boom coincided with a substantial decline in agricultural incomes relatively to non-agricultural incomes. This is hardly surprising, since petroleum revenue is by definition non-

TABLE 7.3: *Nigeria: Agricultural and non-agricultural income, 1970–83* (naira per capita per annum)

	1970	1973	1978	1980	1981	1983
Agriculture	55	63	144	161	167	198
Non-agriculture	251	347	921	1 049	1 115	910
Ratio	4.6	5.5	6.4	6.5	6.7	4.6

SOURCE: Jamal 1986b, p. 10.

agricultural. More instructive of distributional changes is Table 7.4, though the series ends with 1978–79. Here income is divided into rural and urban recipients. As with the agricultural/non-agricultural ratio, we see that the average gap between all urban and all rural households increased. However, the gap between unskilled wage earners and rural households declined. As a result of the oil boom, there was certainly a tremendous increase in urban incomes, but little of this increase filtered down to urban workers. The years shown in the table are when the revenues from oil were the greatest (including the years of large price increases, 1973–74 and 1979). During the period, average urban incomes rose in every year (except 1974–75), increasing by over 30 per cent. At the same time average rural incomes remained more or less constant, so the average rural-urban gap rose from 3.4 in 1973–74 to 4.6 in 1978–79.

However, the ratio of unskilled wage earner incomes to rural incomes did not rise. If one takes 1974–75 as the bench-mark, it fell; and remained about the same on the basis of the 1973–74 value. The large increase in this ratio in 1974–75 reflects the institutional manner

TABLE 7.4: *Nigeria: Measures of rural and urban incomes, 1973–79* (1977–78 naira per annum)

	1973–74	1974–75	1975–76	1976–77	1977–78	1978–79
Rural						
1. Aver. family income	733 (100)	773 (105)	731 (100)	724 (99)	715 (98)	725 (99)
Urban						
2. Aver. family income	2 530 (100)	2 024 (80)	2 809 (111)	3 062 (122)	3 128 (124)	3 378 (134)
3. Aver. unskilled wage	780 (100)	1 388 (178)	1 100 (141)	926 (119)	810 (104)	741 (95)
Ratios (gaps)						
Urban–rural (line 2/line 1)	3.4	2.6	3.8	4.2	4.4	4.6
Wage-rural (line 3/line 1)	1.1	1.8	1.5	1.3	1.1	1.0
Intra-urban (line 2/line 3)	3.2	1.4	2.6	3.3	3.9	4.6

SOURCE: ILO/JASPA 1981b, Jamal 1982 (Nigeria) and revisions.

in which wages are set in Nigeria. Beginning with the Second World War, colonial authorities adjusted wages through the creation of special wage review commissions. This practice continued after independence, with a review about every five years. In consequence, the typical pattern for wage movements in Nigeria is a sudden and substantial money increase, followed by money wage stability and falling real wages (due to inflation). The periodic increases once misled some observers into concluding that Nigerian trade unions in Nigeria have been historically quite powerful and able to win real wage increases in excess of labour market conditions. This view is now largely discredited.[19]

During the 1970s urban wage earners only temporarily improved their position compared to farmers, and lost considerably compared to other urban groups. Since migration during this time exceeded the rate of growth of formal sector employment, it is extremely unlikely that incomes in the urban informal sector grew; in fact, they probably fell (Jamal 1986b). This leaves one with the conclusion that the 'winners' from Nigeria's windfall of oil revenues were the professionals and formal sector entrepreneurs. The latter particularly gained, as a result of buoyant domestic demand and protectionism. Falling urban real wages and declining or stagnant incomes in the informal sector resulted in an increase in urban poverty, from 33 per cent of households in 1973 to 38 per cent in 1978, affecting 5.2 million urban households (ILO/JASPA 1981b, p. 232).

Twenty-two years of price-deflated wages are shown in Table 7.5 and Figure 7.2. Though no strong trend emerges in either the unskilled average wage or the government minimum wage, it is clear that real earnings in the early 1980s were well below their level at the outset of the oil boom (1974–76). Wage restraint and inflation since 1985 have led to further erosion of real earnings. The allegation that Nigerian wage earners were well-paid has been discredited, as said. Indeed, the contrary seems to be true: their pay was low in the 1960s and lower still in the 1980s. Jamal had calculated poverty lines for Lagos at 1978/79 prices for the JASPA mission (Jamal 1982 (Nigeria), Table TP 4.3 and JASPA 1981, Table 56). These figures are reproduced below (Table 7.6) as an added bonus to illustrate the amount of 'water' that goes into calculations of poverty lines – even ones based on a specific number of calories.

The cost ranges from N54.21 to N120.86 per month for a family of 5.6 members, depending on the sort of diet chosen, the first figure being for a diet in which 85 per cent of the calories come from *gari* and

TABLE 7.5: *Nigeria: Unskilled average wage and minimum wage, 1964–85* (indices with 1973 = 100)

Year	Unskilled average wage (nominal)	Deflated	Government minimum wage (deflated)
1964	56	95	93
1968	78	122	122
1970	88	107	113
1973	100	100	100
1974	137	121	109
1975	225	149	134
1976	228	122	110
1977	236	109	98
1978	253	101	84
1979	253	90	77
1980	288	93	106
1981	338	90	110
1982	356	84	100
1983	375	78	85
1984	422	64	61
1985	481	68	58

SOURCE: Jamal 1986b, p. 14.

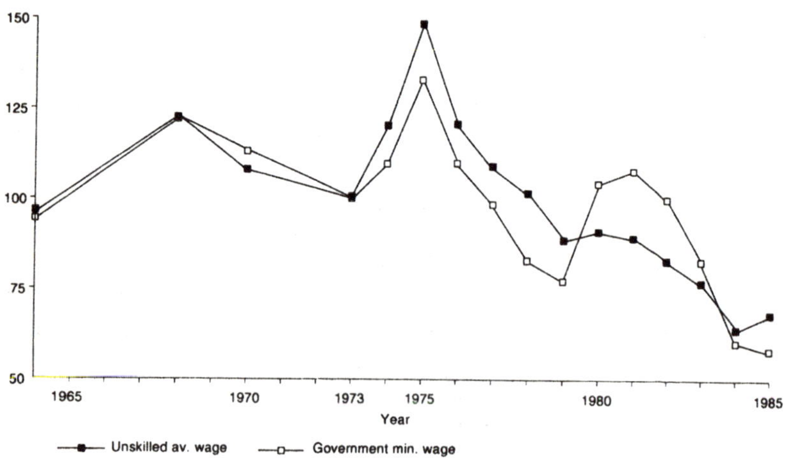

Source: Table 7.5

Figure 7.2 Nigeria: Unskilled average wage and minimum wage, 1964–85 (1973 = 100)

TABLE 7.6: *Nigeria: Cost of various diets in Lagos, 1978–79*

	Composition (per cent of calories)				Cost (kobo per day)			
	D1	D2	D3	D4	D1	D2	D3	D4
Gari	85	70	70	65	28.9	23.8	23.8	22.1
Beans	15	30	25	25	10.7	21.5	17.9	17.9
Fish	–	–	5	5	–	–	18.6	18.6
Meat	–	–	–	5	–	–	–	29.7
Cost per day of 2,700 calories (one adult) (kobo)					39.6	45.3	60.3	88.3
Cost per month (naira)					11.88	13.59	18.09	26.49
Total cost per month for a family of 3 (husband, wife child), or 6,600 calories (naira)					29.04	33.24	44.22	64.75
Total cost for a family of 5.6, or 12,320 calories (naira)					54.21	62.06	82.54	120.86

SOURCE: Jamal 1982 (Nigeria), table TP 4.3, also in ILO/JASPA 1981, table 56.

15 per cent from beans, while the higher figure is for a more varied diet consisting of gari, beans, fish and meat in the ratio of 65:25:5:5. Even the most elementary diet would have exhausted – just the raw ingredients, without any allowance for fuel, let alone non-food items – *90 per cent* of the minimum wage in 1979 (N60 per month) or *80 per cent* of the average unskilled wage (N67.50 per month). At mid-1960s, as may be inferred from Table 7.5, the situation was similar. Then came the wage hikes in the 1970s, but even at its highest the unskilled wage would not have purchased the more varied diet. By 1985 the situation had worsened considerably, with some 55 per cent cut in wages compared to 1975 and the deterioration continued to 1991 when the minimum wage was set at N250 per month. Housing and transport allowances raised this to N460. This implies a decline in the real wage of 10–15 per cent compared to 1985. The ensuing survival strategies are well summarised by Mustapha 1992 (p. 199):

> The urban working class wage is no longer adequate to support the average family, and not even the trading activities of wives can guarantee continued access to minimum levels of sustenance. For millions of Nigerian workers, the answer is to engage in multiple

> modes activities [sic]; not only are working class wives enmeshed in the informal sector, the workers themselves must engage in second, or even more occupations. . . . Firstly, private assets and skills are commercialised. Private motorcycles are periodically converted to taxis . . . Secondly, many other workers, lacking in private assets and skills, simply take a more serious interest in farming. Despite workers' resistance to a return to semi-proletarianisation, many have effectively regressed from proletarians to peasant- proletarians. . . . Thirdly, those lacking access to farmland take to petty trading; clerks and other lower level bureaucrats engage in petty corruption.

The closing of the rural-urban gap is corroborated by Collier (1987, p. 32), who finds that the average urban household sustained a drop of 50 per cent in real income from 1980 to 1985 compared to 27 per cent for the average rural household. He suggests that declining real wages in the 1980s resulted in a reversal of net migration (ibid., pp. 24–25). We are sceptical of this, and data, for whatever they are worth (see Table 2.6), support us. Compared to the rest of Africa, Nigeria has a long urban history, so for a considerable proportion of the urban population 'return' migration is not a viable alternative because of lack of agricultural experience and land. Further, fragmentary evidence suggests that land concentration and consolidation have been going on in the countryside, creating a landless class (Lipton 1985). In any event, there can be no argument that falling real wages had the effect of equilibrating the urban labour market. Throughout the 1980s wages fell but unemployment increased.[20]

LESSONS FROM NIGERIA

Prior to the discovery and production of oil Nigeria was a country characterised by a relatively narrow rural-urban gap, and urban bias was largely in the eye of the beholder. With the oil boom came urban-oriented economic growth, perhaps beyond anything that had occurred in sSA countries up to then. Without question urban groups monopolised the gains from the petroleum rents, but wage earners were not among these, and whatever gains they made were quickly dissipated through inflation. Thus even in a situation in which there were fabulous sums to distribute among urban groups, wage workers benefited very little; the rural-urban gap widened and the incomes of urban wage earners and farmers drew closer together. All this in a situation of the most rapid urban boom in all of Africa.

8 Distributional Dynamics and Trends

The previous chapters documented the general decline in the economies of the countries of the sub-Saharan region, which we argue has been associated with dramatic falls in urban living conditions (particularly of wage earners) compared to rural. In this chapter, we first summarise the major trends of the last decade and then discuss the dynamics of distributional shifts within a general theoretical framework.

TRENDS IN DISTRIBUTION AND LIVELIHOODS

Economic crisis has profoundly changed the character of the sub-Saharan economies, causing a radical shift in the relationship between rural and urban areas, as typified by the living standard between farmers and wage earners. Our case studies identified this process, suggesting a number of trends which are common to the region in varying degrees. In order that these trends not be lost in the specifics of each country study, they are listed and briefly summarised below. In addition, we go beyond the direct evidence in the case studies to draw implications which we feel are justified. This broadening of the discussion reflects our conviction, stated in Chapter 1, that a new stereotype of African countries is required.

The first clear trend is that real wages of urban workers have fallen dramatically during the last 15 years. That this is an Africa-wide phenomenon is important to establish: Table 8.1 and Figure 8.1 attest to this, with data from six Francophone countries, taking as an index the real urban minimum wage (see also Jamal 1992b). Table 8.2 provides further proof on the fall of wages all over Africa. It shows the changes in wages in government service for lowest and highest paid workers. Except for Zimbabwe, the real wages of the lowest paid workers fell in all the countries shown, by an average of 50 per cent, while the real wage of the highest paid workers fell everywhere, including Zimbabwe, for an average of over 60 per cent. In all cases

TABLE 8.1: *Francophone countries: Real minimum wage, 1970–86* (1970 = 100)

	'70	'71	'72	'73	'74	'75	'76	'77	'78	'79	'80	'81	'82	'83	'84	'85	'86
Burkina Faso	100	98	111	103	131	110	184	142	131	142	127	118	133	123	117	110	113
Congo	100	96	87	84	136	116	108	95	86	79	74	63	56	52	50	47	46
Côte d'Ivoire	100	102	101	113	122	109	122	96	106	100	96	88	90	85	82	80	76
Guinea	100	96	111	104	104	101	100	98	95	94	88	80	76	69	62	56	–
Senegal	100	96	91	94	148	113	111	100	97	88	101	100	92	95	85	79	75
Togo	100	94	87	84	75	92	82	77	77	71	70	58	58	53	55	56	54

SOURCE: World Bank 1987a.

TABLE 8.2: *Sample countries: Indices of changes in lowest and highest basic government salaries (also selected sSA countries), 1975–85* (real terms; 1985 with 1975 = 100)

	Lowest	Highest
Kenya	58.2	42.0
Nigeria	42.2	21.9
Sierra Leone	23.4	15.7
Somalia	5.2	4.0
Tanzania	22.9	18.8
Benin	43.2	43.2
Central African Republic	48.9	35.4
Ethiopia	62.6	31.3
Gambia	39.5	36.2
Mauritania	60.6	43.8
Morocco	66.3	52.4
Niger	46.2	46.2
Sudan	30.3	24.6
Togo	58.1	58.1
Zimbabwe	150.6	58.1

SOURCE: Robinson 1990, table 7.D.

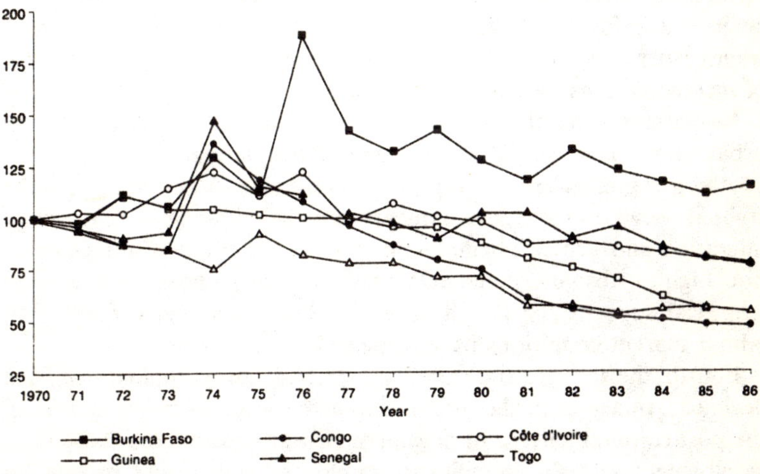

Figure 8.1 Francophone countries: Real minimum wage, 1970–86 (1970 = 100)

(except Benin and Togo) wages of the highest paid workers fell more than those of the lowest, indicating a compression in the wage structure, and to that extent the cause of equity was served, yet declines of 50 per cent or so in the minimum wage cannot be glossed over. With urban labour markets in excess supply, as we have remarked before, the minimum wage has increasingly become the representative wage for many workers. The fall in real wages has pushed a growing proportion of wage-earner households below poverty. The characterisation of the mass of urban workers in the region as an 'aristocracy of labour' clearly no longer applies. In fact, not only has the 'labour aristocracy' disappeared but so also has the wage earning class as a distinct entity. Urban households now extend their outreach over the whole gamut of economic activities to survive, from wage labour to informal sector to even subsistence farming.

Second, there has been a substantial decrease in the income gap between urban wage earners and the rural population. This is the trend which most dictates a radical change in thinking about the dynamics of labour markets in sSA. In most sSA countries, the gap between average rural incomes and average urban incomes has declined. But in one case (Nigeria), an increased gap between these two averages has gone along with a decline in the ratio of wage-earner incomes to the incomes of farmers on smallholdings. The gap between the earnings of unskilled workers and peasant smallholders has declined to the point where it is in favour of the latter in some countries. As a consequence, wage earners have lost relatively to both peasants and the average level of income in urban areas.

Notwithstanding the above two trends, migration from rural to urban areas has hardly abated, and urban labour markets are if anything in greater excess supply than in the past. A key element in the stylised view of sSA development was the hypothesis that urban migration and urban 'unemployment' were the result of wages being 'too high' – absolutely and relatively to rural incomes. There is no empirical support for this hypothesis. Real wages have fallen, but labour market conditions have worsened.

Fourth, the security and stability of formal sector employment have declined. An aspect of the stylised characterisation of sSA countries in the post-colonial pattern of development was to stress the stability of employment and the inability of employers, public and private, to discharge workers. With hindsight, one sees that this characterisation (labour as a 'fixed cost') was a phenomenon of prosperity and expanding employment opportunities (if it existed at all). In most countries of the region private sector employment has declined, and declines in government employment have not been unusual either (although they have been smaller than the decline in Government investment; see Cornia *et al.* 1987). If obtaining a formal sector job in the past involved the expectation of holding that job indefinitely, this is no longer true. In some countries entire industries have closed (e.g. iron mining in Sierra Leone) and in others the entire industrial sector has been devastated (Uganda and Ghana). If protective legislation once made it difficult for private employers to discharge workers, such regulations are now commonly ignored. As a consequence, even the employed face increasing job insecurity.

Fifth, the distinction between the formal and informal sectors is becoming blurred. The difference in incomes to be earned in the two sectors is decreasing, and along with this decrease life-styles and living conditions of households deriving their primary incomes from each sector are becoming similar. Insecurity of employment for formal sector wage earners makes their situation comparable in many ways to that of informal sector operators. With the fall in formal sector employment, erstwhile wage earners have moved into the informal sector, where they probably fare worse than the average worker there.

In consequence of the above, the overall distribution of income in most countries has worsened. Contrary to the conventional wisdom of the past, a narrowed rural-urban income gap has not improved income distribution, but has been at the expense of both wage earners and small farmers. Increasingly, the countries of sSA are not characterised by a split between the privileged urbanites and disadvantaged farmers, but between the rich and the poor, where the latter includes wage earners, informal sector operators and small peasants. Evidence points to a substantial redistribution of income towards private sector entrepreneurs in a number of countries.

The seventh point is made by way of a general conclusion. The dynamics of income distribution in the countries of sSA is not to any degree rural-urban, but rather multi-occupational and multi-sectoral. The common practice of the past to treat income distribution as a rural-urban phenomenon with little reference to the functional distribution of income is no longer appropriate.

The rural-urban fusions that have occurred as part of family survival strategies have important implications for understanding present-day African economies, not least the perplexing numbers that turn up in quantifying them (viz. massive falls in real wages and equally massive increases in food prices). When wage earners resort to growing their own food or collecting it from their rural-based relatives they effectively cease to be just wage earners and become part-time subsistence farmers at the same time, and like them, acquire some immunity from market prices. One suspects it is the latter strategy that dominates and it explains the dramatic changes in rural-urban terms of trade witnessed recently. If rural and urban families were indeed distinct entities such massive changes in relative prices simply could not happen since they imply huge shifts in income, enough if true to engender social unrest. What has happened in African countries is that terms of trade have become 'internalised' within the extended family, straddling the rural-urban physical gap. In this way most of the tension has vanished from relative price changes. This also simplifies the task of the advocates of 'structural adjustment programmes' in demanding massive turnarounds in prices. More and more African countries comply, but if there is any hope that this would lead to genuine 'structural adjustment' – i.e. a shift of labour back to rural areas – that hope remains unfulfilled. Effectively by increasing their production of food and collection of provisions from rural relatives, urban families *have* adjusted structurally; that they would do this by actually going back to the rural areas remains a forlorn hope.

END OF 'URBAN BIAS'?

Having noted the changes that have happened in the rural-urban gap it is only fair that we return to the restrictions in the definition of the gap specified in the opening chapter. This we do to dispel any new doubts that might have arisen in the mind of the reader from the case studies about the territory we are claiming. We have been clear all along that the inequality we are investigating is the inequality between farmers and wage earners – and economic science being what it is and our estimation techniques what they are, we have to confine our measurements to average figures. Our rationale for investigating the farmer-wage gap has also been made clear in terms of its central place in African economic analysis as the major distortion in African economies, with implications not only for migration but more widely even for the pattern of development of African countries. In the current adjustment programmes it is this gap that has to be narrowed or abolished – through higher prices for farmers and reduced incomes for wage earners – to induce a shift of resources (labour, in particular) to rural areas. We have shown through retrospective calculations that most past measurements of the gap – where they were attempted – were erroneous, often based on an unquestioning faith in national estimates of subsistence farm incomes. Thus at no time was the gap as wide as most people asserted; indeed given that at most times the minimum wage purchased no more than the most basic necessities for an average-size urban family, any assertion of a huge gap between such a family and its rural counterpart was bound to be *prima facie* wrong, as it would imply massive starvation in the rural areas. We have also shown that in most cases the alarm about the widening farm-wage gap arose simply from the evidence of increases in the minimum wage in some African countries soon after independence. This was generalised to all African countries and it was asserted that a most dangerous gap was emerging in Africa, thwarting all genuine development.

But what about 'urban bias'? Has it also disappeared with 'the gap'? There are two aspects to urban bias. One is the extraction of surplus through pricing policies – or terms of trade twists – and the other the allocation of government expenditure. We can say with some degree of confidence that the first type of urban bias has now disappeared from African countries. Food crop prices are now almost everywhere decided by market forces while export crop prices are transmitted to the producers without any of the overt surplus extraction represented by export taxes; most African countries have also devalued their currencies extensively and granted price increases to export-crop producers, sometimes over and above those justified by external market conditions. Of course it would be instructive to do calculations of surplus extraction in the past and present,[1] but since at least the late 1970s the evidence from terms of trade analysis indicates the end of overt farm taxation, and the recent-massive devaluations indicate the end of 'exchange rate taxation'.

Urban bias in terms of government expenditure allocation still persists. Although agriculture now receives a higher proportion of government expenditure than before, the past pattern of social services having been urban-biased, their maintenance still means that the urban areas receive more than their share of government expenditure. In this sense there will always be a rural-urban gap in Africa since African urban areas differ so vastly from their rural counterparts.

DISTRIBUTION IN DEMAND-CONSTRAINED ECONOMIES

The most important factor influencing income distribution in sSA countries over the last nearly two decades has undoubtedly been economic decline itself. Its impact has been uneven, however, partly due to the substantial proportion of output in the region which represents non-monetised subsistence production.[2] Decline has tended to depress the monetary sectors of sSA economies more than the subsistence sectors, and this a general law of economic cycles in underdeveloped countries. However, its operation is not as evident as it might seem. The obvious truth in the law arises from the fact that among self-employed producers consuming their own output a form of 'Say's Law' holds. If one has access to the means to produce and is not engaged in exchange to any great extent, supply and demand must coincide since the decision to produce and the decision to consume are one and the same.

At the same time, subsistence production should be viewed in its relationship to activities which bring cash incomes, with subsistence production in part representing a choice forced upon people when the monetary sector contracts. When the demand for cash crops declines, agricultural households may have no other alternative for their surplus capacity than to apply even more of their land and labour to subsistence. Where conditions permit (i.e. access to land), erstwhile wage earners may take up agriculture to survive (Uganda offers an extreme example of this).[3] Thus, the tendency for monetary income to decline relatively to subsistence income is in part due to the basic difference between the two (the latter is immune to demand failures), and also the result of the shift of the labour force from monetary to non-monetary activities in order to survive in periods of economic decline. While subsistence production by and large has held up during the crisis, the decline of the monetary sectors may generate downward pressures on subsistence income, by increasing competition over land. Reports of a reduction in the proportion of land lying fallow is evidence of this pressure.

As a result of monetary sectors contracting relatively to subsistence sectors, economic decline in sSA countries has tended to shift relative domestic income shares (including returns from both monetary and subsistence activities) in favour of the rural sector.[4] Here it is important to stress that the urban informal sector is part of the monetary economy in all sSA countries, so a decline in aggregate demand directly impacts upon informal sector operators as a whole, which is not necessarily the case for rural households taken as a group. The decline of the monetary sectors involves income shifts, not redistribution as such. When the monetary sector contracts, subsistence income rises relatively to cash income, not because one group gains what another loses, but because cash income is by its nature more vulnerable to purely economic shocks. Within the monetary economies, however, important income shifts may arise which involve redistribution as such. These shifts represent what is a basic tendency within the monetary sectors: the tendency for powerful economic agents to gain at the expense of weaker ones. Whether this is a general characteristic of monetary economies is a matter of controversy. The evidence from our case studies indicates that it is an empirical if not an *a priori* law.

Factors generating this tendency (for the weak to lose relatively to the strong) during contractions are well documented in the literature. Both theoretical argument and empirical evidence suggest that larger producers are better able to bear risk and uncertainty and to survive their consequences than smaller producers.[5] Cash-crop producers may incur debts, and the ability to survive indebtedness until market conditions improve is positively related to producers' accumulated wealth. Where land is freely alienable, indebtedness may result in the loss of farms and permanent exclusion from the market for smaller producers. Limited evidence suggests that landlessness is an increasing phenomenon in sSA countries, albeit not as widespread as in Latin America or Asia.[6] For the most part the development of a market for land is not sufficiently advanced in sSA countries for market fluctuations alone to generate bankruptcies and landlessness. However, policies to privatise land could generate this result. Under current land tenure systems, rural households in sSA countries tend to retreat into subsistence when market conditions deteriorate. As a result, market shares of large producers would be expected to rise relatively to the shares of small producers during a period of economic contraction.

Discussion of rural income shifts in response to economic contraction should not be confined to on-farm livelihoods alone. Rural non-farm activities represent a substantial and growing contribution to household incomes, occupying perhaps 20 per cent of the rural labour force in sSA countries in the mid-1980s, particularly important for the poorer segments of the population (ILO 1983 and ILO/JASPA 1991). Most of these non-farm activities are linked to cash crop agriculture and decline sharply when rural money incomes fall; when the latter fall, all sources of money income fall in rural areas. This point has obvious implications for rural-urban migration.

Migration is both the theoretical and actual link between rural and urban incomes, though in a much more complex way than suggested by Todaro-type models. One way to characterise these models is to say that they are general equilibrium systems constrained from reaching full employment by a rigid urban wage. Such analyses derive their inspiration from the general neoclassical one-sector model in which a full employment solution with all markets cleared is the outcome if no variables are constrained. In this formulation, unemployment and migration are wage or income gap phenomena, never demand phenomena. That is, urban employment is constrained by the wage being too high (not by insufficient demand for output), and migration is the result of greater expected earnings in urban areas (not push factors in agriculture). In the 1960s perhaps this was a useful simplification, for most sSA economies grew at rates that kept them pressing against crucial constraints such as skilled labour, rather than product demand. Urban employment could not have been increased by an expansion of aggregate demand alone, even had there been no foreign exchange constraint on growth. However, even in the context of the 1960s, it was questionable to believe that flexible wages would clear the labour market. That belief involves a number of dubious assumptions which have been subjected to severe criticism within mainstream economic theory.[7]

In the present circumstances it is not valid to presume that employment is unconstrained by aggregate demand in sub-Saharan countries, particularly with regard to the urban formal private sector. To judge employment as demand constrained in sSA countries is not to advocate demand-expanding monetary and fiscal policy, a point pursued below. Rather, recognising the demand-constrained aspect of employment is an analytical insight that allows one to understand the dynamic processes determining distribution. One insight it yields is that in a demand-constrained situation a falling rural-urban income differential can induce urban migration, contrary to the predictions of the wage-constrained general equilibrium model. If the relevant decision unit is the extended family then the need to maintain itself above some target minimum poverty level can induce rather than discourage migration even where the relative reward to labour has fallen. This apparently 'perverse' behaviour results because the availability of different forms of livelihood-making is constrained by demand. Thus, income seekers must take what is available and cannot make their choice on the basis of relative rates of return.

Further, in a demand-constrained economy, a falling rural-urban income gap may not have any predictable impact on the evaluation of the advantages of seeking urban and rural livelihoods. If cash crop production is limited by product demand, as it obviously is in sSA countries, then a rise in rural incomes relatively to urban incomes is of limited relevance to urban workers even if they have access to land appropriate for cash crops. In a demand-constrained situation, the consequence of urban workers shifting to agriculture would be a tendency to drive down prices and reduce the returns to rural work.

A common response to the above is to propose that export demand is constrained by the exchange rate (i.e. that the exchange rate is 'overvalued'). This counter-argument assumes that which it seeks to prove: that at the international level there is no demand constraint. This argument is a non sequitur. We take it as self-evident that the world sales of cocoa, for example, are limited by developed country demand, not by the prevailing exchange rates of the cocoa-exporting countries. Were one country, say Ghana, to devalue, it would have no impact on world demand since cocoa prices are fixed in dollars and not cedis. At the most, devaluation would bring higher cedis prices to the farmers. Were Ghanaian farmers thus inspired to increase output, their greater sales would have to come at the cost of cocoa farmers in other countries (since the world price would not have changed). The basic difference in the devaluation argument between the developed country case and the developing country case has not been sufficiently appreciated by protagonists of the devaluation remedy. To pursue the point further, while a developed country's exports may be priced out of the market because of an overvalued exchange rate, a developing country's exports can rarely be, since prices on the international market are not fixed on the basis of internal costs. In such a case increased sales of one country could only come at the expense of other countries. 'Beggar thy neighbour' is a game any one country can play – but not all simultaneously, yet the devaluation remedy is recommended to all and sundry. In a demand-constrained framework swallowing such a prescription would cause the collapse of the cocoa market and beggar all cocoa-producing countries together. Indeed, we feel that recommending case-by-case devaluations without a systematic investigation of the impact on the world market of all of these taken together is highly irresponsible.

To return to distributional dynamics, it is important to recognise that urban incomes have a direct effect upon cash crops produced for the domestic market. Falling wage incomes tend to depress the demand for food crops, decreasing rural employment and incomes. This is further indication that the hypothesis so frequently asserted that wage restraint benefits rural producers is a naive conclusion drawn from the special case of a general equilibrium model with a rigid urban money wage.[8] Demand-constrained situations invalidate virtually all the conclusions drawn from Todaro-type models, though not necessarily yielding opposite ones. If one accepts that sSA economies are demand-constrained, the distributional statics of general equilibrium models do not serve.

More realistic models for the urban areas must incorporate a distinction between public and private activities in the formal sector, and, within the private sector, the distinction between formal and informal activities.[9] With regard to the former, one has observed in sSA countries a fall in private formal activity relatively to public, and with respect to the latter a decline in formal production relatively to informal. These shifts have occurred in the context of an overall fall in urban economic activity, not as allocative changes (i.e. they reflect an aggregate demand constraint). Demand-constrained distributional dynamics occur in the context of a negative sum game in which the ability of groups to protect themselves is closely related to their access to institutionalised political influence as well as economic power. Within the public sector power is particularly relevant. The empirical evidence in the previous chapters shows a tendency for unskilled wages to fall relatively to average wages in a number of cases, as well as redundancies being concentrated among unskilled workers. These tendencies we interpret to be in part the result of the political weakness of unskilled workers compared to skilled workers and professionals.

In the private sector the distributional dynamics involve at least two important processes. First, falling real wages have redistributed income from wages to profits, and entrepreneurial income has tended to rise even in some cases where output has fallen. This redistribution can be explained in terms of the interaction of product and labour markets. On the one hand, private sector real wages have dropped over the last 15 years. On the other, most observers conclude that the product markets are characterised by administered prices. As is well known, one of the aspects of the critique of import-substitution strategies in sSA countries is that they have fostered inefficiency due to lack of competition. Falling real wages combined with administered prices explain the tendency for profit shares to rise.

A second dynamic shift involves the role of the informal sector as the source of last-resort employment. The hypothesis that the inflow of income-seekers drives down informal sector incomes is not new. However, in the context of demand-constrained formal sector employment it does take on a new complexion. The wage-distorted general equilibrium model treats the gap between formal sector wages and informal sector incomes as a phenomenon of misallocation of labour. With demand falling, allocative issues become secondary. We would characterise the demand-constrained dynamics as follows: declining demand for formal sector output results in a fall in the demand for formal sector labour, a fall unchecked by declining real wages, since the possibilities for switching techniques in the short run are limited and entrepreneurs view their output decision as sales-constrained. The primary impact of falling real wages is to depress consumer demand for food crops, formal sector commodities and informal goods and services. With urban wage employment down and rural monetary incomes down, the demand for urban informal activities falls.

This demand-constrained process has severely depressed urban incomes in Africa. Expanded by the inflow of redundant formal sector wage earners and rural migrants in the face of reduced demand for output, the informal sector in sSA countries has become a poverty sector, not just in the sense of low incomes, but also because this is where the unemployed unskilled worker, the landless labourer and the migrant from marginal smallholdings go to survive (ILO/JASPA 1985). This conclusion, that the informal sector in sSA countries over the last decade has been a purgatory of falling incomes and poverty without prospects of improvement, is not to be confused with taking a position in the debate over whether the sector provides productive employment. That debate of the 1970s (Weeks 1975; and Leys 1973), started by the 1972 Kenya mission, referred to the long-run potential of the sector to generate capital accumulation and technical change, not its short-run behaviour under demand-constrained conditions. Whatever the character of the urban informal sector in periods of expanding aggregate demand, when demand is falling and formal sector employment contracting, the informal sector serves to absorb the unemployed at progressively falling income levels. To view the expansion of the urban informal labour force in sSA countries as evidence of reallocative efficiency (shifting labour from capital- to labour-intensive activities) is to make a virtue of growing impoverishment.

The urban informal sector has its own internal distributional dynamics in the context of economic decline. At the risk of oversimplification, agents in the informal sector in sSA countries can be divided into two groups (see also ILO/JASPA 1985). First, there are those who possess assets and skills: e.g. taxi drivers, merchants and artisans. These activities involve substantial barriers to entry and, therefore, suffer least from falling returns when there is an inflow of unemployed, income-seeking labour into the informal sector. The primary income-depressing effect in this case is the drop in consumer demand resulting from a decline in wage employment and cash crop revenue. For the other group, those without assets or relevant skills, it is the increased number of income-seekers, competing over a stagnant or falling quantity of casual employment opportunities, which drives earnings down and generates severe underemployment through work-sharing (voluntary or involuntary).

We have made a number of closely related arguments, which have a common theme: in a demand-constrained situation, income tends to be redistributed regressively within sectors. In the private formal sector, redistribution is from wages to profits; in agriculture from small to large holdings; in the informal sector from 'free entry' activities to restricted occupations. The first two of these involves redistribution in the strictest sense: what one group gains the other loses. The third, within the informal sector, is a shift, since the incomes of the two groups are not drawn from the same revenue pool.

The distinction between a strict redistribution and a shift in income explains our scepticism about alleged rural-urban income redistribution mechanisms and their importance. Given the heavy emphasis in the literature on rural-urban economic interaction, an elaboration of the above distinction is necessary. A fall in private sector wages, other things being equal, results in an increase in profits (assuming rent and interest to be fixed obligations). This is a direct redistribution, requiring no intervening action to achieve it. However, the fall in wages may result in a wider shift in income. If the fall is followed by a fall in prices (e.g. an unchanged profit margin), then all consumers gain. How much they gain cannot be determined until the demand effects of the wage decline is investigated. If the fall in wages provokes a fall in aggregate consumption, then further income declines follow. This is, of course, the 'multiplier' process. Depending on the size of the multiplier, net benefits to consumers as a whole may be substantial, negligible or negative. The impact of wage restraint on rural living standards (and on the informal sector) is an example of the theoretically indeterminate process just described. The final outcome is always an empirical question.

These empirical issues are assumed away in the wage-distorted general equilibrium model. Given that aggregate demand in effect does not vary in the model (in the sense that the multiplier is zero), there is no difference between a direct redistribution and a mediated income shift. Any fall in income in one place in the model must reappear somewhere else as an income gain. This type of argument comes close to assuming what it seeks to prove as a result of what might be called the 'law of conservation of income'. If economies are demand-constrained income lost by one group need not reappear in the hands of another group, but tends to generate further income losses throughout the system. What the size and functional distribution of income will be at the end of the multiplier process cannot be determined *a priori*.

Thus, in the context of demand-constrained economies, hypotheses involving systematic rural-urban income shifts (particularly wage earner-peasant shifts) are singularly unconvincing. The empirical evidence presented in the preceding chapters gives little support for such shifts and considerable basis for sustaining contrary hypotheses. Having placed so much emphasis upon the argument that the economies of sSA countries are demand-constrained, it is necessary by way of conclusion to clarify further this key concept. We are not arguing that African economies are demand-constrained in the sense that idle capacity and unemployed labour could be drawn into production by expansionary fiscal or monetary policy, which is the usual closed-economy Keynesian meaning of the term. Expansionary fiscal and monetary policies would immediately encounter a binding foreign exchange constraint. Indeed, the foreign exchange constraint is the essence of the economic crisis being suffered by the sSA countries. The demand constraint reflects the depressed world market for the region's primary product exports: were export demand to increase, levels of output and employment would expand at prevailing price levels, requiring no significant reduction in the production of non-tradables and requiring no dramatic price changes. In other words, the economies of sSA countries are demand-constrained in that expansion of production, for domestic or foreign markets, is not a relative price/resource allocation problem. Reallocation of resources and relative price changes would be the consequence, not the cause of increased exports. With regard to the ratio most important for this study, declines in urban incomes relatively to rural incomes over the last decade have not represented an equilibrating mechanism, but rather the process of economic contraction and marginalisation of the mass of the population.

9 Aspects of Theory and Policy

INTRODUCTION

Virtually every country in Africa is suffering from an economic crisis, with the intensity varying from the difficult to the catastrophic. It is the view of the IMF and the World Bank that while external factors no doubt contributed to the crisis, most blame should be placed on economic mismanagement. Were only a few countries facing problems, or even were many, but a handful displayed robust economic health, assigning blame to policy errors might have some credibility. But when a crisis situation is universal, suffered by governments of the right and the left, by governments fundamentally committed to letting market forces run and others that seek to limit and restrict market transactions, economic 'mismanagement' explains little.[1] It is for this reason that the IMF's uniform approach with its emphasis upon domestic adjustment is being received with decreasing credibility, perhaps even by economic conservatives.[2] The current depression of economic activity in the African region is not basically a problem of individual countries. Evidence for this is so overwhelming that what is extraordinary is that incantations to 'appropriate policy packages' continue.[3] The singular would be more appropriate because despite many protestations that the IMF and World Bank's prescription for African countries differ according to their structural characteristics they invariably contain the same ingredients under the brand name of 'structural adjustment programmes'. Certainly the proportions vary but the basic formula remains the same. Whether in oil-rich Nigeria or cocoa-dependent Ghana the cure centres on shifting resources to exports – and basically agricultural exports at that. The chosen instrument for this is devaluation and the rationale that past policies have discriminated against the agricultural sector – particularly the export crops – causing the African crisis. We have questioned the applicability of this model to African countries at this stage in their development, as also the efficacy of a shift to agricultural exports in mineral-dominated economies.

DEVALUATION

Notwithstanding the faulty premises of the IMF-WB 'structural adjustment' programmes and notwithstanding the impression that still persists that African countries are reluctant to accept such programmes, most have in fact been forced by their desperate need for foreign exchange into submission.[4] This is best illustrated by the proxy index of devaluation, up to now the item most resisted by African governments. Along with fall in wages, the fall in the exchange rate is another fact of African economies worth recording.[5] Table 9.1 and Figure 9.1 provide the evidence.

It is indeed strange that devaluation should play such an important role in adjustment programmes, since its effectiveness as a policy instrument has been disputed on both theoretical and empirical grounds.[6] Devaluation is recommended to shift relative profitability toward export production. Even were the theoretical underpinnings unambiguously clear (the Marshall–Lerner conditions must hold), and the practical outcome assured (price has to be the binding constraint to increased production), advocating such a policy simultaneously to a large number of countries (recall that Asian and Latin American governments are plied with the same recommendation) is precisely the 'beggar-thy-neighbour' strategy which economists have generally condemned as contributing to the breakdown of world trade during the Great Depression. Fishlow has argued forcefully that such an export-promotion strategy is implicitly based upon a *ceteris paribus*

TABLE 9.1: *Sample countries: Exchange rates (nominal) against the SDR, 1980–87* (1985 = 100)

	1980	1981	1982	1983	1984	1985	1986	1987
Ghana	1 879	2 058	2 172	210	134	100	59.9	26.4
Kenya	184	148	126	123	117	100	92.7	75.7
Lesotho	296	252	237	220	144	100	105.8	102.6
Liberia	86	94	100	105	112	100	89.8	77.4
Nigeria	158	148	149	140	139	100	27.1	18.7
Sierra Leone	420	420	422	218	233	100	13.2	17.6
Somalia	581	637	283	254	183	100	42.2	32.9
Tanzania	174	187	172	139	102	100	28.7	15.3
Uganda	15 854	1 552	1 318	612	302	100	89.8	18.1
Zambia	611	611	611	489	290	100	40.3	55.2

SOURCE: IMF 1989.

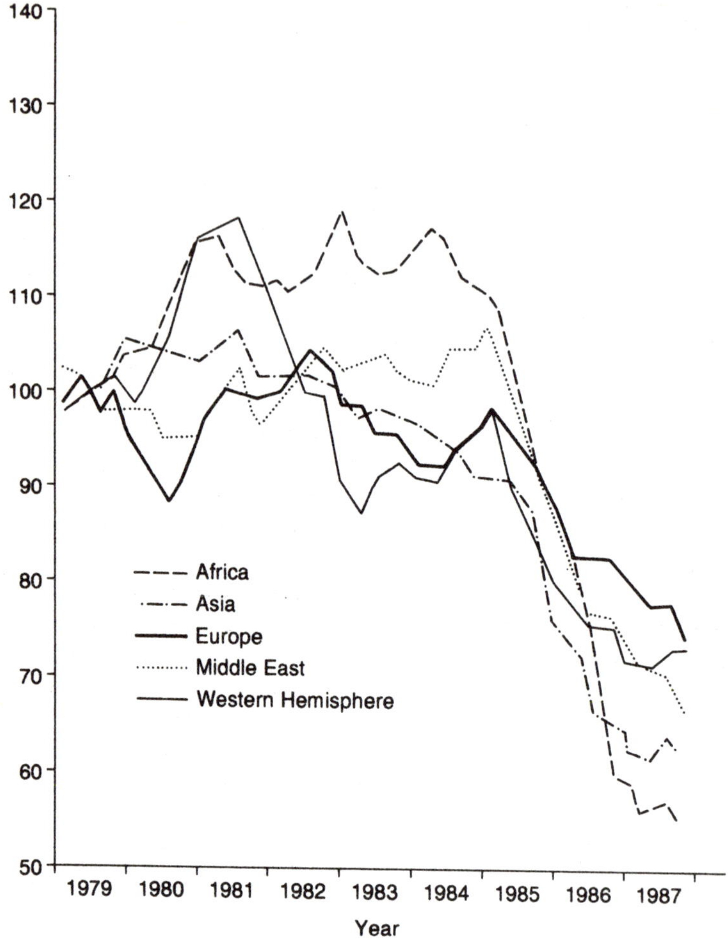

Source: IMF.

Figure 9.1 Africa and others: Real effective exchange rates, 1979–87 (1979 = 100)

presumption that only the country in question will execute it.[7] The allegation that devaluation would unequivocally increase exports of sSA countries because these economies are such small suppliers that they can be treated as 'price takers' is an example of the 'fallacy of composition' argument in its crudest form. If all cotton producers, for example, were to devalue, it is optimistic to think that the net increase in world demand for cotton would sustain the presumed supply response from cotton-producing countries. Models testing the impact of exchange rate adjustment are rare for sSA countries, but an econometric study of the Sudan suggests no gain in exports as a result of devaluation experiments (Hussein and Thirlwall 1984).

If the consequences of devaluation are uncertain in both theory and practice, how does one account for its ubiquitous presence in IMF structural adjustment programmes? There are several possible explanations, at least one of which is ideological. Economic conservatives hold devaluation as a central tenet of the dogma that unregulated markets are self-adjusting and equilibrating. It is the linchpin of such arguments that developing countries will gain from pursuing open-economy policies. When one discovers that in fact terms of trade are moving against African countries and the external account is a barrier to development and a drain upon resources, exchange rate adjustment provides the counter-argument to a reality which conflicts with the predictions of theory. The argument is of course tautological – in a neoclassical framework a balance-of-payments deficit by definition reflects an 'overvalued' exchange rate. If it were accepted that the theory of exchange rate adjustment were indeterminate, a variety of factors such as international monopoly power, the role of reserve currencies in creating asymmetric bargaining power, etc., would have to be entertained. Once one starts down that road, the credibility of the multilateral agencies is thrown into doubt. To be more charitable, there is a second consideration at work here. On three continents the economies of less developed countries are in crisis, even those hailed by conservatives as great success stories a decade ago (Côte d'Ivoire is such an example in Africa). In present circumstances, with world liquidity tight and the OECD countries unlikely to exhibit more than modest expansion in the aggregate, the prospects for even a few less developed countries recovering impressively are slight. In such circumstances, it is hard for one to know what governments should do (or can do to improve the situation substantially). Such a defeatist view, though it may be true, contradicts the tradition of eternal optimism which has been part of Western thought since the Age of Reason and is particularly strong in economics. Devaluation enters here in a ceremonial, almost religious role, supplying a source of optimism in the face of disastrous reality.

Specifically in the African context, we have seen that economic stagnation and decline have brought about many of the changes which devaluation is pledged to achieve. In virtually every country real wages have fallen, presumably more than enough to reduce labour costs substantially. Food prices have risen dramatically and relatively to the general price level, which should by neoclassical analysis stimulate production. In the event neither of these trends seems to have improved matters. To a Keynesian, this is hardly surprising, for in the General Theory it is argued that falling wages herald economic decline, not recovery. With regard to devaluation itself, the trend in 'real exchange rates' as calculated by invariably crude indices of purchasing-power parity,[8] is mixed in the African region, but the export performance of countries does not seem closely correlated with such measures.[9] There are clearly other forces at work which render changes in exchange rates of marginal importance, perhaps reflecting effect rather than cause.[10]

It appears that in present circumstances devaluation in most African countries would worsen income distribution while having little impact on production.[11] This has not always been the case; unlike the IMF we do not think devaluations always and everywhere have the same consequences. In the past rural-urban income differentials were large in some countries, and shifts in relative prices effected by devaluation might have improved distribution and production. But since the mid-1970s at the latest, urban dwellers (except for the élite) have lost almost continuously compared to those living in rural areas. Devaluation would intensify this trend. If one can extrapolate from the evidence in this study, the likely effect of devaluation in many countries of the region would be to redistribute income from workers, peasants and informal sector operators to the wealthy, urban and rural. This does not mean countries can persist with hopelessly 'overvalued' exchange rates for ever; only that the distributional impact may not be as benign as is made out and the output impact less than overwhelming, given the breakdown of these economies.

THE 'CLEARING' OF LABOUR MARKETS

Those who argue for devaluation as a vehicle to 'correct distortions' have a trump card. While real wages may have fallen and the rural-urban gap declined, does it not remain the case that urban labour markets in Africa are characterised by excess supply? And if the answer to this is 'yes', then real wages need to fall more, for their prevailing level is still above the 'market-clearing' rate. One implication of this argument is that while it is perhaps unfortunate that real wages have fallen drastically in a short period in most African countries, such a judgment is subjective; on objective (optimal allocation) grounds, wages should fall even further.

This argument that an excess supply of labour services (or any commodity) implies that its price is too high was discredited even a decade ago, for it is based upon a Walrasian general equilibrium model in which no exchanges occur at disequilibrium prices and (therefore) all adjustment is instantaneous.[12] Its rejuvenated appeal today reflects not an adequate rejoinder to its past critics, but a change in the general political climate in the West that makes such conservative arguments more acceptable, their theoretical shortcomings notwithstanding. One need not go into these esoteric debates to demonstrate the invalidity of this argument for African labour markets.

In African urban areas, unemployment by the definition used in industrial capitalist countries hardly exists. Excess labour supply does not take this form. Those who cannot find formal sector jobs engage themselves in informal activities, including casual labour. Excess urban labour supply has characteristically been considered on the implicit assumption that wage incomes are higher than rural incomes and higher than can be earned in informal activities. But let us consider for the moment the interaction of different labour markets without reference to relative rewards. When wage incomes decline in real terms, households of wage earners can be presumed to seek ways of supplementing their purchasing power. One way to do this is for family members – and perhaps the wage earners themselves – to work in the informal sector. As real wages fall further, this tendency will intensify.[13] Even if wages drop very low in real terms, it would be irrational for those employed to give up their formal sector jobs, unless informal sector earnings per worker rose sufficiently to compensate for the decline in wages (i.e., it is not sufficient that they rise above the average level of wages).

If incomes in the informal sector are in part a function of formal sector performance, then the fall in real wages will drive down the incomes in the informal sector. Thus the dynamics of the labour market will be for wage earners to hold on to their formal sector jobs as part of their strategy for protecting household purchasing power. And informal sector operators will still be attracted to formal sector jobs because of depressed informal sector earnings (even if those earnings rise above the wage level). In this context, a drop in real wages is likely to increase the demand by households for both formal and informal sector income sources. Even should the formal sector wage drop below the level of earnings in the informal sector, the result need not be a shortage of labour in the formal sector. If households seek to protect their standard of living, then they will not make exclusive choices between the returns from different activities as a capitalist does when investing.

The problem with the usual labour market model is that it misspecifies the supply curve. Here we are not considering the trivial case of the 'backward-bending' labour supply curve, but rather how a household responds to a fall in real income. The neoclassical approach presumes that an exclusive choice will be made among income-earning alternatives irrespective of the income level at which the choice must be made. This involves a false analogy with the choices made by a capitalist. The capitalist chooses among alternatives based on their rate of return (or discounted present value), but the absolute income gained from these can always be expanded by merely investing more.[14] The situation of the non-capitalist is entirely different. A wage earner cannot by his or her own action expand the time worked on the job. Nor can he or she usually take a second job of the same type because of the institutional way in which working time is divided. The consequence of the interaction of labour markets is that falling wages need have no tendency to 'clear' markets. On the contrary, an excess supply of labour can signal either that wage levels are 'too high' (attracting the envy of workers outside the formal sector) or 'too low' (attracting labour because the general level of incomes is low in a demand-constrained situation). Thus the general equilibrium model of labour markets with its implicit symmetry between the labour and capital markets may prove misleading for understanding the dynamics of rural-urban interactions in Africa.

POLITICAL CLIMATE AND DEVELOPMENT GOALS

The purpose of this study has been to document the falsity of a stereotyped characterisation of sub-Saharan African countries, a stereotype in which these countries were diagnosed as suffering from extreme rural-urban inequalities. In doing so, we have sought to demonstrate that the primary aspect of income distribution in sSA countries is between rich and poor, be they rural or urban. In the present political context, stressing essentially class aspects of inequality is hardly popular, for we have come light-years from the time when the most prestigious economists in the West argued that distributional considerations should take precedence over the goal of aggregate growth.[15] Indeed, one now sees a 'revisionist' school emerging to tell stories that conclude that attempts to stress distributional considerations and basic needs are self-defeating.

It is unfortunately the case that the brief consensus around the proposition that spreading the gains from growth is as important as growth itself was the product of a period of relative prosperity.[16] The cynic might say that as long as growth was satisfactory and the élites enjoyed increasing privileges, the principle of a more equitable growth pattern could be entertained; however, now that the issue is how losses shall be apportioned, the traditional conservative nature of economic science reasserts itself. Yet distributional issues are now more important than ever: when growth was positive, there was at least some chance that some of it would 'trickle down' to the poor and vulnerable groups; in the 1980s there has been precious little to trickle.

In sub-Saharan Africa there is a development crisis; more profoundly, there is a crisis of accumulating poverty and misery, which now affects urban groups including wage earners to a growing extent. The new consensus in the 'international development community' – with a few individuals and multilateral agencies as exceptions – is to hark back to the traditional *laissez faire* optimism which one would have thought the Great Depression discredited once and for all.[17] It is ironic that the Great Depression of the West brought on a thorough-going reappraisal of accepted economic wisdom, while the Great Depression of Africa has prompted in the West a rejuvenation in development economics of precisely the dogma which the crisis of the 1930s had discredited. This contradiction brings to mind an indictment of the economics profession 30 years ago by Dudley Seers for its myopic view of development.

> Economists seem very slow in adapting themselves to the requirements of the main task of the day – the elimination of acute poverty in Africa, Asia and Latin America – just as the previous generation of economists failed to cope realistically with economic fluctuations until after the depression had brought politically catastrophic results. (Seers 1963, p. 77)

The elimination of acute poverty in Africa – or more modestly the prevention of an intensification of poverty – is as much 'the main task of the day' in the late 1980s as it was in 1963 when Seers wrote. One small but necessary step towards seriously embarking upon that task is to abandon the out-of-date view of African economies as suffering from an enormous rural-urban gap, a view which still continues to guide policy. If generals are always fighting the last war, development agencies are forever using last decade's popular paradigm to understand today's economic realities. The unfortunate thing is their tenacity is haphazard, for while they hold on to past models of development they simultaneously evince undue zeal in discarding some hard-won gains. The rural-urban paradigm still reigns, while notions of equity are being jettisoned. The consequences for developing countries could be tragic.

Notes

FOREWORD

1. For earlier examples of this research see Ghai and Radwan 1983; Ghai and Smith 1987; Greer and Thorbecke 1986; and Jamal 1988c. That such research feeds into advisory services, important for an international organisation, may be gleaned from just a few examples from some recent ILO missions; see in particular ILO 1986a and b, and ILO 1988, being missions to the Sudan, Ethiopia and Tanzania to advise governments on policies to increase food production and achieve growth while safeguarding equity.

PREFACE

1. See, for example, Baker 1990 which refers to our 'seminal study which challenges many of the conventional wisdoms concerning urban and rural conditions [in Africa] . . .' (p. 12). The World Bank, which we critique in the pages that follow, has at least noted our dissenting views (Serageldin 1989 and World Bank 1990a). Smith 1989 writing for the Food and Agriculture Organization of the United Nations (FAO) makes extensive use of our findings on the rural-urban gap while Todaro in the fourth edition of his widely used textbook (Todaro 1990), and the United Nations Development Programme (UNDP) *Human Development Report, 1990* take note of it. Among others who have acknowledged our contribution to the question of falling urban wages, changing income distribution and informalisation of African labour markets have been ILO/JASPA 1989a and 1991, Pinstrup-Andersen 1988a and 1989a and b, Addison and Demery 1989, Nafziger 1988, Iliffe 1987, Mkandawire 1991, Colclough 1991 and Vandemoortele 1991. All subsequent studies of sampled countries have used our findings – e.g. Mamdani 1990 and Loxley 1989 on Uganda, Loxley 1990 on Zambia, Weeks 1990 on Sierra Leone, and Bienefield 1990 and Maliyamkono and Bagachwa 1990 on Tanzania – while the earlier JASPA mission reports too have been widely quoted in subsequent studies.

CHAPTER ONE

1. We shall not deal with the debt crisis here, treating it only as is necessary for our analysis. However, as a background piece of information it is worth retaining that debt/GNP ratio in Africa in 1989 reached 115

compared to only 49 and 28 for Latin America and South and East Asia, respectively. Debt service ratio stood at 27 per cent in 1988 (World Bank 1990b). Elsewhere one of the authors has discussed in some detail the narrowing of policy options as a result of the debt crisis and the ideological shift of the lending agencies (Weeks 1988b; see also Payer 1989 and Campbell 1989). Chapter 7 in UN 1991 contains a review of policies for debt reduction. Among international agencies' annual surveys the UN's is perhaps the least known but deserves more recognition.

2. Actually, the idea that African countries suffer from extreme and debilitating rural-urban income differentials is older than this. W.A. Lewis, while advisor to the government of Ghana in the 1950s warned against policies that might excessively favour urban areas. Later he repeated the point for Nigeria in his 'reflections' on that country's growth record, alleging that rural-urban income differentials were typically around 50 per cent (Lewis 1967, p. 42; and Rimmer 1970 and 1984, where Lewis is quoted). Berg in influential articles in the early 1960s placed heavy stress upon the alleged exalted position of urban wage earners (Berg 1964 and 1966), referring to them as a 'relatively privileged group' (1966, p. 189).
3. 'Terms like "urban bias" and "rural bias" have to be used with the greatest of caution. They can easily become . . . mystifying terms. That is to say, they obscure the real issues, by either ignoring them completely, or misrepresenting them, or grossly oversimplifying them' (Byres 1979, p. 241).
4. Statistical weaknesses may also be responsible. Ghai, *et al.* (1988) have pointed out that these social indicators 'are not observational counts [but] estimates made in national or more generally international offices on the basis of various assumptions and models. . . . These estimated figures may differ markedly from one estimator source to another for the same country' (pp. 14 and 15).
5. Detailed analysis of the technological and ecological conditions of African agriculture is found in FAO 1986.
6. This is a variation on Engel's Law: the lower the income of a household, the higher the proportion of that income that has to be spent on food. If African farmers were fully commercialised – or what is the same thing, if their auto-consumption were properly valued – it would be discovered that they 'spend' up to 75 per cent of their 'income' on food. It should be clarified that we shall use the term 'subsistence production' to refer to output which is directly consumed by the producing unit. Thus, the term 'subsistence production' and 'subsistence producer' do not refer to a standard of living (though a very low standard is generally implied by our usage), but rather to the relationship between production and distribution of that output. That is, by subsistence production we mean neither that the farm family is at the margin of existence nor that its output is completely non-marketed, but that it provides the bulk of its staple food calories from own-farm sources.

CHAPTER TWO

1. An early statement of the African 'mismanagement' hypothesis may be found in the 'Berg Report' (World Bank 1981a). Liebenthal, a Bank staff member, writing in the same year, offered a much more balanced and nuanced view (Liebenthal 1981). The mismanagement thesis was argued in the academic literature by many; for example, Bates (1981 and 1986) attacking market interventions ('food policy in Africa . . . is designed to bring peaceful relations between governments and their urban constituents [at the cost of the farmers].' Bates 1986, p. 49) and Gulhati, Bose, and Atukorala (1986) defending the effectiveness of devaluation. By the late 1980s, 'mismanagement' became an unqualified indictment of African governments in World Bank documents (Serageldin 1988 and 1989; and World Bank, 1989a and b). This emphasis intensified despite a study by the Bank itself that indicated that Bank-Fund adjustment programmes had achieved little success in reviving the African economies (World Bank 1988a). The most objective account of the factors in the African crisis remains Berry 1984. See also Lofchie 1986 for a survey and Jamal 1988b. For a theoretical discussion of adjustment issues see Streeten 1989, and for an analysis of the Third World recession and impact of structural adjustment programmes, the influential book by UNICEF – Cornia *et al.* 1989 – which put the phrase 'adjustment with a human face' in wide currency. Mkandawire 1989 contains several useful studies on factors affecting performance in African agriculture.
2. In its 1988 report on the debt crisis, the World Bank concludes its discussion of the low-income African countries by leaving little doubt where blame should be directed: 'The unfortunate economic policies of the past have already exacted their toll on these countries in terms of declining output, lost investment, and a generation of citizens who have come of age in an era of steadily falling living standards. Those countries that have now adopted rigorous adjustment programs deserve the full support of donors and creditors' (World Bank 1988a, p. xiii).

   Apparently only those countries which have reformed their wayward ways are deserving of help.
3. As Singer 1989 has pointed out, it was the 1970s growth which was spurious, based as it was on debt piling up.
4. A brief summary of the depressing trend in the economies of sub-Saharan African countries is found in United Nations 1986. A recent book by Ghai and Smith (1987) also addresses this issue, as do the two recent *African Employment Reports* by ILO/JASPA (1989a and 1991).
5. For surveys of economic performance in low-income Africa that share our pessimism, see Rose 1985 and United Nations 1986. Mosley and Smith (1989, p. 322) conclude, based on an examination of World Bank data similar to those in Table 2.1 that 'any talk of sub-Saharan Africa having 'turned the corner' as a result of the strong medicine it has recently been given is premature'. Stewart (1991a) concludes that '. . . the "bottom line" is that the [adjustment] policies have not been succeeding in meeting their short-run objectives, and are consequently undermining growth' (p. 433). In another article (1991b) she looks at the impact of

adjustment on equity in African (as well as non-African) countries and finds 'a continued negative impact' (p. 1847).

6. During 1980–84, agriculture, industry and services grew at annual rates of 1.1 per cent, –1.2 and 1.4 respectively, according to World Bank data (World Bank 1986b, p. 156).
7. At the same time, agriculture's share also fell according to World Bank figures, from 42 per cent of GNP in 1973 to 38 per cent in 1984. This estimated decline is difficult to credit in a region where subsistence agriculture is so important, and is probably the result of underestimating non-marketed output. This issue is discussed further in our treatment of survival strategies prompted by the current economic crisis in sSA.
8. In the 1986 *World Development Report* we read: 'If investment is to be restored to sustain growth, many developing countries will have to increase domestic savings. Ultimately, an increase in domestic savings depends on the government's commitment to adopt the policies needed to establish a stable macro-economic environment' (World Bank 1986b, p. 41). It should be clear from the various references here that the World Bank reports contain far-reaching diagnoses and prescriptions. These do not go unchallenged. See for example Singer 1988a and b on 'outward orientation' in *World Development Report, 1987* and the claim to 'human face' concerns in World Bank's annual report of the same year. The assertion of *World Development Report, 1987* of a strong correlation between export orientation and growth too has been challenged by Singer and Gray 1988, and the claim of the World Bank's *Annual Report, 1991* that there is a 'growing consensus' and 'evidence amassed' for the success and correctness of adjustment programmes during the first phase of its special programme for Africa in Singer 1991.
9. This reflects the preponderant importance of exports in their economies. In our sample countries, exports comprised around 10 per cent of total GNP in 1984. Kenya led with 21 per cent, followed by Sierra Leone (16 per cent), Tanzania (10 per cent), Uganda (9 per cent), and Somalia (4.5 per cent). (No data are available for Lesotho, most likely in view of the special role of remittance 'exports'.) Nigeria had 20 per cent of her GNP in exports. Figures for the late-1980s were similar.
10. A 1983 World Bank paper (Singh 1983b), after giving extremely pessimistic projections of world prices, comes to the conclusion that the major determining factor for export growth of sSA countries would be government policies.
11. 'At the root of the poor performance and debt problems of developing countries lies their failure to adjust to the external developments that have taken place since the early 1970s, coupled with the magnitude of the external shocks' (World Bank 1986b, p. 33). There is an implicit admission that 'external developments' have been negative ('external shocks'), but the blame is put squarely on governments for failing to adjust to them! The dismal trends in the terms of trade have been documented in World Bank working papers, but largely ignored in the *World Development Reports*. See Singh 1983a and b.
12. According to IMF data export unit values of sub-Saharan Africa's exports (excluding Nigeria and South Africa) fell in all years of the 1980s,

except 1984, the total decline between 1980 and 1986 being 22 per cent (IMF 1987b, p. 26).

13. The factors he lists are the oil price increases of the Organization of the Petroleum Exporting Counties (OPEC), the rise in dollar interest rates, and the dramatic fall in primary product prices on the international market (Cline 1983). See also the excellent study by Saigal 1990, where quantitative estimates of external shocks are made.
14. East Asian terms fell by only 3 per cent or so in the period under consideration while South Asia's terms improved, by 18 per cent, as did Latin America's, by 28 per cent. The divergent behaviour reflects the composition of the export and import bundles in different regions.
15. Not all international agencies subscribed to the thesis that internal policies were to blame for Africa's ills. The United Nations Conference on Trade and Development (UNCTAD) in its 1989 report on the least developed countries placed primary emphasis on external shocks, as well as questioning the appropriateness of Bank-Fund adjustment packages (UNCTAD 1989b). Extremely strong scepticism also came from the Organization of African Unity (OAU 1988). Perhaps the clearest attack and an alternative policy framework was provided by the Economic Commission for Africa (ECA 1989a).
16. For an argument along these lines see Jamal 1986a. The World Bank has taken the lead in recommending devaluation to African countries. In the light of this it is instructive to read the following in a World Bank staff paper: 'Appropriate price and exchange rate policy would have a relatively small impact on agricultural growth [in sSA countries] . . .' (Cleaver 1985, p. 1). Binswanger (1990, p. 231) in another Bank publication concurs: 'The price elasticity of agriculture overall is very low in the short run because the main factors of production – land, capital and labour – are fixed . . . [D]omestic food supply may not increase rapidly in response to adjustment programmes.' See also UN 1990, pp. 29–33 for a survey of results on supply response.
17. The theoretical debate is summarised in Ghani 1984, pp. 7–12. Some of the ambiguity comes through in World Bank studies. Thus Chhibber (1991, p. 28), summarising results from his research, concedes that nominal devaluations are wiped out by cost-push inflation induced by the devaluations.
18. One reads, 'If developing countries were to adopt policies that encourage domestic savings, increase the efficiency with which they use resources, and increase their links with the world economy, they could raise their growth rates significantly regardless of what the industrial countries do' (World Bank 1986b, p. 3).
19. Looking back at Table 2.1, one sees that the growth rate of per capita income during this period was 3 per cent per annum. Since population was increasing at more than 3 per cent per annum for the region as a whole, the growth rate of real output was in excess of 6 per cent.
20. '. . . Those developing countries that maintained macro-economic stability and implemented policies to make the best of the changing world economy have emerged with strong growth rates and bright prospects . . .' (World Bank 1986b, p. 3).

21. Michael Prowse writing in the *Financial Times* of 8 July 1991 says of the *World Development Report, 1991* that it 'reads like a teaching manual; . . . one gets the impression the bank believes it has found the philosopher's stone of development economics . . . In purely economic terms [economists] may argue that the bank's faith in markets is excessive. After all the bank's own analysis suggests market-oriented structural adjustment programmes in the 1980s had a negligible impact on living standards.'
22. The report of the Advisory Group on Financial Flows to Africa (United Nations 1988) suggests that massive foreign assistance will be necessary to rejuvenate the economies of the sSA region.
23. One misses the anguish of primary producers in terms of trade calculations. Hetmeier (1990) brings this home starkly by showing how much coffee a country would have to give up in December 1989 compared to 1985 to buy a 37–59 KW tractor from Germany – 3.8 tons versus 1.1 tons. There is also an interesting technical point here that is often obscured in terms of trade calculations. During this period the deutschmark was gaining against the dollar, whereas commodity prices are quoted in dollars. For Germany (as for other European countries) with dollar prices of commodities falling, commodities became incredibly cheap in terms of local products.

CHAPTER THREE

1. See, for example, Turgot 1766.
2. The classic statement of the pro-peasant position is found in Sismondi 1819.
3. It is necessary to say 'Black nationals' because many Asians 'Africanised' out of influential positions were also nationals, though in some cases their *de facto* status was ambiguous.
4. Kenya and Zimbabwe, as well as the former Portuguese colonies, had a European landed élite during colonial rule (some of which persists to this day). In northern Nigeria there was a national class based on control of landed property, the Hausa-Fulani élite. Nigeria is somewhat unusual in this regard.
5. Colonial wage and salary policy in three British colonial possessions is discussed in Weeks 1971b. On the relationship between town and countryside in the 1960s see Green 1967.
6. This momentary prestige provoked comments such as, 'the politician is obligated, by reason of the need to stay in power, to compromise with all sorts of conflicting interests – to agree to wage settlements which destroy the income assumptions of the [development] plan.' Leys 1971, p. 109.
7. Influential was Warren's 1966 article on Nigeria, whose emphasis upon the political power of African trade unions was generalised to the region.
8. Excessively high wages were attributed generally to sSA countries by Frank in his much-quoted 1968 article, which can be taken as the seminal work that synthesised previously disparate concerns about rural-urban differentials. Though subsequently overshadowed by several articles by

Todaro, Frank's article effectively set forth the 'urban bias' stereotype for sub-Saharan Africa (Frank 1968).

9. Writings on Nigeria were crucial to forming this generalisation for the region as a whole (e.g. Kilby 1969, where is reprinted his article from the *Journal of Developing Areas*, 'Industrial relations and wage determination: Failure of the Anglo-Saxon model').
10. There were exceptions, of course. Samir Amin argued that judging urban wage earners to be excessively privileged was moralistic (Amin 1969). The late Elimane Kane, Deputy Director-General of the ILO, attending the same conference in which Amin presented his paper, also made comments questioning the widely prevalent view that wage earners had gained immensely in the 1960s: 'It has still to be seen . . . whether [the] increase in wages brought about any comparable improvement in the standard of living of wage earners . . .' (Smith 1969, p. 70).
11. The term seems first to have been used by Lenin to account for the non-revolutionary nature of the leadership of the British working class (but not to the working class itself). It was applied to the entire wage labour force in large establishments in Africa by Arrighi and Saul (1968) to account for what the authors perceived as political conservatism of workers. It is not accidental that this critique from the left coincided with the neoclassicals' emphasis upon the rural-urban gap.
12. This population of petty traders, artisans and casually employed workers came to be known as 'the informal sector'. The term was apparently first used in Hart 1973, and applied in the analytical sense to Kenya in the 1972 ILO mission report. The relevant section is reprinted as 'The informal sector' in Meier 1976 (by John Weeks).
13. The impact of the Lewis model (or Lewis–Ranis–Fei model) is an interesting story in itself, since the model has a number of obvious theoretical inconsistencies that render it invalid; yet it was extraordinarily influential within a profession that prides itself on its analytical rigour. The inconsistencies of the model are discussed in Weeks 1971c.
14. Some of these are: no difference in tastes among trading partners, same technology for each product in each country, homogeneous factor inputs, and no 'factor-reversals' (i.e. reswitching of techniques).
15. These critiques are so standard that references are hardly necessary. It should be noted that the arguments are made now as forcefully as they were 25 years ago. In the *World Development Report, 1986* one reads: 'High wage costs and subsidised capital, especially in the formal economy, reduce output and encourage the substitution of capital for labour' (World Bank 1986b, p. 29). An IMF document puts it more generally, '. . . in the long term a pricing system which departs significantly from underlying market forces is likely to seriously misallocate resources' (IMF 1985, p. 22).
16. The argument is cogently put in Stewart 1972. Weeks (1974) attempts to explain the employment problem in Kenya in the early 1970s using the 'inappropriate technology' hypothesis.
17. The hypothesis that the level of employment was in part a function of the distribution of income was the analytical basis of an ILO report on Colombia in 1970 (ILO 1970).

18. The allegation that African workers in large establishments enjoyed the equivalent of life-long tenure was as false as it was widely believed. In practice labour protection laws in most sub-Saharan countries went unenforced (Gutkind 1968). This is quite an important article, critical of the simplistic 'urban bias' view then emerging, while anticipating some of the insights of the view, such as Todaro's emphasis on the probability of finding a job as a determinant of migration.
19. In a typical judgement, Lewis wrote, '. . . in Nigeria, unskilled urban wages earn much more than twice a farmer's income' (Lewis 1967, p. 92). No calculations were provided to demonstrate this.
20. For example, Hinchcliffe (1974) wrote, 'The urban wage labour force in Nigeria is assumed by many commentators to have moved into a highly privileged position during the 1950s and 1960s relative to rural workers. However, the calculations presented here . . . indicate that in terms of standard of living this "privilege" is not so great'.
21. 'In Eastern Africa [Kenya, Tanzania, Uganda and Zambia] the long-term annual growth rate of real GDP has been about 5 per cent, but the growth of the "modern sector" wage employment has been much slower, at under 3 per cent. What is startling is the exceedingly rapid growth of average earnings . . . [which] represents a 10 per cent growth in real wages. . . If employment growth and equality are to be priority objectives, this sort of situation must be reversed . . .' (Jackson 1971, pp. 532–33).
22. Many authors, particularly sociologists and political scientists, stressed education as the root cause of urban migration. Here the argument was that western-oriented primary and secondary schooling left youth dissatisfied with rural life. The so-called 'school-leaver unemployment problem' does not enter into our discussion in subsequent chapters, so we do not consider this literature.
23. A much more sophisticated, though less mathematical, version of the model is found in Todaro's textbook, where he incorporates other influences (Todaro 1985, pp. 258 ff).
24. This simple calculation requires among others the assumption that jobs are awarded randomly to those in the pool of the unemployed.
25. The literature here is enormous; see for example Turnham and Jaeger 1971 and the studies cited therein.
26. See Elkan 1960 for an excellent early study of migration and income transfers.
27. We refer to some studies of rural-urban income differentials in the next four chapters.
28. For a strict neoclassical presentation of the objections, see Hahn 1984; and for a post-Keynesian point of view, see Leijonhufvud 1981.
29. The neoclassical theory of labour markets is presented and criticised in Weeks 1989.
30. To take another example from the *World Development Report, 1986*, 'In developing countries . . . the burden of higher marginal tax rate falls heavily on agriculture, either implicitly or explicitly' (p. 28). Given the great variety in tax laws among countries, the notorious difficulty of taxing agricultural produce at all directly, and the complexities of the theory of tax incidence, such a blanket conclusion is hardly obvious.

CHAPTER FOUR

1. See Mangat 1969 for a historical treatment of Asians in East Africa.
2. Jamal 1976a and b and 1977b discuss the massive inequalities in Uganda which finally resulted in the expulsion of the Asians. See also Jamal 1991a which puts into a perspective these inequalities in relation to inequalities generated by structural adjustment programmes. That article was in a debate with Mamdani 1990. Mamdani 1991 responds, very dismissively, which is rather a pity for the state of the debate. It is relevant to note that in his 1990 article he used a great part of our thesis on the decline of the wage-earning class in Uganda. See also Jamal 1991b.
3. The fall in export production cannot be estimated accurately because there was considerable smuggling of commodities through Kenya for sale on the world market.
4. This judgement is in contrast to the assessment of the FAO, whose statistics show a sharp decline of 17 per cent between 1972–74 and 1980–82, from 2,141 calories per capita per day to 1,781. Careful inspection of the FAO data shows an underestimation of the 'roots and tubers' group – cassava, sweet potatoes and plantains – which normally provide 40–50 per cent of total calories in Uganda. National figures give 2,382 as the per capita daily calorie availability in 1980–82. The FAO statistics are from the Organization's food balance sheet computer print-outs. The national figures used are from Uganda 1984. For further details see Jamal 1985.
5. In the late 1960s authors referred to Ugandan wage earners as the 'labour aristocracy', not in relation to entrepreneurs, but relatively to farmers (see Knight 1967). Colonial wage policy is treated in Weeks 1971b.
6. The growth rates (percentage per annum) of the four largest towns between 1969 and 1980 were as follows: Kampala 3.2; Jinja -0.7; Mbala 1.7; Tororo 0.5. Compared to this, the overall population growth rate was 2.8 per cent. Up to 1972 the towns were growing at 5–6 per cent per annum. Thus, between 1973 and 1980 all towns (including Kampala) registered lower growth rates than the natural population increase, implying reverse migration. Uganda 1982, Table 1.26, p. 50.
7. It is worth mentioning that one of the authors was a resident of Uganda between 1946–58, 1964–67 and 1972. He returned to Uganda three times after the Asian expulsion – in 1983, 1985 and 1991 – and then several times in 1992. The 'before/after' account of the urban areas draws upon this experience.
8. An important methodological point should be noted. Insofar as urban dwellers switch from purchasing food in the market to obtaining it from their own or relatives' farms, prices and deflation by the consumer price index lose practical significance. What they lead us to is the wage puzzle; how is it that despite catastrophic falls in incomes urban wage earners survive? Imaginatively used they open up to us an insight into the sort of economies African countries are becoming.
9. Developments on adjustment programmes up to 1987 are covered in Banugire 1989.
10. ILO/JASPA entitled its 1982 employment mission report on Tanzania *Basic needs in danger* (ILO/JASPA 1982a).

11. Several studies are available on the performance of the Tanzanian economy. See among others: ILO/JASPA 1978 and 1982a; Green *et al.* 1980; and from a wider perspective Hyden 1980 and Coulson 1982. Excellent papers by Ellis (1982, 1983 and 1984) should also be mentioned. In terms of apportionment of blame, Sharpley 1985 blames internal policies while Stewart 1986 takes a more balanced view. Green 1983, van Arkadie 1983, Singh 1986a, Loxley 1986, and ILO 1988, also make important contributions to the debate, particularly with respect to the pros and cons of standard structural adjustment programmes. Recently Bienefeld 1990 has examined closely the performance of the agricultural sector under the Economic Recovery Programme and found the claims about a turnaround premature. See also Jamal 1986a and 1988d.
12. Beyond this, the policy conditionalities implied a reversal of the direction and priorities of Tanzanian development policy, from a socialist experiment to a market-oriented economy. This point is suggested implicitly in the 1988 ILO report on structural adjustment policies in Tanzania.
13. In the national accounts a production of 100 kg of maize would be counted at Sh. 220 at current prices. In the towns Sh. 220 would buy only 88 kg of maize-meal. Thus, we have to apply a price differential, whose value for other food crops would be much higher than in the case of subsidised maize-meal.
14. A technical paper in ILO/JASPA 1982a deals with subsistence incomes (also published in Jamal 1982 (Tanzania)). One should not think that cash income estimates are any more reliable, as another technical paper in the same publication shows. The Tanzanian authorities have since undertaken a revision of the national accounts.
15. The following prices are assumed: cereals (maize-meal), Sh. 2.50 per kg, equivalent to Sh. 0.69 per 1,000 calories; 'others' at Sh. 3 per 1,000 calories.
16. For an elaboration, see Jamal 1983a, where he treats objections raised by Rugumisa and Semboja 1983.
17. An early estimate of the Tanzanian agricultural sector's terms of trade was done by Jamal for an ILO/JASPA mission (ILO/JASPA 1978, Appendix 2), and updated for another JASPA mission in 1982 (ILO/JASPA 1982a, technical paper 16, also published in Jamal 1982 (Tanzania). Ellis's papers acknowledge this contribution. Bienefeld 1990 contains a critique of Ellis's methodology.
18. Information provided by Mr Hassan Raha, Assistant Director of International Affairs, Organisation of Tanzanian Trade Unions, Geneva, 30 October 1991.
19. Inequality has been noted by many other authors working on Kenya after the celebrated ILO mission of 1972 (ILO 1972) made equity its central theme. See, among others: Leys 1973; Crawford and Thorbecke 1978; Ghai, et. al. 1979; House and Killick 1983; Collier 1984; Greer and Thorbecke 1986; and van der Hoeven 1988.
20. These figures perhaps contributed to the view expressed in the Fourth Five-Year Plan that income distribution had improved between 1969 and 1976 in Kenya. Kenya 1979, Part I, p. 5.

21. Data were collected by Jamal in Kenya between June 1990 and February 1991 when he was detached to work in the secretariat of the Kenya Presidential Committee on Employment (Chairman Philip Ndegwa). See Kenya 1991.
22. Jamal 1982 (Kenya), using a poverty line of the type in Table 4.10, had estimated urban poverty at 8 per cent, compared to 30 per cent in rural areas. Collier and Lal 1980 with a more austere poverty measure concluded that urban poverty hardly existed. The Crawford-Thorbecke report also indicated very little poverty in urban areas.

CHAPTER FIVE

1. Clower *et al.* entitled their 1966 book on Liberia *Growth without development.*
2. This characteristic is less true for the country's other exports, timber, cocoa, and coffee. At least for the last two, some inputs are produced domestically.
3. The expression is Rimmer's (1984, p. 72) in commenting on Clower et. al.'s estimate previously cited. Indeed income distribution profiles are often done by visiting economists and scepticism in using with them would be prudent. The visitors this time were from the World Bank. Perennial optimists, they entitled their report *Growth with development* (World Bank 1975b) – of course a conditional title: *if* Liberia followed World Bank advice, there would be growth as well as development. Unfortunately, 17 years later, there has been neither.
4. See Clower *et al.* 1966. It may be noted that we are talking about the practice that prevailed up to the time Clower *et al.* were writing. This practice has been discontinued since 1970.
5. For Ghana the figure in 1985 was 0.31, for Uganda not available. Figures for some other countries studied here were Kenya, 1.54; Nigeria, 1.29; Tanzania, 1.37; and Zambia, 3.01 (in 1984).
6. In Zambia (as in Kenya) the size distribution of wages was very skewed. The more skewed a distribution, the smaller the percentage of the observations which lie above the mean. In other words, the median wage (the wage level which divides the observations into two groups of equal numbers) was well below the mean.
7. For the years 1960–68 the minimum wage figures are extrapolated from Turner reports and from ILO/JASPA 1981c. For the subsequent years the figures are taken from an unpublished World Bank report (World Bank 1987a). Since the minimum wage varied between different trades, an average figure of some sort seems to have been used in the Bank documents. For example, in 1974 the minimum wage varied between K380–450 (ILO/JASPA 1977, p. 61). In the World Bank source the figure used is K400.
8. Since the producer was a government-owned company, it would presumably produce on the basis of the external price of copper.
9. Not, it should be noted, before undergoing huge devaluations. In 1982 – i.e. before the round of devaluations – the dollar and the kwacha were at

par. Four years later a kwacha could buy only 8 US cents (IMF 1987a). By November 1990 the figure was down to 2.5 US cents (IMF 1991).

CHAPTER SIX

1. An excellent description of Somali pastoral society is found in Cassanelli 1982. For recent developments – though not up to the total destruction of the country in the civil war – see Samatar 1988.
2. Problems arise when using GDP figures to analyse Somalia because of the importance of remittances, whose amount goes largely unmeasured in the national accounts and the balance of payments. See Jamal 1981, 1987 and 1992a.
3. We write in the past tense for reasons of literary style, and also to take account of the major disruption caused by the civil war.
4. A 1978 World Bank paper estimated 70 percent of rural households to be in poverty (Hicks 1978). Less extreme but still too high in our view were the estimates by Hopkins that half of pastoral and two-thirds of farm households were in poverty in 1978 (Hopkins 1978). These estimates are discussed in detail in Jamal 1981. See also Jamal 1990. Jamal's estimates of rural living standards challenged the previous estimates of poverty, and have been confirmed by other work, for example, Hoben *et al.* 1983. See also MNP/UNICEF 1984 where Jamal's estimates have been widely cited.
5. See Haaland and Keddeman 1984 for elaborate estimates of poverty based on missing this vital point. Jamal 1990 points this out in detail.
6. Salaries were so low in the mid-1980s that even the World Bank and the IMF overcame their usual reticence against wage increases. Thus 'Low levels of salaries are a primary determinant of the low morale and motivation of the civil service . . . there is a need to raise public sector salaries to restore the purchasing power of earlier years' (World Bank 1987c, p. 50). See also IDA 1984.
7. For very useful information on foodstuff marketing in Somalia, see Asser *et al.* 1984 – a report by Elliott Berg associates.
8. The world prices of maize and sorghum are those from the Chicago grain market. World urban prices were approximated by the US consumer cost of living index. These calculations are explained in detail in ILO/JASPA 1989.
9. The effect of migration on the South African labour market is treated in Knight 1978.
10. For further details, see Bohning 1981.
11. Wallman, basing her conclusions on research done at the end of the 1960s, puts migration income well above farm income (Wallman 1972, see also Eckert *et al.* 1982).
12. This estimate is based on a population at the end of 1979 of 1.345 million, 10 per cent urbanisation, and five members per household.

CHAPTER SEVEN

1. '. . . [in Ghana] there are signs that the real value of the urban-rural [income gap] may have been reduced by the differential action of inflation since 1974/75, with food prices rising more rapidly than other prices . . .' ILO/JASPA 1982b (Ghana), p. 76.
2. Between 1978 and 1988 Ghana's terms of trade (for practical purposes cocoa's terms of trade, since cocoa comprises two-thirds of Ghana's exports) fell by 60 per cent, while cocoa output fell as a trend between 1973 and 1988 (UNCTAD 1989a, Table 7.2).
3. Space does not permit treatment of the experience of multilateral adjustment policies in Sierra Leone. Lisk 1974 provides a thorough discussion of the IMF programme of the late 1960s, while Weeks 1990 discusses the 1970s and 1980s.
4. For twenty-five years (1950–74) the Sierra Leone exchange rate was virtually unchanged – 1.4 to the US dollar until the Sterling devaluation in 1966, when it dropped to 1.2. As late as 1982 the rate stood at a modest 0.81 to the dollar; by 1986, it had dropped to 0.28 and by the end of December 1990 to .0053! (IMF 1991, p. 464). Although popular image places most African countries in the super-inflation category, in 1984 Sierra Leone's rate at 73 per cent was the second highest in Africa (after Somalia) and in 1986 with 181 per cent, the highest. As a comparison Brazil's inflation was at 145 per cent – highest in the western hemisphere (IMF 1987a).
5. The ratio actually overstates the position of wage incomes, for it makes no allowance for the price differential in commodities between urban and rural areas. Evidence from three household surveys over two decades verifies that urban prices are higher than rural when weighted for consumption patterns. Jamal incorporated this price differential into his calculations and obtained a narrower wage earner/farmer gap for the 1970s than is shown in Table 7.2 (Jamal 1982 (Sierra Leone)).
6. This poverty line calculation is also used in Jamal 1982 (Sierra Leone), and is lower than that found in Lisk and van der Hoeven 1979.
7. This point has been made in Jamal 1988a with respect to Uganda and Jamal 1988b generalised to sub-Saharan Africa as a whole. It is of course a point to which we attach great importance in this study.
8. Derived by dividing the manufacturing wage by the implicit manufacturing price deflator from the national accounts.
9. This by now familiar refrain is particularly worth repeating in the Sierra Leone case since this country never had a pampered wage-earning class behind minimum wages. It did, however, practice quite a severe form of agricultural taxation.
10. These measures compare producers' receipts against 'parity' receipts – i.e. what the farmers actually received for their produce compared to what they could have received had there been no export taxes or marketing board surpluses. See Jamal 1986c.
11. These estimates were derived by assigning export taxes to farm incomes and personal and corporate taxes to non-farmers' incomes – i.e. it was assumed that export taxes are a tax on the farmers only and that the other taxes affected only the non-farmers (Jamal 1986c).

12. According to estimates made by Jamal for the ILO/JASPA mission (ILO/JASPA 1981a, technical paper 1; also published in Jamal 1982 (Sierra Leone)) entrepreneurs and professionals constituted 7 per cent of the urban population in 1975–6 and earned 37 per cent of the urban income. If the same proportions held in 1979–80, this would give the élite groups an average household income of Le 21,700. At this income, according to the income tax schedule they should pay 35 per cent in tax! It may be noted that JASPA's estimates were endorsed by the World Bank in their succeeding mission. See World Bank 1981d. See also Lisk and van der Hoeven 1979, who also use the JASPA income distribution in their widely-quoted poverty study.
13. A balanced assessment of the role of marketing boards in Nigeria is found in Helleiner 1966.
14. An important qualification should be noted. From the fact that imports increased so rapidly the conclusion is often reached that farmers simply lost interest in all food production, giving up on marketing food crops. Actually, juxtaposing the massive urbanisation that occurred in the 1970s and 1980s with imports, one would have to conclude that food marketing increased absolutely although it did not keep pace with the rate of urbanisation. The fact that diets were changing towards rice and wheat is also relevant in explaining the increase in imports. For a more uncharitable view, see Andrea and Beckman 1985.
15. A similar view is implicit in the World Bank country report on Nigeria (World Bank 1981c) and in Jamal 1982 (Nigeria). See also Jamal 1986b and Schatz 1984.
16. 'Allowing that there have been no drastic changes in acreage distribution or (apparently) big increases in the total rural population, this means that there is still very roughly the same number of rural poor. However, there must have been a big increase in the number of urban poor.' ILO/JASPA 1981b, p. 232. The quotation refers to the early 1960s and late 1970s.
17. This may have also been true earlier. See Fapohunda *et al.* 1976, and Reijmerink and van Dijk 1975.
18. A history of the urbanisation of Lagos and description of conditions there in the mid-1970s is found in Fapohunda *et al.* 1976.
19. Rimmer concludes: '. . . the gains won by Nigerian wage earners have been transitory in real terms . . . Real wages and salaries have tended to deteriorate throughout formalised employment.' It is worth noting that he goes on to generalise this to all of West Africa: '. . . institutional forces appear not to have produced, since about 1960, any sustained improvement in the pay of persons in formalised employment, and marked reductions in real wages appear to have occurred in some countries' (Rimmer 1984, pp. 105, 108).
20. In the Todaro model, reverse migration would be the mechanism to equate the expected value of the urban wage to rural income. Collier's study shows that the rate of urban unemployment rose while the urban-rural gap was falling. The urban unemployment rate increased from 5.8 per cent in 1983 to 11.9 in 1986, while urban real wages fell more than average rural incomes (Collier 1987, pp. 24–25). As pointed out by

Olukoshi (1989, p. 228), 'during 1980–83, about one million workers were estimated to have been retrenched from the industrial sector'.

CHAPTER EIGHT

1. Jamal 1989 (also in Jamal 1993) has looked at this question in some detail. He shows that surplus extraction was very much a part of the African agricultural scene in the past and in the modern era extraction operated through overvalued exchange rates. With the massive devaluations that have occurred in the 1980s with their attendant shifts in agricultural prices, it is quite probable that surplus extraction has now disappeared.
2. As before, we shall use the term 'subsistence production' to refer to output which is directly consumed by the producing unit.
3. One must be cautious in this context in referring to urban workers 'returning' to rural areas, for much of the African working class has been in urban areas for at least one generation. The point is important, for it should not be assumed that newly unemployed workers have the knowledge and skills to pursue agriculture successfully.
4. 'Domestic' is stressed because in some countries remittances from abroad make national income significantly different from domestic income. This difference as we saw is quite important for Somalia and Lesotho.
5. The theoretical issues are treated in Weeks 1971d. For empirical evidence, see Lipton (with Longhurst) 1985.
6. African land tenure systems and evidence of landlessness are treated in FAO 1985 and Lipton 1982.
7. The most important of these assumptions is that no 'false trading' can occur (exchanges at disequilibrium prices). See Hahn 1984; Taylor 1983, Ch. 2; and Weeks 1989, Ch. 4.
8. 'Thus . . . [wage restraint] effectively redistributes income from urban to rural households' (World Bank 1983, p. 23). Another example of a study which placed all emphasis on rural-urban differentials and ignored the functional distribution of income, again for Kenya, is Crawford and Thorbecke 1978. See the critique by Jamal 1982 (Kenya), pp. 60–69.
9. As the term is commonly used, 'informal sector' is not an appropriate category for all sSA countries – e.g. Somalia, which for all intents and purposes is an 'informal economy'. We use it without qualification in this chapter.

CHAPTER NINE

1. Recall that a study commissioned by the World Bank itself came to a similar conclusion. Again we quote: '"Appropriate" price and exchange rate policy would have a relatively small impact on agricultural growth in sSA countries. . .' The author went on to say, 'There is no stereotypic price-policy package suitable for all African countries. . .' (Cleaver 1985, p.

1). Binswanger 1990 gives theoretical reasons why rising prices may have limited impact on agricultural output. Balassa (1990) claimed otherwise from an econometric study, showing that a one per cent change in the real exchange rate had about the same impact on the ratio of exports to output. The level of significance of the regression coefficients was low. See also Bose and Atukorala 1985. Commander 1989a shows the limited impact of adjustment programmes on African agriculture, which is borne out by the continuing poor performance of Africa's exports despite major price increases (World Bank 1990c, Table A.8).

2. Even the World Bank in its 1989 report on Africa manages to inject some doubt about the efficacy of adjustment programmes, thus '. . . Africa's economic problems are so deep-seated that conventional stabilisation programmes are inadequate . . . They should evolve to take further account of the social impact of reforms, of investment needs to accelerate growth, and of measures to ensure sustainability' (World Bank 1989b, pp. 62 and 185–186; for a critical review of this report see Stein and Nafziger 1991). This is in sharp contrast to the Bank's report earlier that year which claimed rather triumphantly that adjusting African countries were faring much better than non-adjusting countries (World Bank 1989a), which itself was in sharp contrast to another Bank report (World Bank 1988a). On closer inspection the inflow of external support was mainly responsible for the alleged better performance of the adjusting countries, as the report itself candidly admitted: '. . . as a result of external support, reforming countries have been able to sustain a progressively widening current account deficit . . .' (p. 128) – i.e. they were able to import much-needed raw materials and consumer goods and thus effectively mortgaged themselves out of the crisis, at the cost of accumulating debt. The methodological shortcomings of the Bank's 1989a report were ably exposed in ECA 1989b which resulted in the Bank report being suppressed. See Mosley and Weeks 1993 for a 'revisit'.

3. For example, after being given the following gloomy news in a World Bank report, 'sub-Saharan exports will expand by 3 per cent or more only for tea and tobacco during 1980–1995' (both of which are minor crops for Africa), one comes upon the ritual incantation, 'inappropriate domestic price and incentive policies lie at the heart of the sSA agricultural problem'. Singh 1983a, pp. 7 and 10.

4. In the early and mid-1980s, some 30 sSA countries entered into agreements with the IMF, and at the end of 1986 the region's outstanding obligations to the Fund totalled over US$ 6 thousand million. Williams 1987, pp. 2–3.

5. Members of the Communauté financière africaine are precluded from adjusting their exchange rate with the French franc, so alternative policy tools must be used to achieve the same end. See Devarajan and de Melo 1987.

6. The debate over the impact of devaluation is summarised in Ghani 1984, pp. 7–12. A quite commonsense and non-ideological case for devaluation in sSA countries is found in Gulhati *et al.* 1986.

7. See Fishlow 1985. If all countries followed the World Bank's advice as given in the 'Berg Report' (World Bank 1981a), commodity prices would

surely fall. The response of the Bank is overt 'beggar-thy-neighbour':

First of all, not all countries will follow counsel to expand primary exports. So those that do will capture the markets of those that do not, regardless of their respective comparative advantages. Given this reality, those who stand on the sidelines and urge African States to shun the export sector are in fact handling over market shares to Brazil or Malaysia or Indonesia (Berg 1986).

It is somewhat unfortunate to see a recommendation in which the gains of some countries come at the expense of others. There is a certain Old Testament vengefulness here – let the virtuous prosper and the sinful waste (and the virtuous will be recognised because they prosper) – which seems inappropriate for multilateral organisations.

8. Typically so-called 'real exchange rates' are calculated as the ratio of some index of United States prices to a domestic price index of the sSA country in question. Among other things, this type of measure assumes no distinction between tradables and non-tradables in both countries.
9. Again, one might refer to the Cleaver study (1985), which showed little statistical significance for the exchange rate variable.
10. At the very least, one would have to agree with the following judgement: 'moving towards an equilibrium exchange rate is a necessary but not a sufficient condition for stabilisation and structural adjustment' (Gulhati *et al.* 1986).
11. This certainly seems the case for Tanzania. See ILO 1988, Singh 1986a, and Jamal 1986a.
12. The literature on this issue is vast, taking its inspiration from the work of Clower (1985), Leijonhufvud (1981), and Hahn (1984).
13. Uganda represented an extreme case of this process during the Amin period. See discussion in Chapter 4.
14. The treatment of optimal investment behaviour usually assumes a 'perfect' capital market, so that each agent can borrow and invest up to the point at which the borrowing rate equals the rate of return on the marginal project.
15. In the early 1970s, Hollis Chenery, the highest-ranking economist at the World Bank and perhaps the most influential development economist at the time, wrote: 'It is now clear that more than a decade of rapid growth in underdeveloped countries has been of little or no benefit to perhaps a third of their population . . . While growth policies have succeeded beyond their expectations . . . the very idea of aggregate growth as a social objective has increasingly been called into question' (Chenery 1974, p. xiii).

    One can only marvel at the volatility of ideology in economics. Towards the end of 1991 the World Bank was again swinging back to poverty alleviation as a major concern of development policy, with even a handbook addressed to Bank staff (World Bank 1991a) on how to do poverty assessments.
16. This consensus is analysed in Weeks and Dore 1981.
17. Keynes wrote, 'The celebrated optimism of traditional economic theory, which has led to economists being looked upon as Candides, who, having left this world for the cultivation of their gardens, teach that all is for the

best in the best of all possible worlds provided we will let well alone. . . It may well be that the classical theory represents the way in which we should like our Economy to behave. But to assume that it actually does so is to assume our difficulties away' (Keynes 1936, pp. 33–34).

Bibliography

Addison, Tony and Lionel Demery. 1989. 'The economics of rural poverty alleviation', in Commander 1989b.

Amin, Samir. 1969. 'Levels of remuneration, factor proportions, and income differentials with special reference to developing countries', in A.D. Smith (ed.), *Wage policy issues in economic development*. London: Macmillan.

Andrea, G. and B. Beckman. 1985. *Wheat trap: Bread and underdevelopment in Nigeria*. London: Zed Books.

van Arkadie, Brian. 1983. 'The IMF prescriptions for structural management in Tanzania', in K. Jansen (ed.), *Monetarism, economic crisis and the Third World*. London: Frank Cass.

Arkin, Kwame, Paul Hesp and Laurens van der Laan (ed.). 1985. *Marketing boards in tropical Africa*. London: Routledge and Kegan Paul.

Arrighi, Giovanni and J. Saul. 1968. 'Socialism and economic development in tropical Africa', in *Journal of Modern African Studies*, vol. 6, no. 2.

Asser, Mohamed *et al.* (Elliot Berg Associates). 1984. 'Somalia: Incentives and grain marketing study' (commissioned by the World Bank). Washington, D.C.: IBRD.

Baker, Jonathan (ed.). 1990. *Small town Africa: Studies in rural-urban interaction*. Uppsala: Bohusläningens Boktryckeri.

Balassa, B. 1990. 'Incentive policies and export performance in sub-Saharan Africa', in *World Development*, vol. 18, no. 3.

Banugire, Firimooni R. 1989. 'Employment, incomes, basic needs and structural adjustment policy in Uganda, 1980–87', in Onimode 1989.

Bates, Robert. 1981. *Markets and states in tropical Africa*. Berkeley: University of California Press.

——. 1986. 'The regulation of rural markets in Africa', in Commins *et al.* 1986.

Begg, David K.H. 1982. *The rational expectations revolution in macro-economics: Theories and evidence*. Oxford: Philip Allan.

Bequele, Assefa. 1983. 'Stagnation and inequality in Ghana', in Ghai and Radwan 1983.

Berg, Elliot. 1964. 'Real income trends in West Africa', in M.J. Herskovits and Mitchell Harwitz (eds.): *Economic transition in Africa*. London: Routledge and Kegan Paul.

——. 1966. 'Major issues of wage policy in Africa', in A.M. Ross (ed.), *Industrial Relations and Economic Development*. London: Macmillan.

——. 1986. 'The World Bank's strategy', in J. Ravenhill, ed., *Africa in economic crisis*. Houndmills: Macmillan.

Berry, Sara S. 1984. 'The food crisis and agrarian change in Africa: A review essay', in *African Studies Review*, no. 27, June.

Bienefeld, Manfred. 1990. 'Structural adjustment and rural labour markets in Tanzania'. WEP working paper. Geneva: ILO.

Binswanger, Hans. 1990. 'The supply response of agriculture', in *Proceedings of the World Bank Annual Conference on Development Economics, 1989.* Washington, D.C.: World Bank.

Böhning, W.R. (ed.) 1981. *Black migration to South Africa: A selection of policy-oriented research.* Geneva: ILO.

Bose, Swadesh and Vimal Atukorala. 1985. 'Exchange rate policies in Eastern and Southern Africa, 1965–1983'. World Bank Staff Working Paper, no. 720. Washington: World Bank.

Brewster, Havelock. 1991. 'Medicine without cures for life without growth', in *South-North Development Monitor*, no. 2609, May.

Bryceson, Deborah. 1985. 'Food and urban purchasing power: The case of Dar es Salaam, Tanzania', in *African Affairs*, vol. 84, no. 337, Oct.

——. 1990. *Food insecurity and the social division of labour in Tanzania, 1919–85.* London: Macmillan.

Byers, T.J. 1979. 'Of neo-populist pipe-dreams: Daedalus in the Third World and the myth of urban bias', in *Journal of Peasant Studies*, vol. 6, no. 2.

Campbell, Bonnie. 1989. 'Indebtedness in Africa: Consequence, cause or symptom of the crisis?', in Onimode 1989.

—— and J. Loxley (eds.). 1989. *Structural adjustment in Africa.* London: Macmillan.

Cassanelli, Lee. 1982. *The shaping of Somali society: Reconstruction of the history of a pastoral people.* Philadelphia: University of Pennsylvania Press.

Chenery, Hollis, *et al.* 1974. *Redistribution with growth.* Oxford: Oxford University Press.

Chhibber, Ajay. 1991. 'Tackling inflation during reforms in Africa', in *Finance and Development*, vol. 28, no. 1, March.

Clark, John with D. Keen. 1988. *Debt and poverty: A case study of Zambia.* United Kingdom: Oxfam.

Cleaver, Kevin M. 1985. 'The impact of price and exchange rate policies on agriculture in sub-Saharan Africa'. World Bank Staff Working Paper, no. 728.

Cline, William R. 1983. *International debt and the stability of the world economy.* Washington, D.C.: Institute for International Economics.

Clower, R. 1985. 'The Kenyesian counter-revolution: A theoretical appraisal', in Frank Hahn and F.P.R. Brechling (eds), *The theory of interest rates.* New York: St. Martin's Press.

Clower, Robert *et al.* 1966. *Growth without development.* Evanston: Northwestern University Press.

Colclough, Christopher. 1991. 'Wage flexibility in sub-Saharan Africa: Trends and explorations', in Standing and Tokman 1991.

Collier, Paul. 1984. 'Why poor people get rich: Kenya, 1969–79', in *World Development*, vol. 12, no. 10.

——. 1987. 'Oil shocks and food security in Nigeria'. World Employment Programme Working Paper.

—— and D. Lal. 1980. 'Poverty and growth in Kenya'. World Bank Staff Working Paper 389. Washington, D.C.: World Bank.

Commander, Simon. 1989a. 'Prices, markets and rigidites: African agriculture, 1980–88', in Commander 1989b.

—— (ed.). 1989b. *Structural adjustment and agriculture: Theory and practice in Africa and Latin America.* London: OD1.

Commins, S.K., M. Lofchie and R. Payne (eds). 1986. *Africa's agrarian crisis: The roots of famine*. Boulder, Colorado: Lynne Rienner Publishers.

Cornia, G.A., R. Jolly and F. Stewart. 1987. *Adjustment with a human face: Protecting the vulnerable and promoting growth*. New York and Oxford: Oxford University Press.

Coulson, Andrew. 1982. *Tanzania: A political economy*. Oxford: Clarendon Press.

Crawford, Eric and Erik Thorbecke. 1978. 'Employment, income distribution, poverty alleviation and basic needs in Kenya'. Report of an ILO Consulting Mission. Ithaca: Cornell University.

Devarajan, Shantayanan and Jaime de Melo. 1987. 'Adjustment with a fixed exchange rate: Cameroon, Côte d'Ivoire and Senegal', in *The World Bank Economic Review*, vol 1, no 3, May.

ECA (Economic Commission for Africa). 1989a. *African alternative framework to structural adjustment programmes for socio-economic recovery and transformation*. Addis Ababa: ECA.

——. 1989b. *Statistics and policies: ECA preliminary observations on the World Bank Report – Africa's adjustment and growth in the 1980s*. Addis Ababa: ECA.

Eckert, Jerry (with K.C. Nobe, F.E. Walters, and R.A. Wykstra). 1982. *Towards the year 2000: Strategies for Lesotho's agriculture*. LASA Research Report, no. 10. Colorado: Department of Economics, Colorado State University.

Ellis, Frank. 1982. 'Agricultural price policy in Tanzania', in *World Development*, vol. 10, no. 4.

——. 1983. 'Agricultural marketing and peasant-state transfers in Tanzania', in *Journal of Peasant Studies*, vol. 10, no. 4.

——. 1984. 'Relative agricultural prices and the urban bias model: A comparative analysis of Tanzania and Fiji', in *Journal of Development Studies*, vol. 20, no. 3.

Elkan, Walter. 1960. *Migrants and proletarians: Urban labour in the economic development of Uganda*. London: Oxford University Press.

Fapohunda, O.J. and Harold Lubell (with J. Reijmerink and M.P. van Dijk). 1976. *Lagos: Urban development and employment*. Geneva: ILO.

Fishlow, A. 1985. 'The state of Latin American economics', in Inter-American Development Bank, *Economic and social progress in Latin America*. Report 1985. Washington: IDB.

Food and Agricultural Organization of the United Nations. 1984. *Socio-economic indicators relating to the agricultural sector and rural development*. Rome: FAO.

——. 1985. *Report of the round table on the dynamics of land tenure and agrarian systems in Africa*. Rome: FAO.

——. 1986. *African agriculture: the next 25 years*. Rome: FAO.

Frank, C.R., Jr. 1968. 'Urban unemployment and economic growth in Africa', in *Oxford Economic Papers*, vol. 20, no. 2.

Ghai, Dharam P., Martin Godfrey and Franklyn Lisk. 1979. *Planning for basic needs in Kenya: Performance, policies and prospects*. Geneva: ILO.

—— and S. Radwan. 1983. *Agrarian policies and rural poverty in Africa*. Geneva: ILO.

—— and L. Smith. 1987. *Agricultural prices, policy and equity in sub-Saharan Africa.* Boulder, Colorado: Lynne Rienner Publishers.

——, Michael Hopkins and Donald McGranahan. 1988. 'Some reflections on human and social indicators for development'. UNRISD Discussion Paper. Geneva: UNRISD.

Ghani, E. 1984. 'The effects of devaluation on employment and poverty in developing countries'. World Employment Programme Research Working Paper. Geneva: ILO.

Gibbon, Peter, Yusuf Bangura and Arve Ofstad. 1992. *Authoritarianism, democracy and adjustment.* Uppsala: Scandinavian Institute of African Studies.

van Ginneken, Wouter and Jong-goo Park. 1984. *Generating internationally comparable income distribution estimates.* Geneva: ILO.

Green, Reginald, H. 1967. 'Wage levels, employment, productivity and consumption', in James Sheffield (ed.), *Education, employment and rural development.* Nairobi: East African Publishing House.

——. 1983. 'Political-economic adjustment and the IMF conditionality: Tanzania 1974–81', in J. Williamson (ed.), *IMF conditionality.* Washington, D.C., Institute for International Economics.

—— and Vali Jamal. 1987. 'Paradoxes of private prosperity, poverty pockets, volatile vulnerability and public pauperisation.' Mogadishu: UNICEF.

——, D.G. Rwegasira and B. van Arkadie. 1980. *Economic shocks and national policy-making: Tanzania in the 1980s.* The Hague: Institute of Social Studies.

Greer, Joel and Erik Thorbecke. 1986. *Food poverty and consumption patterns in Kenya.* Geneva: ILO.

Gulhati, R., S. Bose and V. Atukorala. 1986. 'Exchange rate policies in Africa: How valid is the skepticism?', in *Development and Change* vol. 17, no. 3.

Gutkind, P.C.W. 1968. 'African responses to urban wage employment,' in *International Labour Review*, 97 (Feb.).

Haaland, Gunnar and Willem Keddeman. 1984. 'Poverty analysis: The case of rural Somalia', in *Economic Development and Cultural Change*, vol. 32, no. 4.

Hahn, Frank. 1984. *Macroeconomics and equilibrium.* Oxford: Basil Blackwell.

Hart, Keith. 1973. 'Informal income opportunities and urban employment in Ghana', in *Journal of Modern African Studies*, vol. 11, no. 1.

Havnevik, K. (ed.). 1987. *The IMF and the World Bank in Africa: Conditionality, impact and alternatives.* Uppsala: Nordiska Afrikainstituete.

Helleiner, G.K. 1966. *Peasant agriculture, government and economic growth in Nigeria.* Homewood, Illinois: Richard D. Irwin.

Henley, John S. 1973. 'Employment relationships and economic development – The Kenyan experience', in *Journal of Modern African Studies*, vol. 11, no. 4.

Hesp, P. and L. van der Laan. 1985. 'Marketing boards in tropical Africa: A survey', in Arkin, Hesp and van der Laan 1985.

Hetmeier, Heinz W. 1990. 'Drop in commodity prices – Development aid for West Germany', in *Development a Cooperation*, no. 5.

Hicks, Norman. 1978. 'Poverty and basic needs in Somalia'. Washington, D.C.: IBRD (mimeographed).

Hinchcliffe, K. 1974. 'Labour aristocracy – A Northern Nigerian case study', in *Journal of Modern African Studies*, vol. 12, no. 1.

Hoben, A., *et al.* 1983. *Somalia: A social and institutional profile*. African Studies Centre, Boston University.

van der Hoeven, Rolph. 1988. *Planning for basic needs: A soft option or a solid policy? A basic needs similation model applied to Kenya*. Aldershot: Gower.

Hopkins, Michael. 1978. 'Somalia and basic needs: Some issues'. World Employment Programme Research Working Paper, WEP 3–32/WP8. Geneva: ILO.

House, William J. and Tony Killick. 1983. 'Social justice and development policy in Kenya's rural economy', in Ghai and Radwan 1983.

Hussain, N.N. and A.L. Thirwall. 1984. 'The International Monetary Fund supply-side devaluation: An assessment with reference to the Sudan', in *Oxford Institute of Economics and Statistics*, vol. 46, no. 2.

Hyden, Goran. 1980. *Beyond ujamaa: Underdevelopment and an uncaptured peasantry*. London: Heinemann.

International Development Agency. 1984. *Somalia civil service study*. Mogadishu: Ministry of Labour and Social Affairs.

IFAD. 1979. *Report on the special programming mission to Somalia*. Rome: IFAD.

Iliffe, John. 1987. *African poor: A history*. Cambridge: Cambridge University Press.

ILO. 1967. 'Report to the Government of the United Republic of Tanzania on wages, incomes and prices policy'. Turner Tanzania Report 1. Geneva: ILO.

——. 1969. 'Report to the Government of Zambia on incomes, wages and prices in Zambia: Policy and machinery'. Turner Zambia Report 1. Geneva: ILO.

——. 1970. *Towards full employment: A programme for Colombia*. Geneva: ILO.

——. 1972. *Employment, incomes and equality: A strategy for increasing productive employment in Kenya*. Geneva: ILO.

——. 1975. 'Report to the Government of Tanzania on the past, present and future of incomes policy in Tanzania'. Turner Tanzania Report 2. Geneva: ILO.

——. 1978. 'Second report to the Government of Zambia on incomes, wages and prices in Zambia: Policy and machinery'. Turner Zambia Report 2. Geneva: ILO.

ILO (Advisory Committee on Rural Development). 1983. *Promotion of employment and incomes for the rural poor, including rural women through non-farm activities*. Geneva: ILO.

——. 1986a. *After the famine*, Report of the ILO Identification and Programming Mission to the Republic of the Sudan. Geneva: ILO.

——. 1986b. *From crisis to sustainable development: A programme of action*, Report of the ILO Multi-disciplinary Mission to Ethiopia. Geneva: ILO.

——. 1987a. *World Labour Report*. vol. 3. Geneva: ILO.

——. 1987b. *Year book of labour statistics*. Geneva: ILO.

——. 1988. *Distributional aspects of stabilisation programmes in Tanzania*. Geneva: ILO.

ILO/JASPA. 1977. *Narrowing the gaps: Planning for basic needs and productive employment in Zambia*. Addis Ababa: ILO/JASPA. (Same publication specification applies to the rest.)

——. 1978. *Towards self-reliance: Development, employment and equity issues in Tanzania.*

——. 1981a. *Ensuring equitable growth: A strategy for increasing employment, equity and basic needs satisfaction in Sierra Leone.*

——. 1981b. *First things first: Meeting basic needs of the people of Nigeria.*

——. 1981c. *Zambia: Basic needs in an economy under pressure.*

——. 1982a. *Basic needs in danger: A basic needs oriented development strategy for Tanzania.*

——. 1982b. *Rural-Urban gap and income distribution: The case of Ghana, Liberia, Zambia* (3 separate case studies) (by Dudley Jackson).

——. 1985. *Informal sector in Africa.*

——. 1989a. *African employment report, 1988.*

——. 1989b. *Generating employment and incomes in Somalia.* Report of an ILO/JASPA Inter-Disciplinary Employment and Project-Identification Mission to Somalia.

——. 1990. *Alleviating unemployment and poverty under adjustment: Issues and strategies for Sierra Leone.*

——. 1991. *African Employment Report, 1990.*

IMF (International Monetary Fund). 1985. 'Fund-supported programmes, fiscal policy, and the distribution of income'. IMF Fiscal Affairs Department, Washington, D.C.: IMF. (Same publication specification for the rest).

——. 1987a. *International financial statistics.*

——. 1987b. *World economic outlook.*

——. 1989. *International financial statistics.*

——. 1990a. *Annual report.*

——. 1990b. *World economic outlook.* (May).

——. 1991. *International financial statistics.* (Feb.).

Jackson, Dudley. 1971. 'Economic development and income distribution in Eastern Africa', in *Journal of Modern African Studies*, vol. 9, no. 4.

Jamal, Vali. 1976a. 'Asians in Uganda, 1880–1972: Inequality and expulsion', in *Economic History Review*, vol. 19, no. 4.

——. 1976b 'The role of cotton and coffee in Uganda's economic development'. Ph.D. dissertation. Stanford University, Stanford, California.

——. 1977a. 'Data base for basic needs planning in Kenya: Report of a mission.' Addis Ababa: ILO/JASPA.

——. 1977b. 'Taxation and inequality in Uganda, 1900–1964', in *Journal of Economic History*, vol. 38, no. 2.

——. 1981. 'Nomads, farmers and townsmen: Incomes and inequality in Somalia'. Addis Ababa: ILO/JASPA (also issued as Jamal 1982 (Somalia)).

——. 1982. *Rural-urban gap and income distribution: The case of Kenya, Lesotho, Nigeria, Sierra Leone, Somalia, Tanzania* (6 separate case studies). Addis Ababa: JASPA.

——. 1983a. 'Income distribution and poverty: A reply to Rugumisa and Semboja', in ILO/JASPA, *Basic needs and development in Tanzania.* Addis Ababa: ILO/JASPA.

——. 1983b. 'Nomads and farmers: Incomes and poverty in rural Somalia', in Ghai and Radwan 1983.

——. 1983c. 'Poverty and inequality in Sierra Leone'. Addis Ababa: ILO/ JASPA (mimeographed).

——. 1985. 'Structural adjustment and food security in Uganda.' ILO/WEP Research Working Paper, WEP 10–6/WP73.

——. 1986a. 'Economics of devaluation: The case of Tanzania', in *Labour and Society*, vol. 11, no. 3 (special issue: guest editor, Ajit Singh).

——. 1986b. 'Oil, poverty and inequality in Nigeria'. Geneva: ILO (mimeo).

——. 1986c. 'Taxing the peasants in Sierra Leone', in ILO/JASPA, *The challenge of employment and basic needs in Africa*. Nairobi: OUP.

——. 1987. 'Somalia: Economics for an unconventional economy'. Geneva, WEP Working Paper.

——. 1988a. 'Coping under crisis in Uganda', in Jamal 1988c.

——. 1988b. 'Getting the crisis right: Missing perspectives on Africa', in *ibid.*

—— (ed.). 1988c. 'The African crisis, food security and structural adjustment', *International Labour Review*, vol. 127, no. 6 (special issue).

——. 1988d. 'The demise of the labor aristocracy in Africa: Structural adjustment in Tanzania', in Weeks 1988a.

——. 1988e. 'Understanding an unconventional economy', in *Development and Change*, vol. 19, no. 2.

——. 1989. 'The agrarian crisis in Africa: A historical perspective'. Paper presented at ILO/SAREC Conference on Agriculture and Macro-economic Policies, ILO, Geneva, Dec. 1989.

——. 1990. 'Defining poverty in a dualistic subsistence context: A comment on Haaland and Keddeman and an alternative estimate', in *Economic Development and Cultural Change*, vol. 38, no. 4.

——. 1991a. 'Inequalities and adjustment in Uganda', in *Development and Change*, vol. 22, no. 2, April.

——. 1991b. 'The agrarian context of the Ugandan crisis' in Holger Bernt Hansen and Michael Twaddle (eds), *Changing Uganda: The dilemmas of structur-al adjustment and revolutionary change*. London: James Currey.

——. 1992a. 'Somalia: The Gulf link and adjustment' in Kunibert Raffer and M.A. Mohamed Salih (eds), *The least developed and the oil-rich Arab countries*. London: Macmillan.

——. 1992b. 'Wages and implications for structural adjustment – How to survive in Africa?' in Hans H. Bass *et al.* (eds), *Industrialisation based on agricultural development* (African Perspectives Yearbook, 1990/91). Münster and Hamburg: Lit.

——. 1993. 'The agrarian crisis in Africa: A historical perspective' in Ajit Singh and Hamid Tabatabai (eds), *World economic crisis and agriculture in the Third World: The changing role of agriculture in economic development*. Cambridge: Cambridge University Press.

—— and John Weeks. 1987. 'Rural-urban income trends in sub-Saharan Africa'. WEP Research Working Paper, Geneva, ILO.

——. 1988. 'The vanishing rural-urban gap in sub-Saharan Africa', in *International Labour Review*, vol. 127, no. 3.

Jonah, Kwesi. 1989. 'The social impact of Ghana's adjustment programme, 1983–86', in Onimode 1989.

Kenya, Republic of. 1978. *Statistical Abstract*. Nairobi.

——. 1979. *Development Plan, 1979–1983*. Nairobi.

——. 1984. *Statistical Abstract*. Nairobi.

——. 1991. *Development and employment in Kenya: A strategy for the transformation of the economy*. Report of the Presidential Committee on Employment (Chairman Philip Ndegwa).

Keynes, J.M. 1936. *The general theory of employment, interest and money*. London: Macmillan.

Kilby, Peter. 1969. *Industrialization in an open economy*. London: Cambridge University Press.

Knight, John B. 1967. 'The determination of wages and salaries in Uganda', in *Bulletin of Oxford University Institute of Economics and Statistics*, vol. 29, no. 3.

——. 1972. 'Rural-urban income comparisons and migration in Ghana,' in *Bulletin of Oxford University Institute of Economics and Statistics*, vol. 34, no. 2.

——. 1978. 'Labour allocation and unemployment in South Africa', in *Bulletin of Oxford University Institute of Economics and Statistics*, vol. 40, no. 2.

—— and R. H. Sabot. 1982. 'From migrants to proletarians: Employment experience, mobility, and wages in Tanzania', in *Bulletin of Oxford University Institute of Economics and Statistics*, vol. 44, no. 3.

Kuznets, Simon. 1963. 'Quantitative aspects of economic growth of nations: Distribution of income by size', in *Economic Development and Cultural Change*. vol. 11, no. 2, Jan.

Lawrence, Peter. 1986. *World recession and the food crisis in Africa*. London: James Currey.

Leijonhufvud, A. 1968. *Keynesian economics and the economics of Keynes*. Oxford: Oxford University Press.

——. 1981. *Information and co-ordination: Essays in macro-economics*. New York: Oxford University Press.

Lesotho. 1976. *Population census*. Maseru, Government Printer.

——. 1980. *Annual statistical bulletin, 1980*. Maseru, Government Printer.

Levi, J.F.S. 1973. 'Migration from the land and urban employment in Sierra Leone', in *Bulletin of Oxford University Institute of Economics and Statistics*, vol. 35, no. 4, Nov.

Lewis, W. Arthur. 1967. *Reflections on Nigeria's economic growth*. Paris: OECD.

Leys, Colin. 1971. 'Political perspectives', in D. Seers and Leonard Joy (eds.). *Development in a divided world*. London: Penguin Books.

——. 1973. 'Interpreting African underdevelopment: Reflections on the ILO report on employment, incomes and equality in Kenya', in *African Affairs*, vol. 72, no. 289.

Liebenthal, Robert. 1981. 'Adjustment in low-income Africa, 1974–1978'. (A background study for the *World Development Report, 1981*). Staff Working Paper no. 486. Washington, D.C.: World Bank.

Lipton, Michael. 1977. *Why poor people stay poor: A study of urban bias in world development*. London: Temple Smith.

——. 1982. 'Labour and poverty'. World Bank Staff Working Paper.

——. (with Richard Longhurst). 1985. *Modern varieties, international agricultural research and the poor*. Consultative Group on International Agricultural Research Study Paper no. 2. Washington, D.C.: World Bank.

Lisk, Franklyn A.N. 1974. *The political economy of Sierra Leone, 1961–1971, with special reference to the IMF stabilisation programme of 1966 to 1969*. Birmingham, Centre for West African Studies.
—— and Rolph van der Hoeven. 1979. 'Measurement and interpretation of poverty in Sierra Leone', in *International Labour Review*, vol. 118, no. 6.
Lofchie, M.F. 1986. 'African agricultural crisis: An overview', in Commins 1986.
Loxley, John. 1986. 'IMF and World Bank conditionality and sub-Saharan Africa', in Lawrence 1986.
——. 1988. *Ghana: Economic crisis and the long road to recovery*. Ottawa: North-South Institute.
——. 1989. 'The IMF, the World Bank and reconstruction in Uganda', in Campbell and Loxley 1989.
——. 1990. 'Structural adjustment and rural labour markets in Zambia'. WEP working paper. Geneva: ILO.
Maliyamkono, T.L. and M.S.D. Bagachwa. 1990. *The second economy of Tanzania*. London: James Currey.
Mamdani, Mahmood. 1990. 'Contradictions of the IMF programme and perspective', in *Development and Change*, vol. 21, no. 3.
——. 1991. 'A response to critics', in *Development and Change*, vol. 22, no. 2.
Mangat, J.S. 1969. *A history of the Asians in East Africa, c. 1886–1945*. London: Oxford University Press.
Meier, G.M. 1976. *Leading issues in development economics*. Oxford: Oxford University Press. (Third edition).
Mellor, John W. and Raisuddin Ahmed (eds). 1988. *Agricultural price policy for developing countries*. Baltimore: Johns Hopkins University Press.
Mkandawire, Thandika. 1989. *African agriculture*. Dakar: CODESRIA.
——. 1991. 'Crisis and adjustment in sub-Saharan Africa', in Dharam Ghai (ed.) *The IMF and the South: The social impact of crisis and adjustment*. London: Zed Books.
MNP/UNICEF. 1984. *Women and children in Somalia*. Mogadishu: MNP/UNICEF.
Morawetz, D. 1977. *Twenty-five years of economic development, 1958 to 1975*. Washington, D.C.: World Bank.
Mosley, Paul and Lawrence Smith. 1989. 'Structural adjustment and agricultural performance in sub-Saharan Africa, 1980–87', in *Journal of International Development*, vol. 1, no. 3, July.
—— and John Weeks, 1993. 'Has recovery begun? "Africa's adjustments in the 1980s" revisited.' Mimeo.
Muntemba, Dorothy C. 1989. 'The impact of IMF-World Bank Programmes on women and children in Zambia', in Onimode 1989.
Mustapha, Abdul Raufu. 1992. 'Structural adjustment and multiple modes of social livelihood in Nigeria', in Gibbon, *et al.*, 1992.
Nafziger, E. Wayne. 1988. *Inequality in Africa: Political elites, proletariat, peasants and the poor*. Cambridge: Cambridge University Press.
Olukoshi, Adebayo. 1989. 'Impact of IMF-World Bank programmes in Nigeria', in Onimode 1989.
Onimode, Bade (ed.). 1989. *The IMF, the World Bank and the African debt*,

Vol. 1, *The economic impact* and Vol. 2, *The social and political impact*. London and New Jersey: Zed Books Ltd.
Organization of African Unity. 1988. *Africa's mid-term assessment of the implementation of the United Nations Programme of Action for African Economic Recovery and Development*. Addis Ababa: OAU.
Payer, Cheryl. 1989. 'Causes of the debt crisis', in Onimode 1989.
Pinstrup-Andersen, Per. 1988a. 'Food subsidies: Consumer welfare and producer incentives', in Mellor and Ahmed 1988.
——. 1989a. 'Government policy, food security and nutrition in sub-Saharan Africa'. PEW/Cornell Lecture Series on Food and Nutrition Policy, Cornell.
——. 1989b. 'The impact of macro-economic adjustment: Food security and nutrition', in Commander 1989b.
Reijmerink, J. and M.P. van Dijk. 1975. 'Urban development, income distribution and employment in Lagos'. WEP working paper. Geneva: ILO.
Rimmer, Douglas. 1970. 'Wage policies in West Africa'. Faculty of Commerce and Social Science, Occasional Paper, no. 12. Birmingham: University of Birmingham.
——. 1984. *The economies of west Africa*. London: Weidenfeld and Nicolson.
Robinson, Derek. 1990. *Civil service pay in Africa*. Geneva: ILO.
Rose, Tore. (ed). 1985. *Crisis and recovery in sub-Saharan Africa*. Paris: OECD.
Ross, A.M. (ed.). 1966. *Industrial relations and economic development*. London: Macmillan.
Rugumisa, S.M.H. and J.J Semboja. 1983. 'Income distribution and poverty in Tanzania: The ILO/JASPA report reconsidered', in ILO/JASPA, *Basic needs and development in Tanzania*. Addis Ababa, ILO/JASPA.
Saigal, Reshma. 1990. *Policy reforms in sub-Saharan Africa in the 1980s and implications for the agricultural sector*. Rome: FAO.
Samatar, Ahmed 1. 1988. *Socialist Somalia: Rhetoric and reality*. London: Zed Books.
Sawers, Larry. 1989. 'Urban primacy in Tanzania', in *Economic Development and Cultural Change*, vol. 37, no. 4.
Schatz, Sayre P. 1984. 'Pirate capitalism and the inert economy of Nigeria', in *Journal of Modern African Studies*, vol. 22, no. 1.
Seers, Dudley. 1963. 'The limitations of the special case', in *Bulletin of the Oxford Institute of Economics and Statistics*, vol. 25, no. 2.
Serageldin, Ismail. 1988. *Beyond crisis management: The World Bank's comprehensive program for promoting sustained growth with equity in Africa*. Washington, D.C.: World Bank.
——. 1989. *Povery, adjustment and growth in Africa*. Washington, D.C.: World Bank.
Sharpley, J. 1985. 'External versus internal factors in Tanzania's macro-economic crisis: 1973–83', in *Eastern African Economic Review* (New Series), vol. 1, no. 1.
——. 1986. *Economic policies and agricultural performance: The case of Kenya*. Paris: OECD.
Shaw, G.K. 1984. *Rational expectations: an elementary exposition*. Brighton: Harvester Press.
Singer, Hans. 1988a. 'The World Bank: Human face or facelift? Some

comments in the light of the World Bank's annual report'. Farnham: IDS (mimeographed).

——. 1988b. '*The World Development Report 1987* on the blessings of "outward orientation": A necessary correction', in *Journal of Development Studies*, vol. 24, no. 2.

——. 1989. 'Lessons of post-war development experience: 1945–1988'. IDS Discussion Paper, no. 260. Farnham: IDS.

——. 1991. 'Does the World Bank structural adjustment programme in sub-Saharan Africa work?: A troubling doubt'. Farnham: IDS (mimeographed).

—— and Patricia Gray. 1988. 'Trade policy and growth of developing countries: Some new data', in *World Development*, vol. 16, no. 3.

Singh, Ajit. 1986a. 'Tanzania and the IMF: The analytics of alternative adjustment programmes', in *Development and Change*, vol. 17, no. 3.

——. 1986b. 'The world economic crisis, stabilisation and structural adjustment: An overview', in *Labour and Society*, vol. 11, no. 3 (special issue: guest editor, Ajit Singh).

Singh, S. 1983a. 'Sub-Saharan agriculture: Synthesis and trade prospects'. World Bank Staff Working Papers, no. 608. Washington: World Bank.

——. 1983b. 'The outlook for primary commodities'. World Bank Staff Commodity Working Paper, no. 9. Washington, D.C.: World Bank.

Simonde de Sismondi, Jean-Charles-Leonard. 1819. *Nouveaux principes d'economie politique, ou de la richesse dans ses rapports avecla population* (first published in Paris).

Smith, A.D. (ed.). 1969. *Wage policy issues in economic development*. London: Macmillan.

Smith, L. 1989. *Agricultural labour markets and structural adjustment in sub-Saharan Africa*. FAO Economic and Social Development Paper. Rome: FAO.

Standing, Guy and Victor Tokman. 1991. *Towards social adjustment: Labour market issues in structural adjustment*. Geneva: ILO.

Stein, Howard and E. Wayne Nafziger. 1991. 'Structural adjustment, human needs and the World Bank agenda', in *Journal of Modern African Studies*, vol. 29, no. 1.

Stewart, Frances. 1972. 'Choice of technique in developing countries', in *Journal of Development Studies*, vol. 9, no.1, Oct.

——. 1986. *Economic policies and agricultural performance: The case of Tanzania*. Paris: OECD.

——. 1991a. 'Are adjustment policies in Africa consistent with long-term development needs?' in *Development Policy Review*, vol. 9, no. 4, Dec.

——. 1991b. 'The many faces of adjustment', in *World Development*, vol. 19, no. 12, Dec.

Streeten, Paul. 1989. 'A survey of the issues and options', in Commander 1989b.

Svedberg, Peter. 1991. 'The export performance of sub-Saharan Africa', in *Economic Development and Cultural Change*, vol. 39, no. 3.

Tabatabai, Hamid. 1986. 'Economic decline, access to food and structural adjustment in Ghana'. WEP working paper. Geneva: ILO.

Tanzania. 1982. *Economic Survey*. Dar es Salaam, Tanzania: Central Bureau of Statistics.

Taylor, Lance. 1983. *Structuralist macro-economics: Applicable models for the Third World*. New York: Basic Books.

Todaro, Michael. 1969. 'A model of urban unemployment and migration for less developed countries', in *American Economic Review*, vol. 59, no. 1.

——. 1971. 'Income expectations, rural-urban migration and employment in Africa', in *International Labour Review*, vol. 104, no. 5.

——. 1985 and 1990. *Economic development in the Third World.* Third and fourth editions respectively. New York: Longman.

Tripp, Aili Mari. 1989. 'Women and the changing urban household economy in Tanzania', in *Journal of Modern African Studies*, vol. 27, no. 4.

Turgot, Ann-Robert-Jacques. 1766. *Reflexions sur la formation et la distribution des richesses.*

Turner, H.A. 1966. *Wage trends, wage policies and collective bargaining: Problems of underdeveloped countries.* Cambridge,University Press.

Turnham, David and I. Jaeger. 1971. *The employment problem in less developed countries.* Paris: OECD.

Uganda, Republic of. 1982. *Background to the Budget, 1982–83.* Kampala.

——. 1984. *Background to the Budget, 1984–85.* Kampala.

United Nations. 1986. 'The development crisis in sub-Saharan Africa', *World Economic Survey, 1986.* New York: United Nations.

——. 1988. *Financing Africa's recovery: Report and recommendations of the advisory group on financial flows for Africa.* New York: United Nations.

——. 1990. *World Economic Survey, 1990.* New York: United Nations.

——. 1991. *World Economic Survey, 1991.* New York: United Nations.

UNCTAD. 1984 and 1989a. *Handbook of international trade and development statistics.* Geneva: UNCTAD.

——. 1989b. *Self-sustained growth and accelerated development for the least developed countries during the 1990s: Issues for consideration*, Second United Nations Conference on the Least Developed Countries, Geneva.

UNDP. 1990. *Human development report, 1990.* New York: UNDP.

——. 1991. *Human development report, 1991.* New York: UNDP.

——. 1992. *Human development report, 1992.* New York: UNDP.

UNICEF. 1984. *Women and children in Somalia: A situation analysis.* Mogadishu: Ministry of National Planning and UNICEF.

United States Government, Department of Agriculture (USDA). 1981. *Food problems and prospects in sub-Saharan Africa: The decade of the 1980s.* Washington, D.C.: US Government Printing Office.

Vandemoortele, Jan. 1984a. 'Country estimates: Kenya', in Van Ginnekan and Park 1984.

——. 1984b. 'The wage policy in Kenya'. Nairobi: Institute for Development Studies.

——. 1991. 'Labour market informalisation in sub-Saharan Africa', in Standing and Tokman 1991.

—— and R. van der Hoeven. 1982. *Income distribution and consumption patterns in urban and rural Kenya by socio-economic groups.* WEP working Paper. Geneva: ILO

Wallman, Sandra. 1972. 'Conditions of non-development: The case of Lesotho', in *Journal of Development Studies*, vol. 8, no. 2.

Warren, W.M. 1966. 'Urban real wages and the Nigerian trade union movement, 1939–60', in *Economic Development and Cultural Change*, vol. 25, no. 1.

Weeks, John. 1971a. 'The impact of institutional factors and economic forces on urban wages in Nigeria, 1926–1966', in *Nigerian Journal of Social and Economic Studies*, vol. 13, no. 3.
——. 1971b. 'Wage policy and the colonial legacy – a comparative study', in *Journal of Modern African Studies*, vol. 9, no. 3.
——. 1971c. 'The Political economy of labor transfer', in *Science and Society*, vol. 34, no. 2.
——. 1971d. 'Uncertainty, risk and wealth and income distribution in peasant agriculture', in *Journal of Development Studies*, vol. 7, no. 1.
——. 1974. 'Imbalance between the centre and periphery and the employment crisis in Kenya', in 1. Oxaal and A. Barnet (eds), *Beyond the sociology of development*. London: Routledge and Kegan Paul.
——. 1975. 'Policies for expanding employment in the informal urban sector of developing countries', in *International Labour Review*, vol. 111, no. 1.
——. 1976. 'The informal sector', in Gerald M. Meier (ed.): *Leading issues in economic development*. Third edition. New York: OUP.
——. (ed.). 1988a. *Debt disaster? Governments, banks and multilaterals face the crisis*. New York and London: New York University Press.
——. 1988b. 'Losers pay reparations, or how the Third World lost the lending war', in Weeks 1988a.
——. 1989. *A critique of neo-classical macro-economics*. London: Macmillan.
——. 1990. 'Structural adjustment and rural labour markets in Sierra Leone'. WEP working paper. Geneva: ILO.
—— and Elizabeth Dore. 1981. 'Basic needs: Journey of a concept', in Margaret Crahan (ed.), *Human rights and basic needs in the Americas*. Washington: Georgetown University Press.
Williams, Maurice J. 1987. 'Should the IMF withdraw from Africa?' *Policy Focus*. Washington Overseas Development Council, no. 1.
World Bank. 1975a. *Lesotho: A development challenge*. Washington, DC: World Bank. (Same publication specification for the rest unless otherwise indicated).
——. 1975b. *Liberia: Growth with development*.
——. 1979. *Sierra Leone: Country economic memorandum*.
——. 1981a. *Accelerated development in sub-Saharan Africa: An agenda for action*. ('Berg Report').
——. 1981b. *Lesotho: Agricultural sector review* (in two volumes).
——. 1981c. *Nigeria: Basic economic report*.
——. 1981d. *Sierra Leone: Prospects for growth and equity*.
——. 1982. *Liberia: Recent economic developments and medium-term prospects*.
——. 1983. *Kenya: Growth and structural change*.
——. 1984. *Sierra Leone: Agricultural sector review. Main report*.
——. 1985. *Ghana: Towards structural adjustment* (in two volumes).
——. 1986a. *Nigeria: Basic economic report*.
——. 1986b. *World development report, 1986*. New York, Oxford: University Press.
——. 1987a. 'Recent wage-related developments in Sub-Saharan Africa'. Washington, D.C.: World Bank (mimeographed) (Martha A. Starr).
——. 1987b. *World development report, 1987*. New York: Oxford University Press.

——. 1987c. *Somalia: Recent economic developments and medium-term prospects.*

——. 1988a. *Report on adjustment lending.*

——. 1988b. *World debt tables and external debt of developing countries.* Volume 1: Analysis and summary tables.

——. 1988c. *World development report, 1988.* New York: Oxford University Press.

——. 1989a. *Africa's adjustment and growth in the 1980s.*

——. 1989b. *Sub-Saharan Africa: From crisis to sustainable growth.*

——. 1990a. *Making adjustment work for the poor: A framework for policy reform in Africa.*

——. 1990b. *World debt tables, 1989–1990*, vol. 1.

——. 1990c. *World development report, 1990.* New York: Oxford Univeristy Press.

——. 1991a. *Poverty reduction handbook.*

——. 1991b. *World development report, 1991.* New York: Oxford Univeristy Press.

——. 1992. *World development report, 1992.* New York: Oxford University Press.

Index